D1188447

INTERETHNIC
COMMUNICATION

INTERNATIONAL AND INTERCULTURAL COMMUNICATION ANNUAL

Volume X   1986

Editor
Young Yun Kim
Governors State University

Consulting Editors for Volume X

Richard Allen
University of Michigan

Fred L. Casmir
Pepperdine University

William Davey
Arizona State University

Huber Ellingsworth
University of Tulsa

William B. Gudykunst
Arizona State University

L. Brooks Hill
University of Oklahoma

Sarah S. King
Central Connecticut State University

Felipe Korzenny
San Francisco State University

Joe Pilotta
Ohio State University

Larry Sarbaugh
Michigan State University, Emeritus

Robert Shuter
Marquette University

Stella Ting-Toomey
Rutgers University

Joanne S. Yamauchi
American University

INTERNATIONAL AND INTERCULTURAL COMMUNICATION ANNUAL
VOLUME X   1986

INTERETHNIC COMMUNICATION
CURRENT RESEARCH

edited by

Young Yun KIM

Published in Cooperation with
The Speech Communication Association
Commission on International and Intercultural Communication

SAGE PUBLICATIONS
The Publishers of Professional Social Science
Newbury Park   Beverly Hills   London   New Delhi

For information address:

SAGE Publications, Inc.
2111 West Hillcrest Drive
Newbury Park, California 91320

SAGE Publications Inc.
275 South Beverly Drive
Beverly Hills
California 90212

SAGE Publications Ltd.
28 Banner Street
London EC1Y 8QE
England

SAGE PUBLICATIONS India Pvt. Ltd.
M-32 Market
Greater Kailash I
New Delhi 110 048 India

Printed in the United States of America

International Standard Book Number 0-8039-2836-X

International Standard Book Number 0-8039-2837-8 (pbk.)

International Standard Series Number 0270-6075

FIRST PRINTING

Contents

Preface

This is the tenth volume of the *International and Intercultural Communication Annual.* This publication is sponsored by the Speech Communication Association's (SCA) Division of International and Intercultural Communication. Beginning with Volume VII, the annual has been focusing on specific themes as indicated in the volume titles: *Intercultural Communication Theory* (Volume VII), *Methods for Intercultural Communication Research* (Volume VIII), and *Intercultural Communication in Organizations* (Volume IX).

This volume deals with the theme of interethnic communication. It is the first anthology on interethnic relations that consists entirely of communication-focused studies. To represent maximally the interdisciplinary nature of interethnic communication research, calls for papers were placed in newsletters of all major behavioral-social science associations. Additionally, calls were mailed to over 1000 individuals identified for their academic or professional interests in interethnic communication and related areas.

Approximately 80 papers were submitted, of which 11 were selected for inclusion. Many were rejected because their subject matter was beyond the immediate concern of this volume, that is, *individual-level* analyses of communication-interaction between members of different ethnic groups *within* societal boundaries. Primarily, studies in this volume deal with interethnic communication in the United States, except the study by Giles and Johnson conducted in Great Britain. Chapter 1 details the theme and the chapters.

The members of the Consulting Editorial Board generously gave their time and expertise evaluating the papers, for which I am deeply grateful. While the value of this book ultimately rests on the quality of the individual studies, the assistance of the consulting editors was crucial in selecting the best available studies. Also, their detailed comments were invaluable to the authors in finalizing their manuscripts.

I wish to thank the staff of Sage Publications for their enthusiasm, support, and help in the making of this volume. The continuous support of William Work, Executive Director of SCA, of the members of the Division of International and Intercultural Communication, and of my colleagues at Governors State University, has been a major source of my commitment to excellence. My special thanks go to Gordon Craigo for his many hours of assistance in proofreading. His thorough and efficient checking of the manuscripts greatly expedited the copy-editing process.

Most of all, this volume owes its worth to the talent, dedication, and labor of the authors. I thank them for what they have accomplished and for what may yet be realized by them and by others in coming years. I take pride in having had the opportunity to work with them and to have played a role in promoting the scientific understanding of interethnic communication—a "ground-level" process of sociocultural integration in all multiethnic nations.

—*Young Yun Kim*
Steger, Illinois

1

Introduction
A Communication Approach to Interethnic Relations

YOUNG YUN KIM • Governors State University

This chapter presents an overview of Volume X by describing its purpose, definition, and focus. Volume X is designed to facilitate research in understanding the process of communication and relationship development between individuals of different ethnic backgrounds. This communication approach to interethnic relations emphasizes interpersonal contact and interaction. The term ethnicity *is used here to accommodate both the traditional sociological meaning of a social category and the psychological meaning of ethnic identity. The eleven studies presented in this volume are briefly introduced, followed by an overall theoretical and methodological assessment.*

Problems of interethnic relations seem particularly acute in today's world. The emergent cultural formation of historically "minority" groups are challenging the definitions of the standard and the dominant in many societies.[1] At the time of this writing, the turmoil of conflict between Whites and Blacks is threatening the stability of South Africa; its impact is felt in many other parts of the world as well.

The political and social importance of ethnicity and interethnic relations generates unceasing public debates and academic interests. To the extent that societies regard harmonious interethnic relations as a significant social issue, systematic research is needed to help understand the ways individuals and groups with different ethnic backgrounds interact with, and relate to, each other. We need to strive to find ways of promoting effective communication and cooperative relationships across ethnic boundaries.

Hence this volume—an attempt to bring together some of the current inquiries consistent with the present theme and to facilitate the further development of our scientific understanding of the dynamics of interethnic relations. The guiding principle in preparation of this volume was to present studies that bear direct relevance to interethnic *contact* and *interaction* of individuals. Thus, the *communication*-related concepts such as perception, attitude, language, verbal behavior, nonverbal behavior, and interpersonal relationship development take the central place in the studies presented in this volume.[2]

As this volume emphasizes communication aspects, macroscopic analyses of the historical, political, and economic dimensions of interethnic relations are beyond its scope. Without discounting the enormous importance of these broad issues, effective communication is viewed here as the viable mechanism through which interethnic differences and conflicts may be constructively voiced and managed. Communication, indeed, offers the alternative to violence in attempting to reduce any relational problem, interethnic or otherwise.

DEFINITIONS

A major problem in interethnic communication studies is to define the key terms. There have been numerous attempts to make fine distinctions between terms such as *international communication, intercultural communication, interracial communication,* and *inter-ethnic communication* (e.g., Kim, 1984; Rich, 1974). Without repeating the controversy of definitions, *the term* interethnic communication *is employed here as a subset of intercultural communication within a societal boundary that applies to communication between individuals who differ in ethnicity.*

Ethnicity needs elaboration. In the sociological tradition, ethnicity has been used primarily in an "objective" sense as a label to designate a social *group* and to distinguish it from other groups, based on such symbolic markers as race, religion, language, national origin, and combinations of them (Feagin, 1984). In this definition, ethnicity becomes the character, quality, or condition of belonging to an ethnic group as well as the ethnic group itself. This is the way Glazer and Moynihan (1970), for example, use the term, stressing both the condition of group belongingness and the character of the group.[3]

On the other hand, psychological studies of ethnicity often have defined ethnicity as the "subjective" identification of *individuals* with an ethnic group, that is, the identity felt by members of the ethnic group (compare Burgess, 1978, p. 268). Implied in this definition is the variability of ethnicity across individuals and, accordingly, the variability of interethnic communication. This variability of interethnic communication is comprehensively explained by Tajfel and Turner (1979) in their conceptualization of intergroup-interpersonal continuum of interaction. Here, interethnic relationships are viewed not as dichotomously distinct from intraethnic relationships, but as varying in degrees of "intergroupness" (or "interpersonalness") in the way the individuals relate to each other.

> At one extreme . . . is the interaction between two or more individuals which is fully determined by their interpersonal relationships and individual characteristics and not at all affected by various social groups or categories to which they respectively belong. The other extreme consists of interactions between two or more individuals (or groups of individuals) which are fully determined by their respective memberships of various social groups or categories, and not at all affected by the individual personal relationships between the people involved. (Tajfel & Turner, 1979, p. 34)

The present communication approach integrates both the objective and subjective definitions of ethnicity and interethnic communication. It acknowledges, first, the usefulness of labeling the boundaries and distinctions drawn by ethnic markers such as language, religion, national origin, and race. Indeed, these markers represent within-group commonalities and between-group differences in individuals' experiential backgrounds. The communication approach further recognizes that no two individuals in an ethnic group are identical in personal attributes, including ethnic characteristics and subjective identification with the ethnic group.

To understand an interethnic encounter, therefore, the participants' subjective experiences of ethnicity as well as their ethnic characteristics need to be taken into consideration. The objective-subjective ethnicity distinction is viewed here as only a conceptual one reflecting two different perspectives. In reality, both are integral to a person's disposition influencing how he or she communicates with members of another ethnic group.

THE COMMUNICATION APPROACH

Literature within the field of interethnic relations falls within two broad traditions: one concerned with ethnic relations, the other with minority communities. The countless instances of work within the area of interethnic relations deals minimally with interethnic relations, and more with studies of ethnic communities, without apparent connectedness of two or more groups. Many of the anthropological studies that describe cultural characteristics of ethnic groups belong to this category. (See Bentley, 1981, and Ross, 1978, for a bibliographical guide.)

Studies with direct relevance to interethnic relations have been conducted primarily in sociology and psychology (or social psychology). Each research tradition has helped answer questions on interethnic relations from its disciplinary perspective. Briefly, questions concerning social-structural issues (e.g., minority-majority power dynamics, social-economic stratification and inequality, and structural assimilation or segregation of minority/immigrant groups) have been primarily the domain of the sociological perspectives (e.g., Blalock, 1967, 1982; Laumann, 1973; Marrett & Leggon, 1979, 1980). The psychological studies, on the other hand, have been focusing mainly on individuals' cognitive and attitudinal orientations toward in-group and out-group members. Such concepts as prejudice, ethnocentrism, stereotypes, intergroup distances, and ethnic identity have been predominant in these studies (compare Turner & Giles, 1981).

The central research focus in the communication approach to interethnic relations is the communication process itself, that is, the process of contact and interaction between individuals of differing ethnicity through sending, receiving, and interpreting verbal and nonverbal messages. This communication perspective conceives the social order as a communicative order, whereby such phenomena as interethnic relations are conducted in interactive terms. The observable patterns of cognitive, affective, and behavioral processes are a built-in feature of the conduct of interethnic communication (or any other set of interactive relations). The study of the orderly use of language, for example, can give us an access to how interethnic relations are carried out by members through interpretative work. It is through communicative activities that we collaboratively conceive of interethnic relations for what they are.

Another crucial aspect of interethnic communication research is the relatively high degree of differences in the experiential backgrounds of the communicators because of cultural, religious, linguistic, historical, and biological dissimilarity. These differences are, after all, what make interethnic communication a unique challenge to both researchers and nonresearchers alike. Thus, identifying critical differences between ethnic cultures and communication patterns is a crucial aspect of interethnic communication research: It presents insights into understanding how individuals relate to members of other ethnic groups.

The communication approach clearly overlaps with, or incorporates, the above-mentioned psychological and anthropological approaches. Understanding psychological attributes such as stereotypes, ethnocentrism, and ethnic identity of individual communicators contributes to the understanding of the overall communication process. Also, findings of anthropological studies are critically valuable to interethnic communication research by providing information about the individual communicator's experiential background. Understanding the key differences between the communicators' worldviews, values, norms, language, and verbal and nonverbal patterns characteristic of their respective ethnic culture will doubtlessly help understand potential communication barriers and the ways individuals manage, or fail to manage, such differences.

Additionally, the communication approach benefits from sociological knowledge as it presents information about the larger socioeconomic-political context in which specific interethnic encounters take place. A basic premise of the sociological approach to interethnic relations is that the conditions of structural inequality between particular ethnic groups systematically influence the interethnic behaviors of the individuals within those groups (see, for example, Blalock, 1967, 1982). The sociological information thus serves as a group-level understanding of interethnic relations in studying the communication patterns at the individual level.

The communication approach to interethnic relations is, indeed, a multidisciplinary or interdisciplinary venture. While it focuses on the communication process (the encoding and decoding of messages), it demands a multidimensional understanding of psychological and social contexts as well. Focusing on communication to study interethnic relations, therefore, presents a difficult challenge—a challenge of having to use a broad conceptual/theoretical perspective to utilize and integrate input from more than one academic field. At the same time, this approach provides a unique opportunity to integrate the diverse disciplinary perspectives.

THE STUDIES

The eleven studies presented in this volume demonstrate the above-mentioned interdisciplinary-multidisciplinary nature of interethnic communication research. Focusing on specific aspects of interethnic communication, these studies incorporate a wide range of varied perspectives and theories for analyses. The studies are generally arranged from the most intrapersonal (psychological) to the most interpersonal (social).

The first four studies are analyses of message-decoding patterns. Specifically, they deal with ethnic patterns of cognitive and affective orientation in the context of interethnic communication. McNabb (Chapter 2), using the participant-observation method as well as anthropological literature, focuses on common stereotypes about Eskimos and examines possible sources of some misconceptions by observing the interaction conventions of Eskimos in comparison with the corresponding conventions of non-Eskimos. Similarly, Albert (Chapter 3) examines the differences between Hispanics and Anglo-Americans in attributional patterns. Specifically, the cognitive reasoning processes by teachers and students in the two groups are compared. Albert reports her findings on the ways Hispanics and Anglo-Americans differ in emphasizing "shame" as a focal difference between two groups' attributional patterns.

From a slightly different angle, Tzeng and his associates (Chapter 4), using Osgood's *Atlas of Affective Meanings*, compare in detail Black and White adolescents' affective orientation, specifically their subjective intergroup distances. Ting-Toomey's analysis (Chapter 5) of Black and White college students focuses on the strategies used by the two groups in dealing with situations of interpersonal conflict. Her interethnic comparison is further elaborated by the male and female differences within each ethnic group, refining previous research findings on this comparison.

The next five studies focus on language and verbal and nonverbal behavior in interethnic interactions. The research by Giles and Johnson (Chapter 6) consists of two experiments attempting to discern how and why Welsh speakers manage their language behavior in the English-speaking environment. Examined here is the role of intervening variables—degree of ethnic commitment and the speaker's ethnicity—on the subject's language orientation. Next, Starosta and Coleman (Chapter 7) present an interethnic rhetorical analysis based on the controversial case of "Hymietown" remarks by presidential candidate Jesse Jackson during the 1984 election campaign. This particular case is analyzed as a series of interethnic communication activities (between Blacks as represented by Jackson and Jews at large). Kochman's ethnographic analysis (Chapter 8) elaborates on the Black verbal style, "verbal dueling," and discusses implications of this verbal style in specific communication encounters between Blacks and Whites.

Next we observe ethnographic, observational studies of multiethnic classroom interactions, in the chapters by Rubin (Chapter 9) and Hanna (Chapter 10). Both studies describe the communication dynamics as they occur between/among teachers and students with different ethnic backgrounds. Rubin's study (Chapter 9) focuses on the verbal aspect of interaction, specifically the classroom questioning typically used by teachers based on an Anglo-Saxon pedagogical style. Rubin analyzes how this mode of questioning affects communication processes in multicultural classrooms. Hanna (Chapter 10), on the other hand, analyzes Black children's nonverbal behavior, specifically dance movements, as expressions of their ethnic identity in dealing with White children. This analysis of dance as a form of interethnic communication offers a unique insight into the ways children relate to one another across ethnic boundaries.

The final two chapters examine the role of ethnicity in interpersonal relationship development across ethnic groups. Based on uncertainty reduction theory, Gudykunst (Chapter 11) examines whether ethnicity influences the patterns of self-disclosure and attributional confidence in interpersonal relationships between persons of the same and of different ethnic group membership. Taking a somewhat different research focus, Hammer (Chapter 12) explores the interpersonal relationship development taking into consideration ethnic and attitude similarity and difference in initial encounters.

CONCLUSION

These eleven studies are presented as a sounding board for current research in interethnic communication. They are by no means a complete representation of the state of the art. Each focuses on a specific aspect of communication such as cognitive attribution, verbal behavior, and relationship development. Yet these studies as a whole show the key research aspects that promise potential usefulness in understanding the communication process between individuals of different ethnic backgrounds. Further development in this line of inquiry lies in the hands of those who may be encouraged by these studies to do additional research, attempting to test and expand the current understanding of interethnic communication.

As pointed out earlier, the present studies are based on diverse theoretical perspectives. Each study interprets its results in terms of the selected concepts or variables considered important to a particular theoretical perspective organizing the particular phenomenon observed. Each study, consequently, is limited in its scope and power to describe and explain the actual interethnic communication process in its totality and the interrelatedness among its elements. There is clearly a need to develop broader theoretical perspectives that integrate a number of particular theories and balance the detail of particular observations. More general theories would enable researchers to include a wider range of research variables and thus to develop more comprehensive knowledge about interethnic communication.

A noticeably healthy development in these studies is the diversity of research methods employed that roughly balance the "ethnographic-holistic-contextual" methods to the "quantitative-analytic-reductionist" methods. Readers may, of course, compare the effectiveness of the methodological approaches in addressing the respective research questions. Ultimately, the methodological assessment of empirical research must be determined by the usefulness of knowledge and insights a particular method generates. Meanwhile, different methodological approaches must be encouraged to be developed fully, as has been the case in this volume. (See Kim, 1984, for a fuller discussion on this point.)

All in all, neither theoretical nor methodological syntheses seem imminent based on the present studies. The process of interethnic communication will likely continue to be examined from a variety of perspectives using a wide variety of data sources. Yet, continued research promises to move our systematic understanding of interethnic communication closer to realism and completeness. To this end we must contribute, finding ways to solidify the often troublesome interethnic relations.

NOTES

1. See Heisler (1977), Hunt & Walker (1974), and Kang (1976), for surveys of interethnic relations in various parts of the world.

2. The communication emphasis in studying interethnic relations was the theme of another volume. In 1978 Ross edited *Interethnic Communication*, based primarily on the key symposium of the Twelfth Annual Meeting of the Southern Anthropological Study.

This volume represented the first concerted effort to focus on the study of interethnic communication and to the application of knowledge in solving problems of communication breakdown. Some authors dealt exclusively with analytical questions, while others dealt with the everyday difficulties of living in an ethnic neighborhood, of organizing communities, or of facilitating interpersonal communication across cultural boundaries. Readers are encouraged to compare the present volume with this earlier one.

3. This definition of an ethnic group is somewhat different from the way many anthropologists have used focusing mainly on national cultures. (See Ross, 1978, for a discussion of the term.) Note also that because ethnicity is often closely aligned with racial background, the terms *interethnic communication* and *interracial communication* have been used by researchers interchangeably. In this volume, *interethnic communication* is preferred throughout as it allows a broader interpretation than racial group membership.

REFERENCES

Bentley, G. C. (1981). *Ethnicity and nationality: A bibliographical guide.* Seattle: University of Washington Press.

Blalock, H. M., Jr. (1967). *Toward a theory of minority-group relations.* New York: Wiley.

Blalock, H. M., Jr. (1982). *Race and ethnic relations.* Englewood Cliffs, NJ: Prentice Hall.

Burgess, M. E. (1978, July). The resurgence of ethnicity: Myth or reality? *Ethnic and Racial Studies, 1,* 265-285.

Feagin, J. R. (Ed.). (1984). *Racial and ethnic relations* (2nd ed.). Englewood Cliffs, NJ: Prentice-Hall.

Glazer, N., & Moynihan, D. P. (1970). *Beyond the melting pot* (2nd ed.). Cambridge: MIT Press.

Heisler, M. O. (Ed.). (1977). Ethnic conflict in the world today. *Annals of the American Academy of Political and Social Science, 433,* 1-5.

Hunt, C. L., & Walker, L. (1974). *Ethnic dynamics: Patterns of intergroup relations in various societies.* Homewood, IL: Dorsey Press.

Kang, T. S. (Ed.). (1976). Ethnic relations in Asia. *Journal of Asian Affairs, 1.*

Kim, Y. Y. (1984). Searching for creative integration. In W. B. Gudykunst & Y. Y. Kim (Eds.), *International and intercultural communication annual, Vol. VII. Methods for intercultural communication research* (pp. 13-30). Beverly Hills, CA: Sage.

Laumann, E. O. (1973). *Bonds of pluralism.* New York: Wiley.

Marrett, C. B., & Leggon, C. B. (1979). *Research in race and ethnic relations* (Vol. 1). Greenwich, CT: JAI Press.

Marrett, C. B., & Leggon, C. B. (1980). *Research in race and ethnic relations* (Vol. 2). Greenwich, CT: JAI Press.

Osgood, C. E., Miron, M. S., & May, W. H. (1975). *Cross-cultural universals of affective meanings.* Chicago: University of Illinois Press.

Rich, A. L. (1974). *Interracial communication.* New York: Harper & Row.

Ross, E. L. (1978). Interethnic communication: An overview. In E. L. Ross (Ed.), *Interethnic communication* (pp. 1-12). Athens: University of Georgia Press.

Tajfel, H., & Turner, J. C. (1979). An integrative theory of intergroup conflict. In W. G. Austin & S. Worchel (Eds.), *The social psychology of intergroup relations.* Monterey, CA: Brooks/Cole.
Turner, J. C., & Giles, H. (1981). Introduction. In J. C. Turner & H. Giles (Eds.), *Intergroup behavior* (pp. 1-32). Chicago: University of Chicago Press.

I

ANALYSES OF
MESSAGE DECODING PATTERNS

2

Stereotypes and Interaction Conventions of Eskimos and Non-Eskimos

STEVEN L. McNABB ● *Social Research Institute, Anchorage*

Communication research in several fields suggests that most, if not all, behavioral dimensions of communication are structured and may vary across ethnic groups. The cognitive elements of these structures are problematic. Whether ordered variability across groups reflects differences in character and personality or merely variance in social conventions, stereotypes about ethnic groups based on observed interaction patterns nonetheless emerge and persist. An interactional and sociolinguistic approach is used in a case study of communication between Eskimos and non-Eskimos in northwest Alaska. Observational records of interethnic communication are quantified, and bivariate and ANOVA analyses are conducted in order to identify common patterns and differences in communication routines. Stereotypes and dispositional judgments about Eskimo character are identified and explained as products of faulty inferences about the meanings of communication conventions.

Interethnic communication processes have received vigorous attention in recent years in a number of fields, including linguistics, psychology, sociology, and anthropology, to name only a few. To the extent that these processes are any different from more generic types of communication, their special status is usually thought to hinge on what are termed cultural values, mores, worldview, and more general sets of expectations, assumptions, or social orientations that exert significant influences on communication and vary across ethnic groups. Such underlying patterns shape distinctive forms of communication and may imbue these forms with a characteristically ethnic "flavor."

It is generally recognized that tacit assumptions exert their influences by establishing patterned agendas, sequences, message forms, and social relations for the conduct of communication. These patterns are termed *value orientations* in the Values/Communication model, and comprise a set of cultural patterns, life scripts, regulative rules, and operators in the Coordinated Management of Meaning approach (Cronen & Shuter, 1983). In the fields of psychology, artificial intelligence, linguistics, anthropology, and sociology, these patterns are often labeled *schema, scripts, frames, structures of expectations;* ancillary terms such as *appropriateness criteria, situational use rules*, and *accounting procedures* are used. (See Tannen, 1979, for a concise review of disciplinary overlaps in terminology and concepts.)

Frames (to use Goffman's term, which is suitably general for this discussion; see Goffman, 1974) prefigure perceptions of social groups. Most analyses of communication acknowledge that formulation of identity and interpersonal relations is a constructive act that occurs in an interactional context, which is guided by and in turn guides the selection and use of appropriate frames. Since frames vary across ethnic boundaries, structured presuppositions about persons will vary also.

These issues are addressed in a case study of interethnic communication between Inupiaq Eskimos in northwest Alaska and their non-Eskimo, largely Anglo neighbors who are temporary residents in this setting. The Inupiaq Eskimos, although an ethnic minority in the state, are a majority population in northwest Alaska. The non-Eskimo population is small, transient, and engaged in highly specialized and confined tasks. They are primarily teachers, administrators, and technicians involved in social services and governance. Social and economic polarities are great. Inupiaq Eskimos still hunt and fish to sustain their families but they also work in blue- and white-collar jobs, live in villages linked by the latest telecommunications technology, and send their children to local schools equipped with modern video and computer hardware. These factors, unique to Inupiaq Eskimos, may inhibit generalization to other interethnic situations, but they provide the basis for a rich and illuminating case study.

STEREOTYPES AND CONVENTIONS
IN INTERETHNIC COMMUNICATION

A stereotype is any categorical generalization about persons or social groups that ignores individual and social variability. Although the term *stereotype* commonly refers to pejorative beliefs and assertions, it is used here in a broader and neutral sense. Stereotypes may evolve and persist through the same means by which any person anywhere derives inferences about the meanings of interaction. Seemingly warranted conclusions are drawn through the application of situational principles of the organization of talk and gesture, which are based on apparently meaningful histories and precedents of personal behavior and observed interaction. These conclusions are stereotypes. They are inferences about persons, places, and relations that are a shorthand for more complex situations. They prefigure our interactions and allow them to proceed briskly. We use them constantly.

However, situational principles of interaction organization that underlie frames are different among Eskimos and non-Eskimos. Their respective communication conventions reflect different ideals or targets for interaction impressions and interpretations, thus they may seek different accounts of the same events. They do this in part by applying different "appropriateness criteria" (i.e., implicit standards for proper, well-formed interactions that yield coherent and intended results; see Garfinkel, 1967; Kendon, 1977).

Stereotypic inferences commonly attribute personality or character qualities to the opposite group. Because appropriateness standards are apparently violated, such inferences seek to account for this violation by reference to the ability, intention, or motivation of the other group. However, since ultimate feelings and motivations are inaccessible to the observer, and furthermore because communication itself is the common basis of all inferences of this sort, the patterning of expressive behavior may provide the evidence from which stereotypic generalizations are derived. Ethnic caricature and stereotypes, therefore, may be more a description of expressive convention than of mass psychology or group personality. Because communication conventions establish structured and widely shared habits for organizing topics, persons, and message forms, the forms of communication generated by these conventions may, and often do, influence the idiosyncratic meanings "felt" by individuals. Structured communication styles entirely unrelated to affect or psychology may in fact produce the "feel" that is so often associated with ethnic groups.

Character Generalizations About Inupiaq Eskimos

A sample of character generalizations about Eskimos is offered below. This sample is derived mainly from scholarly literature and is intended to illustrate the sort of character statements that may evolve through the process described earlier. The sample is by no means comprehensive and omits numerous lay stereotypes that are less benign than those listed here.

Eskimos are nearly never described as impassioned, excitable, or intense. They are normally described as passive, slow-paced and quiet, phlegmatic and indifferent, shy, deliberate, reserved, and noncommittal (Chance, 1966; Coles, 1977; Collier, 1973; Foulks, 1972; Kleinfeld, 1978; Oswalt, 1963). Inupiaq Eskimos are also said to be group-oriented, social, nonegocentric, egalitarian, agreeable, and self-effacing (Spencer, 1959, p. 254); tactful and nonindividualistic (Spencer, 1959, p. 253); permissive and affirmative (Oswalt, 1963, p. 31) or indulgent toward children (Chance, 1965, 1966); cheerful, cooperative, attentive, and responsive to others (Kleinfeld, 1978, pp. 43-44); noncompetitive (Chance, 1966; Spencer, 1959; Kleinfeld, 1978, p. 62); and nonaggressive (Briggs, 1970; Chance, 1966; Hughes, 1960). This is a rather complex generalization since a premium on individual prowess is said to parallel a group orientation that stresses sublimation of individual inclinations. Personal strength and tenderness, altruism and attainment, wisdom and great modesty coexist side by side in the Inupiaq scheme of things.

Eskimos are also said to be stoic, capable of great mental and physical endurance, tolerant, deliberate, restrained, calm, reserved, purposeful, and calculating (see Briggs, 1970; Brody, 1970; Brower, 1980; Chance, 1966; Coles, 1977; Hughes, 1960). In contrast, some stereotypes assert that Eskimos lack self-control (see Brower, 1980, p. 113) and are impulsive, temperamental, capricious "children of nature" (Rasmussen, 1932, p. 17). This last point illustrates that contradictions and inconsistencies among dispositional statements, or stereotypes, are not uncommon. One scholar of Eskimo studies remarks: "Argumentative and quarrelsome persons were ignored. If there were boasting, it was always tinged with good humor" (Spencer, 1959, p. 160). Yet twenty years later the same scientist stated: "Competition marked by aggression was the clear keynote of the traditional society" (Spencer, 1979, p. 72).

Both Eskimos and non-Eskimos often give serious and protracted thought to such generalizations and have even broadcast them through public channels. One recent controversy concerning the "true" nature of Eskimos grew into a public debate between two non-Eskimos that even reached the pages of the *New York Times*; one person's argument was titled "Alaskan Eskimos' Hatred of Whites," while the rebuttal was headlined "The Warm and Friendly Inupiaq People" (see Brower, 1980, pp. 106-107, for a brief analysis of this specific controversy).

THE STUDY

Methods

The data for this study are interaction episodes recorded over an eight-month period in 1979 in 11 villages in northwest Alaska. These data are complemented by linguistic and ethnographic materials collected in 1975, 1976, and 1979-1984. The episodes were observed in naturalistic settings without intervention. Interactions were recorded using a standardized observation protocol. The raw data and subsequent scores for each of several communication variables correspond to analytic categories used in sociolinguistics (see Gumperz & Hymes, 1972; Hymes, 1974), the ethnography of communication (see Bauman & Sherzer, 1974; Gumperz & Hymes, 1964, 1972; Hymes, 1964), and discourse analysis (see Coulthard & Montgomery, 1982; Freedle, 1979).

Nine variables were defined. Two variables are identifier labels for data management. The remaining seven variables consist of a formality and privacy index based on Gumperz and Hymes's (1972) and Irvine's (1979, p. 778) definitions, a setting index that specifies the environmental boundaries of the episode, a participant index that rates the extent of stratification among participants, three simple numeric variables (the number of participant roles enacted during the episode, the number of topics of communication contained in the episode, and the duration in minutes of the episode), and a final variable that denotes whether or not the episode involved non-Eskimo participants (see McNabb, 1985, for a full discussion of these variables and the following methodology).

Bivariate linear analyses of all variables were undertaken in order to determine if, and to what degree, attributes of these variables covaried in a systematic fashion. These analyses were conducted with both the entire data set and the subsets composed of (1) episodes involving Eskimos alone and (2) episodes involving both Eskimos and non-Eskimos together. The objective of these analyses was to detect regularity in communication routines and then to determine how this regularity is expressed in actual communication forms in each of the two subsets. The ultimate goal is to discover whether or not Eskimo and non-Eskimo interaction behaviors are truly different, as stereotypes suggest, and whether or not detectable differences can be attributed to the underlying character differences asserted by common stereotypes. These differences were assessed using analysis of variance (ANOVA) methods.

The interactional data analysis was complemented by linguistic analysis designed to illustrate the means by which speech sustains this interaction and conveys social meanings in its own right. Analysis of speech is important in this connection since numerous lay stereotypes concern the creolized English dialect spoken by most Eskimos. Use of this dialect, which is a vernacular with simplified grammar and syntax and many non-English phonological patterns, is widely considered by non-Eskimos to be a sign of limited mental proficiency, hence speech itself may engender prejudicial attitudes.

An implicational analysis (see Berdan, 1975; Bickerton, 1973; DeCamp, 1971, 1973; Fasold, 1975) was performed to describe the parameters of linguistic and situational covariation as a single system of speech behavior. This method requires a formal linguistic analysis of the phonological and grammatical features of the vernacular dialect, termed *village English*, abbreviated VE. Since each nonstandard feature alternates with other nonstandard or standard features, the object is to determine the conditions under which alternations take place. Furthermore, certain features may imply the presence of others, and to the degree that this is so, such features become "trademarks" of a speech style used under particular circumstances. To oversimplify but clarify the method we only need to recall occasional uses of slang; this approach would seek to describe the linguistic structure of the slang and the situations during which persons revert to slang expressions.

Results

With few exceptions the interaction variables intercorrelate well. This is generally predictable. In speech, regular correspondences between sounds and language categories make communication possible since they underlie a systematic phonology, grammar, syntax, and semantic structure. Similarly, broader interaction meanings are contingent on regular covariations between types of interaction contexts, categories of persons, kinesic and proxemic patterns, and other linguistic and nonlinguistic circumstances. Communicative routines are in fact one of several means humans use to regularize and synchronize their own behavior, thus intercorrelation should be expected.

In order to illustrate the bivariate relations as well as characteristics of each subset (Eskimo/Eskimo communication and Eskimo/non-Eskimo communication), subset distributions have been superimposed on scatterplots of the entire data set. In the following figures the statistical summaries describe characteristics of the entire sample. The oval boundaries encircle the subset distributions within a one standard deviation limit, and X and Y axis mean intercepts for each subset are marked.

Figures 2.1 and 2.2 display the relationships between the formality index and two other variables: participant characteristics and the number of participant groups. These figures illustrate the typical pattern found in all comparisons, although the linear relationships are insignificant in these (and only these) two cases. The subset distributions tend to overlap, but the attributes of the variables are not uniformly distributed across both subsets. The variables are expressed differently depending on situational circumstances: Communicational encounters between

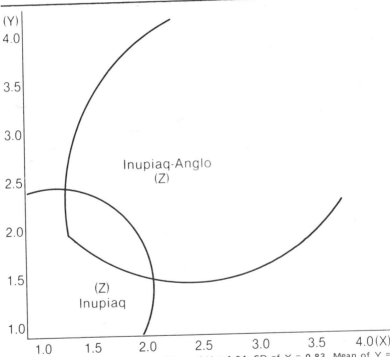

(Z) = intercept of subset means. Mean of X = 1.84; SD of X = 0.83. Mean of Y = 2.02; SD of Y = 0.91. N = 251. Pearson's r = 0.33; significance of r = n.s. (p > 0.05); standard error of r = 0.06.

Figure 2.1 Bivariate Correlation and Subset Distributions: Formality/Privacy (X) and Participant Characteristics (Y)

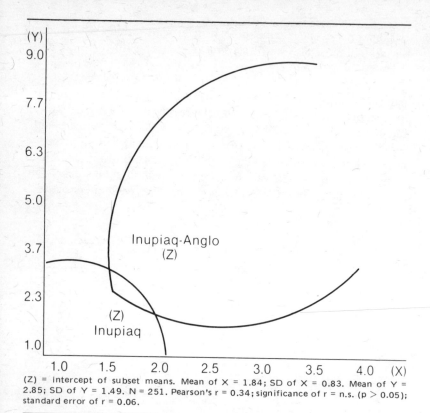

(Z) = intercept of subset means. Mean of X = 1.84; SD of X = 0.83. Mean of Y = 2.85; SD of Y = 1.49. N = 251. Pearson's r = 0.34; significance of r = n.s. (p > 0.05); standard error of r = 0.06.

Figure 2.2 Bivariate Correlation and Subset Distributions: Formality/Privacy (X) and Participant Groups (Y)

Eskimos alone are less stratified and less formalized than those involving Eskimos and non-Eskimos in joint encounters.

Figures 2.3 through 2.8 illustrate correlations that are uniformly significant. Setting characteristics, participant characteristics, episode duration, participant groups, and topics are significantly intercorrelated. Although the variables are salient for each subset, they are expressed differently as the subset distributions demonstrate. The evidence suggests that (1) Eskimos differentiate between communication contexts and audiences and modify their communication habits depending on such circumstances; (2) Eskimos exercise great flexibility and range in their interactions, since they employ all possible combinations of variable attributes depending on specific circumstances; and (3) their

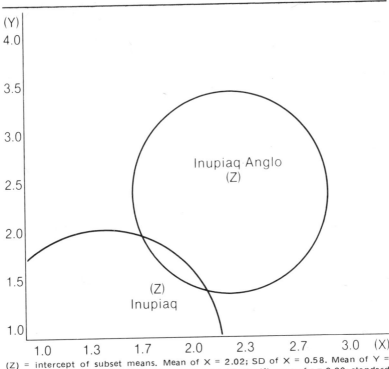

(Z) = intercept of subset means. Mean of X = 2.02; SD of X = 0.58. Mean of Y = 2.02; SD of Y = 0.91. N = 251. Pearson's r = 0.37; significance of r = 0.00; standard error of r = 0.06.

Figure 2.3 Bivariate Correlation and Subset Distributions: Setting Characteristics (X) and Participant Characteristics (Y)

counterparts (non-Eskimos) exhibit a confined range, represented by and large by the higher values of the variables.

These differences are measured and summarized in Table 2.1. The results convincingly demonstrate that the subsets are fundamentally different except in terms of formality patterns (which were ambiguous in the bivariate analyses as well) and duration. Nonetheless the F statistics are significant in all cases, and further analysis of the duration variable suggests that it too distinguishes between the subsets if it is transformed into a set of interval categories (McNabb, 1985, p. 205).

The results of linguistic analysis reveal a pervasive pattern of code-switching among Eskimos. Relatively few Eskimos are fully competent in the traditional Inupiaq language, but nearly all Eskimos speak a

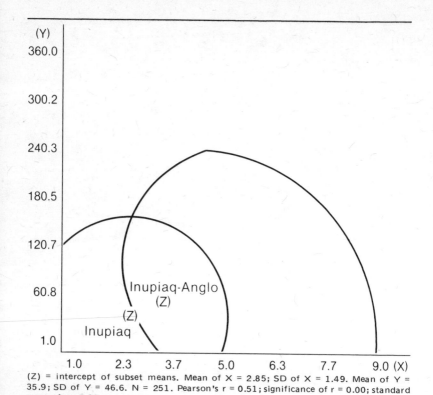

(Z) = intercept of subset means. Mean of X = 2.85; SD of X = 1.49. Mean of Y = 35.9; SD of Y = 46.6. N = 251. Pearson's r = 0.51; significance of r = 0.00; standard error of r = 0.06.

Figure 2.4 Bivariate Correlation and Subset Distributions: Participant Groups (X) and Duration in Minutes (Y)

creolized dialect of English, which is heavily influenced by Inupiaq phonological and grammatical structures. Few of the 19 distinctive linguistic elements identified during analysis are consistent and defining features of this speech form. These elements are ordered along a continuum such that the dialect is more or less conspicuous depending on speaker habits and specific environmental contexts. Forms of the dialect that approximate standard English are typically used in conversation with non-Eskimos, whereas more "accented" dialect forms are commonly used with other Eskimos. Potent social meanings are signaled by variation along this dialect continuum. Among its speakers, VE is considered more intimate and private, while standard English is considered pedantic and tedious. For Eskimos, VE as well as the

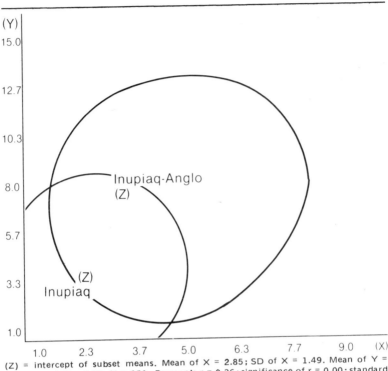

(Z) = intercept of subset means. Mean of X = 2.85; SD of X = 1.49. Mean of Y = 5.63; SD of Y = 2.87. N = 251. Pearson's r = 0.36; significance of r = 0.00; standard error of r = 0.06.

Figure 2.5 Bivariate Correlation and Subset Distributions: Participant Groups (X) and Topics (Y)

Inupiaq language evoke sentimental associations, Eskimo values, and solidarity; among non-Eskimos, VE is widely thought to be barren, imprecise, and childlike. Comprehensive treatments of this dialect are reported elsewhere (Kaplan & McNabb, 1981; McNabb, 1981, 1985; Vandergriff, 1982).

Figure 2.9 integrates the interaction and speech analysis findings. The Eskimo and mixed Eskimo/non-Eskimo subset characteristics are outlined, the ranges of their interaction participation are indicated, and the continuum of creolized speech use (ranging from VE through standard English, or SE) is superimposed across the subsets.

The subset distributions are generalized in this figure. Non-Eskimos participate in only a portion of all interactions, specifically those with

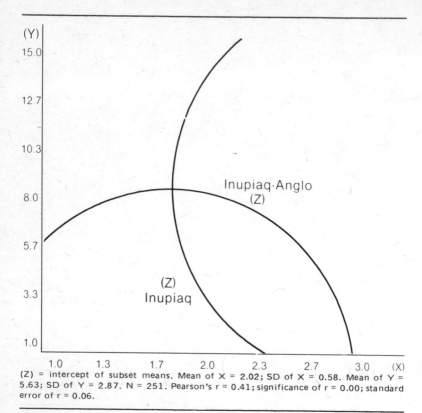

(Z) = intercept of subset means. Mean of X = 2.02; SD of X = 0.58. Mean of Y = 5.63; SD of Y = 2.87. N = 251. Pearson's r = 0.41; significance of r = 0.00; standard error of r = 0.06.

Figure 2.6 Bivariate Correlation and Subset Distributions: Setting Characteristics (X) and Topics (Y)

high attributes along each variable. Inupiaq Eskimos either participate with other Eskimos alone or in groups that include some non-Eskimos. The VE-SE speech continuum provides a "bridge" that spans these differences and provides a mechanism for Eskimos to accommodate different language habits among varying audiences or to resist accommodation and express ethnic solidarity through the use of a divergent dialect.

DISCUSSION

Because participation is fragmented in the manner noted earlier, opportunities for employing and refining interaction techniques and

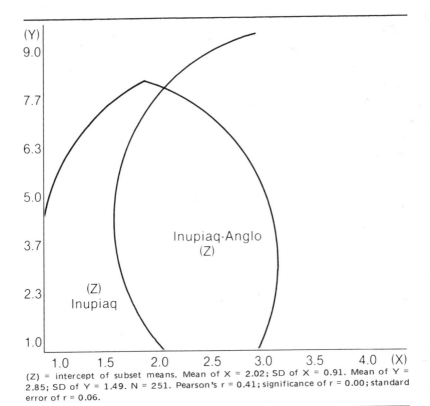

(Z) = intercept of subset means. Mean of X = 2.02; SD of X = 0.91. Mean of Y = 2.85; SD of Y = 1.49. N = 251. Pearson's r = 0.41; significance of r = 0.00; standard error of r = 0.06.

Figure 2.7 Bivariate Correlation and Subset Distributions: Participant Characteristics (X) and Participant Groups (Y)

situational use principles are unequally distributed. Non-Eskimos are severely constrained from learning appropriate rules of interaction since they do not generally apply in their orbits of interaction. Eskimos manipulate the full range of variable attributes while their counterparts do not. To the extent that these variable patterns represent the products of appropriateness criteria and situational use rules, the Eskimo repertoire is clearly more varied; keyed to multiple uses, settings, persons, and circumstances; and, to their counterparts, potentially more opaque. Eskimo frames are more inclusive and represent kinds of interaction assumptions that non-Eskimos simply do not experience or apply.

These factors make it unlikely that all participants and observers will grasp the fact that, although different in important respects, their modes

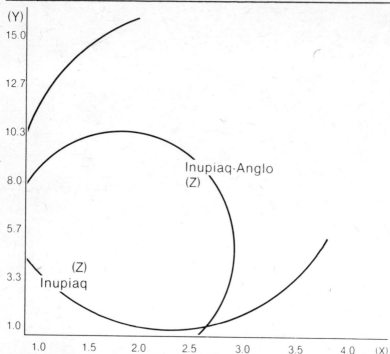

(Z) = intercept of subset means. Mean of X = 2.02; SD of X = 0.91. Mean of Y = 5.63; SD of Y = 2.87. N = 251. Pearson's r = 0.53; significance of r = 0.00; standard error of r = 0.06.

Figure 2.8   Bivariate Correlation and Subset Distributions: Participant Characteristics (X) and Topics (Y)

of interaction are born of the same underlying principles. The same variables are salient for each but not in the same ways. Either pole of the continuum is, for many persons situated at the other end, a rare interaction style. Rarity itself aids in creating a sense of "difference."

These conditions are predicted by attribution theory. Unfamiliarity may spur closer perceptual and interpretive attention on the part of an observer, and the mere fact of such "fine rating" may lead to a greater incidence of dispositional judgments about observed persons (e.g., the cause of behavior is someone's "character," or ability, or competence) and a high level of confidence about these dispositional explanations. *Fine rating* is a term popularized by Newtson (1973) to describe close attention and the division of behavioral "strips" into small segments of

TABLE 2.1

Analysis of Variance in Interaction Determined by Ethnic Composition of Participant Groups

Variable	Source of Variation[1]	DF	Sum of Squares	Mean Squares	F	p	t	p
Formality/ Privacy	Ethnicity	1	12.22	12.22	14.4	0.00	n.s.[2]	
	Residual	249	211.5	0.85				
Setting Characteristics	Ethnicity	1	12.86	12.86	44.5	0.00	6.7	0.02
	Residual	249	72.04	0.29				
Participant Characteristics	Ethnicity	1	69.97	69.97	124.5	0.00	11.2	0.006
	Residual	249	140	0.56				
Participant Groups	Ethnicity	1	46.81	46.81	23	0.00	4.8	0.04
	Residual	249	507	2.0				
Topics	Ethnicity	1	817	817	162.3	0.00	12.7	0.004
	Residual	249	1253	5.0				
Duration	Ethnicity	1	9410	9410	4.38	0.04	n.s.	
	Residual	249	535K	2150				

Notes: 1. Ethnicity: homogenous Inupiaq versus heterogeneous Inupiaq-Anglo. 2. Significance test level: 0.05.

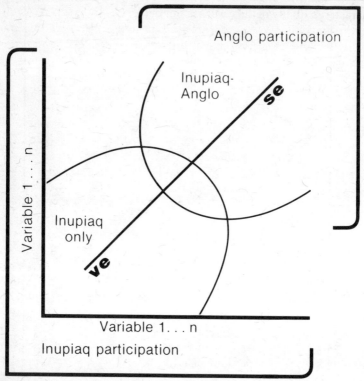

NOTES: The VE (village English) – SE (standard English) speech gradient overlies the nonverbal behavioral patterns that distinguish Inupiaq from mixed Inupiaq-Anglo interactions. VE is a vernacular English dialect heavily influenced by Inupiaq phonology and grammar. Intermediate points along the gradient represent blends of VE and standard English. "Variable 1 . . . n" along each axis signifies that a general linear relationship depicted here is common to all variables. Higher variable values coincide with more frequent non-Inupiaq participation and more frequent use of standard English (or diminished VE use). Lower variable values coincide with more frequent VE use and less frequent non-Inupiaq participation (or more frequent exclusive Inupiaq participation).

Figure 2.9 A Model of Verbal and Nonverbal Dimensions of Interethnic Communication in Northwest Alaska

short duration for cognitive analysis. Similarly, attribution research shows that anxiety, uncertainty, and opacity may quickly generate fine rating. Under circumstances of uncertainty (or its counterpart, fine rating), persons tend to attribute personal causes (dispositions) to others while making external attributions (circumstances, luck) about oneself.

Thus, when affairs turn ambiguous, it is not due to the flaws of character or ability in the audience but to one's own sheer bad fortune. Furthermore, if events are perceived in a positive light, personal attributions are made to oneself, and circumstantial attributions are inferred for others. Hence one's own mishaps are momentary lapses or accidents, while one's own rewards are well earned (Fischoff, 1976; Jones & Nisbett, 1972).

Finally, attribution research has uncovered "primacy effects"; when fine rating occurs, people tend to create dispositional explanations that they will maintain tenaciously. The earliest encounters tend to leave the longest-lasting effects (Kanouse, 1972). Short-term non-Eskimo residents, new to the north and thrown into alien settings and possessed of narrow repertoires for interaction in such settings, are prone to all these effects. Although empirical evidence demonstrates few uniform properties of Eskimo interaction, uniform character stereotypes can nonetheless be generated and maintained by their audiences.

There are two results of the intersection of speech variations and interaction differences. The intersection provides a solution to obstacles to communication by providing a verbal channel for communication that is correlated to subset differences. It also introduces a complicating factor that exaggerates the sense of uncertainty and difference between the subsets. However, the addition of a verbal countersign to the interaction differences described above may exaggerate already notable differences and create a doubly marked, redundant sense of divergence between the ethnic groups. Strong and often negative attitudes about VE prevail among non-Eskimos, and code-switching on the part of Eskimos, in concert with interaction variations, may unwittingly encourage stereotyping.

Table 2.2 illustrates the association between conventional expressions, functions of messages, and readings of these expressions and messages. The column on the left lists conventions of speech and gesture among the Inupiaq Eskimos. The center column identifies the function of these expressions in the Inupiaq communication system, and the column at the right lists common non-Eskimo interpretations of these messages.

The center column identifies the use of forms generated through conventions on the left. These are functions of conventional expressions. Non-Eskimos witness behavioral forms that are generated through conventions on the far left. They have far less access to the functions in the center column and are by and large oblivious to them, since in fact they are able to create entirely congruent explanations by interpreting

TABLE 2.2
Functions and Interpretations of Eskimo Communication Conventions

Conventional Gesture	Inupiaq Function	Anglo Interpretation
Tactful Compliance	de-escalation, avoidance, appeasement	passivity, submission, gullibility
Solicitude	social vigilance, conscientiousness, fair play	group orientation, egalitarianism, devotion
Taciturn Reserve	delay of commitment, await consensus, diminish or censor excitation and emotionalism	apathy, animosity, procrastination, withdrawal, patience
Ambivalence/ Equivocation	avoidance of commitment of public disclosure, maintain indefinite circumstances, evade determination of cause, effect, or responsibility	fatalism, indecision
Effacement	evasion of self-referral, anticipate and avoid charges of egoism, anticipate and reject personal responsibility (or) invite self-referral, accept personal responsibility through indirect means	shyness, egalitarian style, nonassertion

patterned but "raw" forms through the situational use rules and appropriateness criteria already familiar to them. These interpretations are similar to the messages contained on the left but are nonetheless inaccurate. In some cases the interpretations approximate the general conventional theme (as in the Anglo interpretation of "effacement" = "shyness"), but for the most part they overlook the function of conventional expressions. Whereas non-Eskimos usually conclude that Eskimos are shy, the meaning of the convention is that it is "appropriate" and fitting to express shyness.

If stereotypes were due exclusively to differences in codes, people would quickly adapt to these differences and overcome them. But situational use patterns and conventional expressive themes are so thoroughly internalized that they are apt to be treated not merely as codes but rather as final arbiters in the meaning of behavior. For interactors who use them, they are only in the rarest circumstances treated as conventions. They are instead statutory guides to the "way things really are." Interactors, when faced with ambiguous situations, tend to cling stubbornly to these conventions and instead inspect the more neutral codes or the behaviors of the co-communicators for solutions and answers.

A brief summary of findings is in order. First, many inconsistent stereotypes about Eskimo character exist. It is unlikely that valid psychological traits are expressed by the behaviors that underlie these stereotypes, since these behaviors are conventional habits that are performed over and over again as they are appropriate. Social and cultural standards determine when they are appropriate. However, since observers rarely share the same standards, the logic that makes these behaviors commonplace to Eskimos is not readily apparent. Instead, psychological explanations are invoked to account for them. Second, Eskimo verbal and nonverbal behavior patterns are extremely sensitive to social context and vary tremendously, hence they defy simple characterizations. Although these facts allow Eskimos to cope with widely divergent audiences and interaction settings, it makes their behavior seem less consistent, less predictable, and, paradoxically, more opaque to non-Eskimos. In turn, this ambiguity encourages further stereotyping.

In conclusion, personality, character, and cultural values are reflected in behavior only insofar as they are communicated. To be communicated they must be codified, and these codified forms embody expressive conventions that are far more reflective of uniform communication habits than of uniform psychological or character traits. Observers, as members of (normally) different speech communities, are not apt to possess the situational usage skills and implicit knowledge of appropriateness criteria that are necessary to decode and encode these conventional messages and discern them from others. They are therefore apt to employ divergent situational usage skills and appropriateness criteria, which commonly leads to the apprehension of patterned behaviors that are nonetheless misconstrued. Simple processes of perceptual detection, attention, and memory, the core issues of attribution theory (Schneider & Shiffren, 1977), account for the development and persistence of dispositional judgments (or, in short, stereotypes) about persons and social groups under these circumstances.

REFERENCES

Bauman, R., & Sherzer, J. (1974). *Explorations in the ethnography of speaking*. London: Cambridge University Press.

Berdan, R. (1975). The necessity of variable rules. In R. Fasold & R. W. Shuy (Eds.), *Analyzing variation in language* (pp. 11-27). Washington, DC: Georgetown University Press.

Bickerton, D. (1973). Quantitative versus dynamic paradigms: The case of Montreal, Que. In C. Bailey & R. W. Shuy (Eds.), *New ways of analyzing variation in English* (pp. 23-44). Washington, DC: Georgetown University Press.

Briggs, J. (1970). *Never in anger*. Cambridge, MA: Harvard University Press.

Brody, H. (1970). *The people's land*. New York: Penguin.

Brower, W. C. (1980). *Ethnic identity and revitalization: psychocultural adaptation among the Eskimos of North Alaska*. Ph.D. dissertation, Anthropology Department, University of Colorado.

Chance, N. (1965). Acculturation, self-identification and personality adjustment. *American Anthropologist, 67,* 372-393.

Chance, N. (1966). *The Eskimo of North Alaska*. New York: Holt, Rinehart & Winston.

Coles, R. (1977). *Eskimos, Chicanos and Indians*. New York: Atlantic Monthly Press.

Collier, J. (1973). *Alaskan Eskimo education*. New York: Holt, Rinehart & Winston.

Coulthard, M., & Montgomery, M. (Eds.). (1982). *Studies in discourse analysis*. London: Routledge & Kegan Paul.

Cronen, V. E., & Shuter, R. (1983). Forming intercultural bonds. In W. B. Gudykunst (Ed.), *Intercultural communication theory* (pp. 89-119). Beverly Hills, CA: Sage.

DeCamp, D. (1971). Toward a generative analysis of a post-creole speech continuum. In D. Hymes (Ed.), *Pidginization and creolization of languages* (pp. 349-370). New York: Cambridge University Press.

DeCamp, D. (1973). What do implicational scales imply? In C. Bailey & R. W. Shuy (Eds.), *New ways of analyzing variation in English* (pp. 141-148). Washington, DC: Georgetown University Press.

Fasold, R. W. (1975). The Bailey wave model: A dynamic quantitative paradigm. In R. Fasold & R. W. Shuy (Eds.), *Analyzing variation in language* (pp. 27-58). Washington, DC: Georgetown University Press.

Fischoff, B. (1976). Attribution theory and judgment under uncertainty. In J. H. Harvey et al. (Eds.), *New directions in attribution research*. New York: John Wiley.

Foulks, E. F. (1972). *The arctic hysterias of the North Alaskan Eskimo*. Washington, DC: American Anthropological Association.

Freedle, R. (Ed.). (1979). *New directions in discourse processing*. Norwood, NJ: Ablex.

Garfinkel, H. (1967). *Ethnomethodology*. Englewood Cliffs, NJ: Prentice-Hall.

Goffman, E. (1974). *Frame analysis*. New York: Harper & Row.

Gumperz, J. J., & Hymes, D. (Eds.). (1964). The ethnography of communication. *American Anthropologist, 66* (part 2).

Gumperz, J. J., & Hymes, D. (1972). *Directions in sociolinguistics: The ethnography of communication*. New York: Holt, Rinehart & Winston.

Hughes, C. C. (1960). *An Eskimo village in the modern world*. Ithaca, NY: Cornell University Press.

Hymes, D. (1964). *Language in culture and society*. New York: Harper & Row.

Hymes, D. (1974). *Foundations in sociolinguistics.* Philadelphia: University of Pennsylvania Press.

Irvine, J. (1979). Formality and informality in communicative events. *American Anthropologist, 81,* 773-790.

Jones, E. E., & Nisbett, R. E. (1972). *The actor and the observer: Divergent perceptions of the causes of behavior.* Morristown, NJ: General Learning Press.

Kanouse, D. E. (1972). Language, labeling and attribution. In E. E. Jones (Ed.), *Attribution: Perceiving the causes of behavior.* Morristown, NJ: General Learning Press.

Kaplan, L., & McNabb, S. (1981). *Village English in Northwest Alaska.* Paper presented at the annual meeting of the Society for Applied Anthropology, Symposium on Cross-Cultural Education in Alaska, Denver, April.

Kendon, A. (1977). *Studies in the behavior of face-to-face interaction.* Lisse: Peter de Ridder Press.

Kleinfeld, J. (1978). *Eskimo school on the Andreafsky.* New York: Praeger.

McNabb, S. (1981). *Achieving logical misunderstandings: Cross-cultural communication in North Alaska.* Paper presented at the annual meeting of the American Anthropological Association, Los Angeles, December.

McNabb, S. (1985). *Interaction conventions and the creation of stereotypes in Northwest Alaska: An ethnography of communication.* Ph.D. dissertation, Anthropology Department, Brown University.

Newtson, D. (1973). Attribution and the unit of perception in ongoing behavior. *Journal of Personality and Social Psychology, 28,* 28-38.

Oswalt, W. (1963). *Mission of change in Alaska.* San Marino, CA: Huntington Library.

Rasmusson, K. (1932). *Report of the fifth Thule expedition* (Vol. 9). Copenhagen: Nordisk Forlag.

Schneider, W., & Shiffrin, R. M. (1977). Controlled and automatic human information processing: detection, search, and attention. *Psychological Review, 84,* 1-53.

Spencer, R. F. (1959). *North Alaskan Eskimo* (Bureau of American Ethnology Bulletin 171). Washington, DC: Government Printing Office.

Spencer, R. F. (1979). Play, power and politics in Native North America. In E. Norbeck & C. F. Farrer (Eds.), *Forms of play of Native North Americans* (pp. 67-76). Los Angeles: West.

Tannen, D. (1979). What's in a frame? Surface evidence for underlying expectations. In R. Freedle (Ed.), *New directions in discourse processing.* Norwood, NJ: Ablex.

Vandergriff, J. (1982). Kotzebue Inupiaq English. In H. G. Bartelt (Ed.), *Essays in Native American English.* San Antonio, TX: Trinity University Press.

3

Communication and Attributional Differences Between Hispanics and Anglo-Americans

ROSITA DASKAL ALBERT • University of Minnesota

This chapter describes research undertaken to explore communication and attributional differences between Hispanic and Anglo-American teachers and pupils. A brief account of the conceptual framework is presented, followed by a description of five phases of the procedure of a large-scale research project on Hispanic-Anglo interactions. Data analyses and results are presented for a subset of the data focusing on an important cultural difference between Hispanics and Anglos: the greater Hispanic emphasis on attributions of shame. Implications of the findings for both theory and training are discussed.

Interpersonal encounters between persons from different ethnic and cultural backgrounds are often fraught with misunderstanding and conflict. The difficulty stems in part from the fact that individuals from different cultures tend to expect different kinds of behavior in a given interaction situation and to interpret the same behavior differently. The expectations, perceptions, and experiences that persons from different cultural backgrounds bring into social interaction situations sometimes create obstacles to effective and satisfactory communication.

Because cultures exist in different ecologies, they differ in conceptions of what behaviors are appropriate and desirable. When individuals from two different cultures interact, they may find that their conceptions of behavior are incompatible. Misunderstandings occur primarily because: (1) we expect the other person to behave differently from the

AUTHOR'S NOTE: *The research on which this chapter was based was supported in part by grants from the Illinois Office of Education (Bilingual Education Section) to Harry C. Triandis and Rosita D. Albert, and from the National Institute of Education (NIE-G-80-0188) and the University of Illinois Research Board to Rosita D. Albert. The author wishes to thank Harry Triandis, H. Ned Seelye, Peter Imrey, and Charles Bantz for invaluable contributions, and John Adampoulos, Angela Ginorio, Angelica Schultz, Barbara Anderson, David Brinberg, Paul Golstein, Steve Wise, Alok Goswami, and Nancy Hynes for competent research assistance.*

way that he or she in fact behaves, or (2) we use different standards to evaluate his or her behavior. For example, complimenting someone can be seen as an attempt to manipulate, providing information can be interpreted as an attempt to misdirect, and a gift can be perceived as a bride (Albert & Triandis, 1979).

Interpersonal differences caused by variations in cultural assumptions about, and interpretation of, behavior can be understood in terms of the *attributions* that a person makes about the causes of the other's behavior. According to Heider (1958), individuals try to understand the world and render it more predictable by making inferences about the causes of observed behavior. They act in some ways as scientists do and seek to "explain" behaviors by attributing causes to their own behaviors as well as to those of others. The attributions we make can have important consequences for our own behavior toward others: If we see a compliment as an attempt to "butter us up," we are likely to react very differently than if we see it as a way to acknowledge our special contributions. Depending on the attributions we make, we may react extremely favorably, in a neutral manner, or extremely unfavorably.

In analyzing intercultural difficulties it is particularly helpful to focus on attributions since discrepancies in attributions are more likely when two individuals (P and O) belong to different cultures. Such discrepancies may result in misunderstandings, low interpersonal attraction, rejection, and even overt hostility and conflict. If P is to understand O's behavior, it is helpful, and sometimes essential, for P to analyze the situation in a manner that is similar to the way in which O analyzes the situation (Triandis, 1975, 1977).

The present research constitutes an attempt to use some of these ideas to investigate Hispanic-Anglo differences in perceptions and interpretations of intercultural interactions and to use the findings for the development of effective cross-cultural training materials. This chapter describes the procedure for the entire project and reports findings for a subset of the research focusing on situations involving attributions of shame. This aspect of interpersonal behavior was chosen because of its importance in the socialization of Hispanic children. Specifically, we were interested in the following questions:

(1) Do Hispanics differ from Anglos in the attributions made in a given intercultural interaction?
(2) Do teachers differ from pupils?

(3) Are there interactions in which attributional preferences depend on both the ethnic background (Hispanic-Anglo) and the pupil-teacher status of the respondents?

RESEARCH PROCEDURE

The research, conducted in naturalistic settings, employed both emic and etic perspectives, and used a variety of methods, including interviews, structured and unstructured questionnaires, and observations. (See Kim, 1984, for a recent statement about the desirability of integrating several research methodologies in intercultural communication.) It consisted of the following phases:

Phase I

Interviews were conducted with samples of 10- to 15-year-old Hispanic students (N = 150, including approximately equal numbers of Mexican Americans, Puerto Ricans, Cubans, and "other Hispanics," that is, Hispanics from other Latin American countries) from 15 public schools in a northern state. Whenever possible, we interviewed pupils who had come to the continental U.S. recently. Interviews were also conducted with 70 Anglo-American teachers from the same schools who taught Hispanic pupils. Teachers and pupils were from schools in rural as well as urban areas. The proportions of Hispanic pupils, as well as the total enrollments, varied among the schools. Principals and bilingual coordinators were invited to share with the investigators their experience and knowledge about cultural differences in school settings. In addition, naturalistic observation of classroom interactions and of other interactions conducted at a number of different schools provided important information about potential cross-cultural differences.

Phase II

Transcripts of the interviews and notes from the observations were used to generate 146 "critical incidents" in the form of simple stimulus stories. These stories presented a wide variety of school-related situations and behaviors and usually depicted problematic interactions between a Hispanic pupil and an Anglo teacher. Sometimes parents, principals, Anglo pupils, and other Hispanic pupils were also depicted. The following is an example:

Maria could not speak English very well, but she was learning little by little. During English class the teacher was talking and asking the children some questions on grammar. Maria raised her hand, but the teacher did not see her. Maria wanted to answer so badly that she began to give the answer out loud.

Phase III

Sets of stories, each followed by one or more questions (e.g., Why did Maria begin to give the answer even though the teacher had not called on her? What did the teacher do when Maria gave the answer?), were administered in the form of booklets to samples of Hispanic students (N = 300, primarily Mexicans and Puerto Ricans, but also other Hispanics) and Anglo teachers (N = 62) in 10 schools. Control groups of Anglo students (N = 100) and Hispanic teachers (N = 42) were also employed.

Approximately 20 Hispanic students, and 10 to 12 persons from each of the other groups (Anglo students, Hispanic and Anglo teachers), responded to each stimulus story. Hispanic participants received booklets in Spanish and English, and Anglo participants received them in English. Participants were asked to read each story carefully and then to answer in their own words the questions posed at the end of the story. The questions focused primarily on the behaviors, but also on the feelings and cognitions of Hispanic pupils and Anglo teachers in the stimulus stories. Approximately 50 answers or free attributions were obtained for each of the 246 questions asked.

Phase IV

The approximately 12,500 free attributions obtained from the participants in Phase III were examined by a bicultural, bilingual panel of four judges. These judges attempted to synthesize the answers obtained by selecting for each question three or four attributions which fulfilled a number of criteria specified in advance, including frequency of mention by each cultural group and likelihood of a cultural basis for the attributions. In most cases the judges tried to select two attributions that they felt were predominantly Hispanic, and two that they considered to be predominantly Anglo or North-American.

A final set of episodes, each consisting of a story followed by a question and by three—or, more commonly, four—attributions, was constructed. The three or four attributions were presented in a paired-comparison format so that each attribution was paired with each of the others. Thus, when four attributions were presented, attribution 1 was paired with attributions 2, 3, and 4, attribution 2 was paired with attributions 3 and 4, and attribution 3 was paired with attribution 4. This yielded either six paired comparisons (for four attributions) or three paired comparisons (for three attributions) for each episode.

There were 176 different episodes and a total of 987 paired comparisons in the final set. The episodes were randomly assembled into small booklets and their order within the booklets was counter-balanced. In addition, nine randomly selected episodes were used for a reliability check and were presented four times throughout the final set.

Phase V

New samples of fifth- through ninth-grade students (Hispanics N = 208, Anglos N = 256) and teachers (Anglos N = 18, and Hispanics N = 18) were given booklets containing the episodes with the paired attributions. For each pair of attributions they were asked to select the attribution that they felt best answered the question at the end of the story. Hispanic participants received booklets in Spanish or English, and Anglo participants received them in English. Each of the teachers rated the entire set of 176 episodes, which contained 987 paired comparisons. Each of the students rated approximately 8% to 10% of the total set of episodes.

ANALYSES

Demographic Characteristics of the Participants in Phase V

Almost all the Anglo teachers and pupils were born in the United States. The Hispanic pupils were primarily of Mexican origin, although our sample also included a sizable number of Puerto Ricans and a few students from other Latin American countries. The Hispanic teachers came from a variety of Latin American countries including Mexico, Ecuador, and Cuba. For analysis purposes all Hispanics were combined into one group because of the small number of subjects: Only 18 Hispanic teachers and an average of 15 Hispanic pupils rated each story. Although phase I data had been gathered from four subgroups of Hispanics, it was not possible to obtain sufficiently large samples to analyze for subgroup differences in later phases.

Most of the Hispanic pupils (72%) reported having been in the continental United States for less than 2 years; the remaining 28% indicated they had been here longer. Students ranged in age from 8 to 16, with an average age of 13 for Hispanic pupils and 12 for Anglo pupils. Their grade levels ranged from fourth to ninth, with a preponderance of seventh and eighth graders.

Reliability Checks

As previously mentioned, nine stories of the total set were repeated (two times in two different booklets) in order to check the reliability of the choices made by the respondents. Reliability indices were obtained for each group of subjects by dividing the number of agreements (instances in which subjects chose the same alternative in the two repetitions appearing in the same booklet) by the total number of choices made. The average reliability was .819 for Anglo pupils, .932 for Anglo teachers, .792 for Hispanic pupils, and .921 for Hispanic teachers. These reliability scores were considered relatively high, particularly for pupils.

Preliminary Analyses

The proportions of Hispanic pupils, Anglo pupils, Hispanic teachers, and Anglo teachers choosing each attribution in each of the paired comparisons per episode in phase V were obtained. Tests of the difference between two proportions were performed for differences between each group of subjects (e.g., Anglo teachers) and each of the other groups (e.g., Hispanic students, Hispanic teachers, Anglo students).

All possible comparisons between groups of subjects for all pairs of attributions resulted in a total of 5922 comparisons, of which 3948 were cross-cultural (between Hispanics and Anglos). Of these comparisons, 751 were statistically significant, far exceeding the number expected by chance alone (197). A total of 1974 comparisons in the data set were intracultural, and 401 of these were significant. (See Albert, 1983b, for a summary of the tests made and the significant comparisons found.)

The preliminary analyses showed four times as many significant differences overall as would be expected by chance. The greatest number of differences, as expected, was found between Hispanic pupils and American teachers. One indication of this is provided by the finding that, out of 176 episodes used in this phase of research, 141 showed a significant difference in one or more comparisons between Hispanic pupils and Anglo teachers.

Aggregate Analyses

The preliminary analyses suggested that there were a number of important cross-cultural as well as teacher-pupil differences that deserved to be examined more thoroughly. Rather than looking at 36 comparisons per story, the data were aggregated for each story to answer the following questions: Do the four groups of subjects (Anglo teachers, Hispanic teachers, Anglo students, Hispanic students) differ with respect to the kinds of attributions they prefer in a given interaction situation? Do Hispanics differ from Anglos, and do teachers differ from pupils in their choices? Are there interactions between the Hispanic-Anglo factor and the Teacher-Pupil factor?

The methods of Imrey, Johnson, and Koch (1976) were utilized to summarize the data for each question and to assess the level of statistical significance associated with the Anglo-Hispanic and the teacher-student dichotomies, as well as the interaction between them. Basically, preference parameters that summarized the preferences of each group were obtained. Chi-square tests of significance were then performed on these preference scores for the Hispanic-Anglo factor, the Teacher-Pupil factor, and the interaction.

A Bradley-Terry model (Bradley & Terry, 1952) was fit to the observed choice proportions within each of the four groups by the method of weighted least-squares. This model allows summarization of the choice propensities of the members of each group and makes it possible to determine the degree of statistical significance of group-asso-ciated variation by standard multivariate linear statistical models. Bradley-Terry preference parameters are the best estimates provided by the model of how each group perceived each of the four attributions across all comparisons.

There were 104 stories which fit the Bradley-Terry model. (These yielded nonsignificant chi-squares for model fit.) These stories were analyzed for the effects of the cultural factor (Hispanic versus Anglo), the status factor (Teachers versus Pupils), and the interaction between the two factors.

The stories that did not fit the model were examined by marginal analysis. For each item, the proportions of individuals selecting that item from each of the paired comparisons were averaged. For inference and smoothing, these observed marginal preference proportions were analyzed using a log-linear model involving the main effects of Hispanic versus Anglo and Teacher versus Student dichotomies. Variances and covariances of the marginal preference proportions were estimated from the data and weighted least-squares fitting methods used. Resulting Wald (1943) tests for no interaction and for the main effects of Anglo versus Hispanic and Teacher versus Student dichotomies were calculated. Statistical computing was accomplished using the computer program GENCAT (Landis, Stanish, & Koch, 1976).

RESULTS

In order to examine differences in episodes containing attributions of shame, criteria had to be devised for the selection of appropriate stories. For a story to be included it had to have at least one attribution that specifically mentioned the words "shame" or "ashamed." In addition, two judges working independently had to agree that the story should be included. Finally, all stories with attributions mentioning shame would have to be included. There were 12 stories in the total set that fulfilled these criteria.

For each story chi-squares based on the preference parameters were computed for a Hispanic-Anglo main effect, a teacher-pupil main effect, and an interaction. Table 3.1 presents the results of these analyses.

As shown in Table 3.1 there were five significant differences for the Hispanic-Anglo factor, six for the Teacher-Pupil factor, and two significant interactions. Of the 12 stories, 10 had one or more significant chi-squares. Each of these significant differences is discussed below by examining the specific preference parameters obtained. These parameters are the best estimates priovided by the Bradley-Terry model of how each group perceived each of the four attributions. The parameters not only rank the alternatives by preference, but also provide an estimate of the degree of preference for that attribution relative to the other three attributions. (Note that the sum across the four attributions is 1.00 for each group of respondents.) Preference parameters for attributions to the 12 stories are presented in Table 3.2.

Below, Hispanic-Anglo differences are presented first, followed by Teacher-Pupil differences. For each story, differences with respect to the attribution of shame are described, followed by other differences suggested by the preference parameters.

Hispanic-Anglo Differences

Significant differences between Hispanics and Anglos, with Hispanics selecting attributions of shame more frequently than Anglos, were expected. There were five stories—11B, 17B, 48, 52, and 139C—which

TABLE 3.1
Chi-Squares for Stories with Shame Attributions

Story Number	Analysis	Anglo-Hispanic Effect	Teacher-Pupil Effect	Interaction
11B	Marginal	56.46***	3.93	3.96
14	Bradley-Terry	4.23	12.33**	1.78
17B	Marginal	7.61*	18.63***	2.17
18A	Bradley-Terry	6.18	27.16***	6.25
32B	Bradley-Terry	3.24	4.20	3.71
48	Marginal	17.77***	6.98	4.28
52	Marginal	30.11***	7.36	8.69*
74	Marginal	.19	13.12***	21.51***
108	Marginal	4.75	36.10***	2.10
138B	Bradley-Terry	6.22	15.08***	2.63
139A	Marginal	2.43	7.25	3.28
139C	Bradley-Terry	24.05***	5.44	4.17

*$p < .05$; **$p < .01$; ***$p < .005$.

showed significant Hispanic-Anglo differences. Preference parameters for these stories indicate that, with the expection of story 11B, Hispanics had higher preferences for the shame attribution than did Anglos.

In story 17B, which described how Jesus really felt about being late for class, Hispanic students had a very strong preference for attribution 4 (ashamed about being late), whereas Anglos, as well as Hispanic teachers, found this the least preferable alternative. Anglos preferred attribution 2 (surprised because he did not understand why it was such a problem) and 3 (that he was not doing something wrong). In both instances, their preferences were higher than the Hispanic preferences.

Similarly in story 48, which was about why Carlos felt uncomfortable when Mrs. Bates praised or corrected him in front of the class, the shame attribution was second in preference among the Hispanics, but last among the Anglos. Although both Anglos and Hispanics chose attribution 4 (he thought the other children were going to make fun of him) more than other alternatives, Anglos were higher in their preference than were Hispanics.

In story 52, which discusses why Antonia does not speak up in front of her classmates, the biggest difference beteween Hispanics and Anglos occurred in their responses to attribution 1 (she is ashamed), with Hispanics choosing this alternative more than Anglos. This occurred even though the ashamed attribution was the third choice for both cultural groups. Anglos more than Hispanics preferred attribution 2

TABLE 3.2
Preference Parameters for Stories with Shame Attributions

Stories and Attributions	AP	AT	HP	HT
11B. Marisa goes to the washroom without permission because:				
1. She is in a hurry and does not have time to ask permission.	.33	.36	.17	.22
2. She has bad manners.	.28	.26	.16	.18
3. She is ashamed to say where she is going.	.37	.37	.26	.30
4. She wanted to chew gum.	.02	.01	.41	.30
14. Estela left the group of non-Spanish-speaking children midway through the exercise because:				
1. They did not know Spanish and she did not know English.	.28	.14	.37	.26
2. She felt frustrated because the assignment was too hard for her.	.17	.42	.20	.25
3. The children did not want to work with her.	.13	.05	.09	.04
4. She was ashamed that she could not talk very well with the other children.	.41	.38	.35	.45
17B. Jesus was stopped by the principal for being late for class and told that the principal wanted to see his mother. About being late, Jesus really felt:				
1. Scared because his mother would scold him.	.25	.31	.19	.30
2. Surprised because he did not understand why it was such a problem.	.28	.35	.18	.30
3. That he was not doing something wrong.	.28	.28	.18	.23
4. Ashamed about being late.	.19	.06	.45	.17
18A. Jorge does not want to go to his teacher's desk after she told him he could not go without raising his hand because:				
1. He is ashamed after being scolded in front of the class.	.23	.50	.30	.35
2. He feels rejected by the teacher.	.32	.42	.21	.38
3. He is a very sensitive child.	.22	.06	.21	.20
4. He thinks the teacher is too strict.	.23	.03	.27	.07
32B. Ramon, a fifth-grade student, was upset about having to use a fourth-grade book when he was in a mixed fourth, and fifth-grade class because:				
1. He did not want to fall behind.	.17	.15	.40	.18
2. He thought that the teacher was flunking him.	.35	.35	.19	.45
3. He felt insulted and ashamed.	.48	.51	.41	.37
48. Carlos was uncomfortable when Mrs. Bates praised or corrected him in front of the class because:				
1. The teacher made him feel different from the other children.	.24	.28	.23	.26

(continued)

TABLE 3.2 Continued

Stories and Attributions	AP	AT	HP	HT
2. He was nervous.	.20	.19	.19	.17
3. He was ashamed.	.15	.18	.23	.27
4. He thought the other children were going to make fun of him.	.41	.35	.35	.30
52. Antonia doesn't speak up in front of her classmates because:				
1. She is ashamed.	.18	.16	.28	.24
2. She is shy.	.34	.37	.27	.30
3. She is afraid that her classmates will make fun of her.	.31	.31	.35	.35
4. She was taught that girls do not speak in front of a group.	.17	.16	.10	.11
74. Mario did not go to school during his suspension from the school bus because:				
1. He was ashamed.	.29	.23	.29	.24
2. His parents thought he was suspended from school, too.	.30	.29	.31	.30
3. His parents did not care if he went to school.	.20	.15	.21.	.16
4. His parents were angry at the bus suspension and decided not to send him to school.	.21	.32	.18	.29
108. Ramon does not want to take a slip home about the school's open house because:				
1. He is afraid the teacher will complain about him to his parents.	.23	.25	.22	.27
2. He is ashamed to bring his parents to the open house because they do not speak English.	.23	.37	.21	.37
3. He knows his parents are not interested in an exhibition of children's work.	.23	.26	.16	.20
4. His work for the exhibition is not good and he does not want his parents to see it.	.32	.12	.41	.16
138B. Pancho does not want to go to class, and after trying to calm him, his mother hits him in front of other people because:				
1. She wanted to make him feel ashamed, so that he would never disobey her again.	.18	.23	.28	.21
2. She thought that Pancho did not want her to meet his teacher.	.17	.11	.13	.09
3. She was ashamed of Pancho's behavior.	.51	.41	.42	.19
4. She was so angry, she could not control herself.	.14	.26	.16	.52
139A. Cristina had not told her teacher that she had not understood him earlier because:				
1. She was afraid that the teacher would get angry.	.27	.32	.30	.35
2. She was ashamed.	.29	.33	.31	.33

TABLE 3.2 Continued

3. The teacher had not given her the opportunity to ask him.	.25	.24	.27	.25
4. She did not think it was important enough to bother the teacher.	.19	.11	.12	.07
139C. When her teacher told her that if she had not understood she should have told him earlier, Cristina feels:				
1. Angry.	.15	.13	.06	.04
2. Ashamed.	.30	.23	.53	.62
3. Humiliated.	.32	.58	.26	.23
4. Frightened.	.23	.07	.15	.11

NOTE. The stories have been maximally condensed here only to provide information that is essential for understanding the attributions. AP = Anglo Pupils; AT = Anglo Teachers; HP = Hispanic Pupils; HT = Hispanic Teachers.

(she is shy), and Hispanics more than Anglos (although by a small margin) preferred attribution 3 (she is afraid that her classmates will make fun of her).

In story 139C, Hispanics chose attribution 2 (ashamed) in answer to how Cristina felt when the teacher told her she should have told him earlier that she had not understood him. This Hispanic choice is extremely strong for both teachers and pupils, and greater than the Anglo preference for this alternative by a high order of magnitude (preference parameters were .53 and .62 for Hispanic students and teachers respectively, and .30 and .23 for Anglo students and teachers). Anglos, on the other hand, chose attribution 3 (humiliated) more than Hispanics. The alternative "angry" was the least preferred by both cultures and was rarely chosen by Hispanics.

The one exception to the trend of Hispanics choosing attributions of "ashamed" more than Anglos occurred in story 11B. In response to why Maria goes to the washroom without permission, the Anglos chose attribution 3 (she is ashamed to say where she is going) more than the Hispanics. Nevertheless, the "ashamed" attribution was the second choice for Hispanic pupils and was tied with attribution 4 (she wanted to chew gum), for first choice among Hispanic teachers. Hispanic pupils found attribution 4 more compelling.

Thus, in four out of five stories that exhibited significant differences between Hispanics and Anglos, the Hispanics showed a higher preference for attributions of shame than did the Anglos. Furthermore, this attribution was often preferred to other attributions by Hispanics. In several instances the preference ratings given to this attribution showed the largest differences between Hispanics and Anglos.

Seven stories did not exhibit a significant Hispanic-Anglos effect: 14, 18A, 32B, 74, 108, 138B, and 139A. When the preference parameters for these stories were examined, it became apparent that parameters for the attribution of shame were very high for Hispanics. The apparent difference between these stories and the ones with significant Hispanic-Anglo effects was that for five out of the seven stories (14, 18A, 32B, 108, and 138B), Anglos as well as Hispanics gave their highest preference to the shame attributions. By comparison, Anglos gave their lowest or next to lowest ratings to the shame attribution for three of the stories that showed a significant Hispanic-Anglo difference (17B, 48, and 52). Apparently, in these three situations, Anglos found other attributions (detailed earlier for each story) more compelling. For most of the stories, the shame attribution was highly preferred by the Hispanics. Significant differences occurred primarily when Anglos gave it a lower preference rating relative to other attributions.

Teacher-Pupil Differences

There were six stories for which significant differences in Teacher-Pupil preferences were observed: stories 14, 17B, 18A, 74, 108, and 138B. For three of these stories (14, 18A, and 108), Teachers had higher preference parameters than Pupils, while for the other three (17B, 74, and 138B),Pupils had higher parameters than Teachers. Overall, neither group had a greater preference for attributions of shame.

Story 14 concerned Estela's leaving a group of non-Spanish speaking girls during an exercise. When asked why Estela left the group, all groups had high preference scores for attribution 4 (she was ashamed that she could not talk very well with the other children), with teachers' (especially Hispanic teachers') scores being slightly higher. Pupils, particularly Hispanic pupils, preferred attribution 1 (they did not know Spanish and she did not know English) more than teachers did, and teachers (particularly Anglo teachers) preferred attribution 2 (she felt frustrated because the assignment was hard for her) more than pupils did. For this story, differences between teachers and pupils as evidenced by preference parameters were greater for attributions 1 and 2 than for the shame attribution.

Story 17B, mentioned above in connection with Hispanic-Anglo differences, also showed teacher-pupil differences: Pupils, especially Hispanic pupils, preferred the attribution that Jesus really felt ashamed about being late for class more than teachers. Teachers preferred alternative 2 (Jesus really felt surprised because he did not understand why it was such a problem), and alternative 1 (Jesus really felt scared because his mother would scold him) more than pupils.

Story 18A dealt with why George did not want to go to his teacher's desk after the teacher told him he could not do it without raising his hand. Teachers chose attribution 1 (he is ashamed after being scolded in front of the class) more than pupils did, and this was the attribution preferred by Anglo teachers above all other attributions. Teachers preferred attribution 2 (he feels rejected by the teacher) more than pupils. Pupils, on the other hand, preferred attribution 4 (he thinks the teacher is too strict) and attribution 3 (he is a very sensitive child).

Story 74, which dealt with the reasons why Mario did not go to school during the five days in which he was suspended from the school bus, showed both a main effect for the Teacher-Pupil factor and an interaction. Students were more likely than teachers to choose attribution 1 (he was ashamed) and attribution 3 (his parents did not care if he went to school), while teachers were more likely than students to prefer attribution 4 (his parents were angry at the bus suspension and decided not to send him to school). Attribution 2 (his parents thought he was suspended from school) showed no differences between the groups.

Attributions to story 108, in which Ramon is reluctant to take home a slip about the school open house, revealed two major differences. Teachers preferred attribution 2 (he is ashamed to bring his parents to the open house because they do not speak English) more than pupils. The largest difference between teachers and pupils was found for attribution 4 (his work for the exhibition is not good and he does not want his parents to see it), with pupils preferring it much more, and teachers preferring it much less, than all other alternatives.

Story 138B centered on why Mrs. Garcia finally hits her son Pablo in front of other people when he doesn't want to go to school. This story had two attributions involving the notion of shame: (1) She wanted to make him feel ashamed, so that he would never disobey her again, and (3) she was ashamed of Pablo's behavior. Attribution 3 was preferred by pupils more than teachers, and attribution 1 did not exhibit a clear teacher-pupil difference. Large differences occurred for attribution 4 (she was so angry, she could not control herself), with teachers, particularly Hispanic teachers, preferring it more than pupils.

There were six stories (11B, 32B, 48, 52, 139A, and 139C) that did not have significant teacher-pupil differences. The preference parameters for these stories indicate that both teachers and pupils had high scores for the shame attribution in four of these stories (11B, 32B, 139A, and 139C). No significant differences occurred between pupils and teachers in these stories; both groups had similar ratings for most attributions, including the shame attribution.

In summary, 10 of the 12 stories that had one or more explicit attributions involving shame showed significant differences. Five of these differences were Hispanic-Anglo differences, with Hispanics demonstrating higher preference parameters for the attributions involving shame than did Anglos. Six of the significant differences were teacher-pupil differences, with teachers having higher preference parameters in three of the stories, and pupils having higher preference parameters in the other three. A number of other significant findings regarding a variety of other attributions were also reported. In most of the 12 stories, the shame attribution received very high preference parameters compared to other attributions.

DISCUSSION

The results presented (as well as those obtained in the remainder of the study) have both theoretical and practical implications. Theoretically, the study contributes to the discovery of attributional differences significant for Hispanic-Anglo interactions. This finding is important not only for understanding Hispanic-Anglo interactions but also for developing integrative theories of intercultural relations based on empirical data.

Experimental (Kagan, 1977) as well as longitudinal evidence (Holtzman, Díaz-Guererro, & Swartz, 1975) suggests that Hispanics are more interpersonally oriented than the Anglo-Americans. What is needed is empirical and conceptual work that delineates components of this dimension. This is indeed what we have begun to provide with the analysis presented in this chapter. The present data suggest that "shame" is an important component of Hispanic-American interpersonal orientation and presents specific instances in which differences with respect to attributions of shame occur between Hispanics and Anglos. The present data further suggest the possibility that, in at least some situations, Anglos may not view "shame" with the same importance as Hispanics. The salience of this concept may be higher for Hispanics because of their collectivistic culture (Triandis, in press) which contrasts with the individualistic Anglo culture of the United States. Clearly these ideas deserve further investigation. The present data are limited, offering only the first steps toward the empirical discovery of components of the interpersonal orientation.

The findings of the present study also have important implications for training. If Anglos and Hispanics are to interact effectively, they must understand how the other ethnic group views a wide variety of situations. For example, Anglo teachers may learn that Hispanic pupils are likely to feel shame more frequently than Anglo pupils do and react differently than Anglo pupils in certain situations.

Hispanics are one of the largest ethnic groups in schools in the United States. They have the highest dropout rate of any group. Training Anglo-American teachers to understand the Hispanic cultural background, and helping Hispanic pupils to understand the Anglo perspective, therefore, is an important educational issue. Toward this goal, episodes in which significant differences were observed between Hispanic pupils and American teachers have been selected for inclusion in two intercultural sensitizers (ICS) or culture assimilators. (See Albert, 1983a, for a discussion of the ICS as a method for intercultural training.) One of these intercultural sensitizers (Albert, 1984a), is addressed primarily to American educators as well as to other persons who work closely with Hispanic pupils. The other (Albert, 1984b) is addressed primarily to Hispanic pupils.

These materials have been used in two field experiments designed to assess their effectiveness in sensitizing Anglo-American teachers to the attributions made by Hispanic children (Albert & Crespo, 1982; Albert, Triandis, Brinberg, Ginorio, & Anderson, 1979; Crespo, 1982). The results indicated that the ICS and role-playing exercises based on the ICS were both significantly more effective than either a control condition or "self-insight" training (Kraemer, 1973, 1978) in affecting the attributions made by Anglo teachers to the behaviors of Hispanic pupils.

A variety of other propositions regarding significant dimensions of cultural difference between Hispanics and Anglos are being tested with the data. It is hoped that these and other similar efforts will contribute to a greater understanding of differences which may create obstacles to effective communication between Hispanics and Anglo-Americans in the United States.

REFERENCES

Albert, R. D. (1983a). The intercultural sensitizer or culture assimilator: A cognitive approach. In D. Landis & R. Brislin (Eds.), *Handbook of intercultural training, Vol II: Issues in training methodology* (pp. 186-217). New York: Pergamon Press.

Albert, R. D. (1983b). Mexican-American children in educational settings: Research on children's and teachers' perceptions and interpretations of behavior. In E. E. Garcia (Ed.), *The Mexican-American child: Language, cognition and social development* (pp. 1983-194). Tempe: Arizona State University.

Albert, R. D. (1984a). *Communicating across cultures.* Manuscript submitted for publication.

Albert, R. D. (1984b). *Understanding North Americans: A guide for Hispanic pupils.* Manuscript submitted for publication.

Albert, R. D., & Crespo, O. I. (1982, March). *Cross-cultural sensitization of teachers of Hispanic pupils: New procedures and an experimental evaluation of their effects in naturalistic settings.* Paper presented at the meeting of the American Educational Research Association, New York.

Albert, R. D., & Triandis, H. C. (1979). Cross-cultural training: A theoretical framework and some observations. In H. T. Trueba & C. Barnett-Mizrahi (Eds.), *Bilingual multicultural education and the professional: From theory to practice* (pp. 181-194). Rowley, MA: Newbury House.

Albert, R. D., Triandis, H. C., Brinberg, D., Ginorio, A., & Anderson, B. (1979). *Measurement procedures for evaluating cross-cultural training programs.* Unpublished manuscript.

Bradley, R. A., & Terry, M. E. (1952). Rank analysis of incomplete block designs. I: The method of paired-comparisons. *Biometrika, 39,* 324-345.

Crespo, O. I. (1982). *Effects of cross-cultural training on the attributions and attitudes of students in a teacher-training program.* Unpublished doctoral dissertation, University of Illinois.

Heider, F. (1958). *The psychology of interpersonal relations.* New York: Wiley.

Holtzman, W. H., Díaz-Guerrero, R., & Swartz, J. D. (1975). *Personality development in two cultures.* Austin: University of Texas Press.

Imrey, P. B., Johnson, W. D., & Koch, C. G. (1976). An incomplete contingency table approach to paired-comparison experiments. *Journal of the American Statistical Association, 71,* 614-623.

Kagan, S. (1977). Social motives and behaviors of Mexican-American and Anglo-American children. In J. L. Martinez, Jr. (Ed.), *Chicano psychology* (pp. 45-85). New York: Academic Press.

Kim, Y. Y. (1984). Searching for creative integration. In W. B. Gudykunst & Y. Y. Kim (Eds.), *Methods for Intercultural Research. International and Intercultural Com-*

munication Annual (Vol. VIII, pp. 13-30). Beverly Hills, CA: Sage.

Kraemer, A. J. (1973). *Development of a cultural self-awareness approach to instruction in intercultural communication* (HumRRO Technical Report 73-117). Alexandria, VA: Human Resources Research Organization.

Kraemer, A. J. (1978). *Teacher training workshop in intercultural communication. Instructors guide* (revised).

Landis, J. R., Stanish, W. M., Freeman J. L., & Koch, G. G. (1976). A computer program for the generalized chi-square analysis of categorical data using weighted least squares (GENCAT). *Computer Programs in Biomedicine, 6,* 196-231.

Triandis, H. C. (1975). Cultural training, cognitive complexity, and interpersonal attitudes. In R. Brislin, S. Bochner, & W. Lonner (Eds.), *Cross-cultural perspectives on learning* (pp. 39-77). New York: Sage/Halsted/Wiley.

Triandis, H. C. (1977). *Interpersonal behavior.* Monterey, CA: Brooks/Cole.

Triandis, H. C. (in press). Collectivism vs. individualism: A reconceptualization of a basic concept in cross-cultural social psychology. In C. Bagley & G. K. Verma (Eds.) *Personality, cognition and values: Cross-cultural perspectives of childhood and adolescence.* London: Macmillan.

Wald, A. (1943). Tests of statistical hypotheses concerning several parameters when the number of observations is large. *Transactions of the American Mathematical Society, 54,* 426-482.

4

Subjective Intergroup Distances of Blacks and Whites

OLIVER C.S. TZENG   •   C. J. DUVALL   •   ROGER WARE   •
ROBERT NEEL   •   ROBERT FORTIER   •
Purdue University School of Science

This study investigates differences in Blacks' and Whites' affective attributions to three intergroup distances: alienation, separatism, and favoritism. For this purpose, semantic differential ratings of Blacks and Whites on 10 concepts that define the contents of these intergroup distances were obtained from Osgood and associates' Atlas of Affective Meaning. Data were collected from some 650 teenage males in both cultures and were analyzed for (1) bicultural comparisons on individual affective components (Evaluation, Potency, and Activity) for each concept, (2) comparisons of indigenous cultural factor structures for the 10 concepts, (3) comparisons of structural relationships among the three affective components, and (4) comparisons of personal self with two collective (in- and outgroup) selves. Results indicate that the two cultures differed significantly in all comparisons pertaining to social alienation, within-group favoritism, and between-group hostility. To facilitate intercultural interactions, the nature of these differences is discussed in the realms of socioeconomics, racial hostility, social environment, and implicit affective attribution.

The present study investigates three types of intergroup distances between Blacks and Whites in the United States—alienation, separatism, and favoritism. Here, *alienation* refers to the consequence of thoughts regarding rejection, indifference, and detachment from the members of the other group or from the environment as a whole; *separatism* represents the attitudinal dichotomization between the two groups with respect to various issues; and *favoritism* denotes the tendency toward a favorable evaluation of those ideas, values, and actions that are in alignment with the interest of one's own group.

In studying *alienation* among Blacks and Whites, Shingles (1979) and Suen (1983) reported that Black students on a predominantly White campus felt more alienated than did White students. Similarly, Allen (1982) found that many Black students in a predominantly White university lacked the coping mechanisms and felt alienated from the environment. Generally, studies have reported a higher level experience of alienation by Blacks, particularly Black youths, than among their White counterparts. Schuman and Hatchett (1974) found that alienation occurred most among young Blacks with the lowest or highest education in a predominantly White environment. Also, Turner and Wilson (1976) reported a higher level alienation among young Blacks with low occupational status.

Many investigators have also shown the existence of *separatism* in the two groups. For example, Campbell (1971) found that young Blacks tended to be separatistic in their attitudes toward White society and willing to use violent means for social change (see also, Brown, Nordlie, & Thomas, 1977, and Schuman & Hatchett, 1974 for similar findings). This finding does not necessarily suggest that Blacks and Whites differ in their values, goals, and racial tolerance. In fact, Landis and his associates (1976) reported that Blacks and Whites had similar goals and ideals in education, employment, and economic success. In addition, when members of both groups shared the same values, they made similar judgments of other Blacks and Whites (O'Gorman, 1979).

Other comparisons of Blacks and Whites have indicated within-race *favoritism*. Studies have generally shown that Blacks evaluated Blacks more favorably than Whites, and Whites evaluated Whites more favorably than Blacks (Longshore, 1979; Scontrino, Larson, & Fiedler, 1977). Jarmon (1980), however, reported a finding that indicated a tendency among Blacks to evaluate Blacks even more negatively than Whites did.

Research so far has been unsuccessful in providing any clear, conclusive information about how Blacks and Whites differ in their subjective experiences of intergroup distance. Notably, no work has been reported in the literature that delineates the interrelatedness of the three psychological attributes within a single theoretical system and compares the two ethnic groups along these dimensions simultaneously. The present study is an initial attempt to bridge this missing link.

Subjective Culture and Affective Attribution

Human behavior is viewed to be influenced by at least two aspects of culture (Tzeng & Osgood, 1976; Tzeng, 1983). The first aspect is *objective culture*, which contains such social indicators as names (concepts) of things, ethnicity, gender, age, education, economic background, employment, and housing. These indicators are recognizable characteristics of people in a given social environment. The other aspect is the *subjective culture,* which contains such social indicators as feeling, believing, conceiving, judging, hoping, intending, and meaning. These indicators represent the mental characteristics of members of a culture that cannot be directly observed. Interactions between these two aspects of culture involve evaluation processes and behavioral intentions with respect to various life experiences. Therefore, the subjective characteristics of cultural members reflect the attributional profiles of the objective culture.

Through the processes of social learning and interactions with life-environments, individuals assimilate the subjective characteristics of each culture. They develop two systems: (1) the *cognitive system* (denotation), which represents a person's descriptive (referential) attributions or categorizations of objects and events, and (2) the *affective system,* which represents a person's emotional and autonomic attributions toward objects (e.g., distinguishing a person as being *good* or *bad*). Due to the mental processes involved in metaphorizing new life events with old experiences, affective attribution usually includes semantic generalizations across a wide range of life contexts and social situations. Thus, affective attribution significantly influences the individual's overt behaviors and dispositions (Osgood, Miron, & May, 1975).

Individuals within a cultural group share common cognitive and affective characteristics that may be different from those of other cultural groups (Triandis, 1972). Therefore, when members of two cultural (ethnic) groups interact, the dissimilarity between their subjective cultural characteristics tends to increase intergroup distance, which, in turn, tends to irritate interracial relations. The resultant difficulties include stereotyping, prejudice, racism, discrimination, and poor communication (see Allen, 1982; Deutsch, Katz, & Jensen, 1968).

In this study, the subjective characteristics of the Black and White ethnic cultures will be explored. Specifically, it compares the two cultures in terms of three indices of intergroup distances: alienation, separatism, and favoritism.

METHOD

To study these intergroup distances, data from Osgood, Miron, and May's (1975) *Atlas of Affective Meaning* for Black and White cultures in the United States were used to generate within-culture profiles and between-ethnic group comparisons. The *Atlas of Affective Meaning* is briefly described below.

Osgood and his associates developed the *Atlas of Affective Meaning* to investigate affective attributions of conceptions in and across 30 language/culture communities around the world (Osgood et al., 1975). Three functional phases were used to compile the *Atlas*.

The first phase was the *tool-making phase*, in which culturally indigenous semantic markers were constructed to represent three pan-cultural (i.e., functionally equivalent) affective components: Evaluation (E: represented by such scales as good/bad), Potency (P = strong/weak), and Activity (A = active/passive).

The second phase was the *tool-using phase*, which included three operational steps: (1) identification of some 620 cross-culturally common concepts that tap diverse conceptual domains of human life experiences, (2) semantic differential ratings of these concepts by some 650 teenage males in each of the 30 communities, (3) analyses of subject ratings for compilation of an *Atlas* table for each community including the "raw" factor scores (E, P, and A) and the "standard" factor scores of each concept. The standard factor scores were obtained from normalizing the raw factor scores with respect to the means and standard deviations of all 620 concepts (E-Z, P-Z, and A-Z). Additional statistical indices were also derived, including Standardized Familiarity ratings, Meaningfulness, Polarization, and Cultural Instability measures (Osgood et al., 1975; Tzeng, 1983).

The third phase involved *category analysis*. The 620 *Atlas* concepts were organized into some 50 conceptual categories, each representing an important domain of human experiences. For the present study, the Ingroup/Outgroup category was used because affect attribution to the concepts in this category were considered closely related to the issues of alienation, separatism, and favoritism.

For the present study, factor scores of ten concepts were selected from the Ingroup/Outgroup category in the *Atlas of Affective Meaning* for both the Black and White cultures in the United States. These concepts were I-Myself, Most People, Person, Enemy, Foreigner, Friend, Family, Stranger, White Race, and Black Race. For each concept, the measures obtained from the *Atlas* included the raw factor scores on E, P, and A, and the standard factor scores E-Z, P-Z, and A-Z. While the raw factor scores depict within-culture characteristics, the standard factor scores serve as the quantitative basis for between-culture comparisons.

Analysis of the data was performed first by evaluating the Black-White differences in the standard factor scores for each concept. A deviation of .50 or greater in scores was considered a "significant" difference (see Osgood et al., 1975). To compare the conceptual structures between Blacks and Whites, principal components analysis with varimax rotation was performed for each group based on the intercorrelations among the ten concepts, computed across the E, P, and A components simultaneously. Also, to identify the structural relationships among affective components within each culture, correlation coefficients were computed between the E, P, and A components across all 10 concepts and then factor analyzed through principal component analysis with varimax rotation. Finally, results from all analyses were integrated and interpreted in terms of the differences in the two cultures with regard to both the affective responses to the selected concepts and the structural relationships among the concepts and the affective components.

RESULTS

Differences in Affective Attribution

The standard factor scores of the concepts for both cultures are reported in Table 4.1. Comparisons of the scores on the individual affective components reveal a number of similarities and differences between the two cultures. On the *Evaluation* component, three observations can be made: (1) For both groups, the race concept of the indigenous culture was positively evaluated, whereas the race concept of the other culture was negatively evaluated. (2) The concept I-Myself was positive for the White group but close to neutral for the Black group. (3) The concepts Foreigner and Stranger were negatively evaluated by both the Black and White ethnic groups, with Foreigner being more negative for the Black than for the White and Stranger being more negative for the White than for the Black.

On the Potency component, the Black and White cultures differed on six concepts: (1) Two ego-related concepts (I-Myself and Friend) were positively rated by both cultures, but the Black had much higher intensities. (2) Two concepts representing unfamiliar individuals (Most People and Stranger) were negatively rated by both cultures, but the White has a stronger negative tone. (3) The concept Foreigner also had negative ratings from both groups, but the Black revealed a higher

TABLE 4.1
Bicultural Comparisons on Affective Attribution

Concepts	E - Z		P - Z		A - Z	
	White	Black	White	Black	White	Black
I-Myself	.49	-.01	.37	1.14	2.09	-.54
Most people	.00	.32	-.78	-.23	1.31	1.09
Person	.22	.41	-.11	.13	.75	-.96
Enemy	-2.67	-3.12	-.38	-.23	-.10	3.30
Foreigner	-.03	-.97	-.96	-1.70	.58	.19
Friend	.72	.57	.31	.89	1.87	-.40
Family	.77	1.04	.65	.89	1.07	.70
Stranger	-1.14	-.47	-.64	-.14	.11	.72
White race	.49	-.97	1.22	-1.90	.90	2.84
Black race	-.87	.50	-.11	.20	.37	1.43

NOTE: Values in this table are standard factor scores of each concept on Evaluation (E), Potency (P), and Activity (A) components. The underlined pair of values indicates bicultural difference with a magnitude of .50 or more.

intensity. (4) On the concept Black Race, the two cultures did not differ significantly (both with neutral scores). (5) On the concept White Race, within-culture endorsement by the White subjects and between-culture negativism by the Black subjects were clearly indicated.

On the Activity component, the Black and White cultures were different in several ways: (1) Three ego-related concepts (I-Myself, Friend, and Person) were distributed in two opposite semantic polarities, with the White anchoring on the positive pole and the Black on the negative pole. (2) Conversely, the concept Enemy was close to neutrality for the White culture (A-Z = – 10) but extremely active in the Black culture (A-Z = 3.30). (3) While the two race concepts (Black Race and White Race) received positive Activity values from both cultures, White Race was rated twice as active as Black Race by both Black and White cultures. (4) The Black culture rated both race concepts three times greater than did the White culture (A-Z = 2.84 versus A-Z = .90 on White Race, A-Z = 1.45 versus A-Z = .37 on Black Race).

Of the 30 bicultural comparisons on the standard factor scores in Table 4.1, 18 were significantly different by a minimum magnitude of .50. The other 12 comparisons indicated congruent (not significantly different) affective attributions to the concepts that had virtually universal connotation. For example, both groups considered Family as generally good (+ E), potent (+ P), and active (+ A), Friend as good (+ E), and Enemy as extremely bad (–E) and moderately weak (–P).

Differences in Conceptual Structures

Structures of all concepts from factor analysis for each culture are shown in Table 4.2. Two dimensions were obtained for the Black group. In order to facilitate the interpretation of each dimension, the codings of the 10 concepts on various denotative components were retrieved from the Ingroup/Outgroup category in the *Atlas* (e.g., the Duration component in the Time Unit category; see Tzeng & Osgood, 1976). This analysis helped to identify the underlying cognitive base for factorial structure of salient concepts on each dimension.

For the Black culture, the first dimension was characterized by the concepts I-Myself, Person, and Friend on one pole and Most People, Foreigner, Stranger, White Race, and Black Race on the other pole. This dimension, coded by the Immediacy (intimate versus remote) component represents personal and peer alienation and separatism from social institutions. It is interesting to note that the concept Black Race was not positively associated with the ego concepts I-Myself and

TABLE 4.2
Rotated Factor Structures of Concepts

Black Culture				White Culture			
Dimension 1 (Alienation)		Dimension 2 (Separatist/Social Hostility)		Dimension 1 (Social Interactions)		Dimension 2 (Social Hostility)	
Most people	.91	Enemy	.96	Most people	.99	Enemy	.98
Foreigner	.90	Stranger	.89	Person	.99	White race	.91
Black race	.82	White race	.60	Foreigner	.98	Black race	.90
White race	.79	Black race	.56	Family	.98	Stranger	.77
Stranger	.45			Friend	.97		
I-Myself	-.99	Family	-.96	I-Myself	.91		
Friend	-.82	Person	-.86	Stranger	.63		
Person	-.50	Friend	-.56				

NOTE: Two factor analyses were conducted, one for each culture, on the standard scores on E, P, and A. The values in this table are salient factor loadings.

Friend. It seems to suggest a lack of within-ethnic group identification for the Black youth. Therefore, this dimension may be labeled *Alienation.*

The second dimension was characterized by the concepts Family, Person, and Friend on one pole and Enemy, Stranger, White Race, and Black Race on the other pole. This dimension, coded by the Ingroup/Outgroup component, seems to reflect social hostility and separatism across races with a tendency to choose close ties with family and peers. This dimension was labeled *Separatism/Social Hostility.*

Two dimensions were also obtained for the White culture. The first dimension was characterized on one pole by the concepts Most People, Person, Foreigner, Family, Friend, I-Myself, and Stranger, clearly representing a nonseparatist or socially interactive characteristic. Therefore, it was labeled as a *Social Interactions* factor. The second dimension was also a unipolar factor, characterized by the concepts Enemy, White Race, Black Race, and Stranger. Like the second factor of the Black culture, this dimension seems to suggest the existence of hostility and conflict associated with racial interactions. Therefore, it was labeled a *Social Hostility* factor.

Interrelationships Among E, P, and A Components

A single dimension emerged from factor analysis of correlations among the E, P, and A components for the Black culture, with high positive factor loadings from the Evaluation and Potency components (.87 and .77, respectively) and a high negative factor loading from the Activity component (–.86). This factor suggests that the attitudinal judgments (Evaluation and Potency) were opposite to the behaviors (Activity). Such bipolarity may reflect incongruent attributions between value judgments and daily life experiences. This phenomenon was further supported by the standard factor scores; the concepts Enemy, Foreigner, Stranger, and White Race were rated bad (–E), quite impotent (–P) but very active (+A); see Table 4.1. Therefore, it can be identified as the *Affective Components Incoherence* factor.

A single dimension was also obtained for the White culture, but with high positive factor loadings from all three components (.91, .77, and .88 for E, P, and A, respectively). It clearly suggests congruent attributions between attitudinal judgments (E and P) and behavioral activities (A). This factor, in contrast to the polarization nature of the Black culture, can be called an *Affective Components Coherence* factor.

INTERPRETATION

As expected, the Black and the White cultures differed significantly in many aspects of affect as indicated by (1) 18 (63%) significant differences in a total of 30 comparisons (Table 4.1) and (2) concept structure differences both in dimensional polarization and content characteristics (Table 4.2). The nature of these differences, which have significant impact on interethnic communications, can be discussed in terms of (1) differences in affective attributions to self-concepts, (2) differences in social institutions, and (3) differences in implicit affective attribution.

Attribution Differences in Personal and Collective Selves

In order to identify the linkage between affective differences and subjective intergroup distances, the standard factor scores of the concepts that represent the personal self (I-Myself) and two collective (ingroup and outgroup) racial selves for Blacks and Whites (Black Race and White Race) were depicted in triangle displays (Figure 4.1). The magnitude of the differences between any two concepts on each component is distinguished by either > (a minimum of .50 difference) or >> (a minimum of 1.00 difference).

In the literature on Black self-concept (e.g., Clark & Clark, 1947; Coopersmith, 1967; McCombs, 1985; Natanson, 1972; Wright, 1985), the Evaluation component has been considered as the self-esteem system that represents a person's personal regard, worth, and value. Therefore, negative values on Evaluation would represent self-rejection or dissociation from a particular life experience or a series of experiences. Similarly, the Potency and Activity components can be considered as the motivational system (significance or strength from Potency and dispositional activation from Activity) that links psychological and sociological needs with life experiences and subsequent behaviors. Under this conceptualization, comparisons of the affective attributions to the personal self and the two collective racial selves facilitate our interpretation of the behavioral dynamics involved in interracial relations and conflicts.

For the Black culture, the three concepts were significantly different on each of the three affective components. Also, the hierarchical orders among the three concepts were also different across the three affective components: Black Race > I-Myself > White Race on self-esteem (Evaluation), I-Myself > Black Race >> White Race on affective intensity or significance in motivation (Potency), and White Race >>

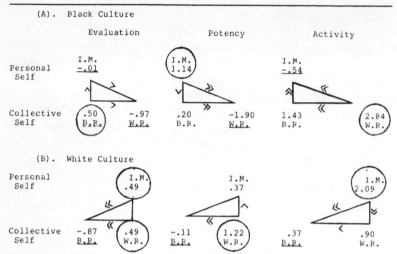

NOTE: Three concepts are abbreviated as I.M. for I-Myself, B.R. for Black Race, and W.R. for White Race. The largest value in each triangle is circled and the smallest value is underlined. Between each pair of the three concepts, the double inequality sign (>>) indicates the existence of an extremely significant difference between two standard factor scores with a magnitude of 1.0 or higher, and the single inequality sign (>) indicates a very significant difference with a magnitude between .50 and 99.

Figure 4.1 Comparisons of Personal Self with Two Collective Selves

Black Race >> I-Myself on perceived encountering frequency (Activity). These results clearly suggest: (1) The Black culture tends to reject the White on both racial-esteem (E) and racial-significance (P); (2) the cultural experiences of the White are perceived most prevalent in the Black social environment (A); and (3) the personal self is considered more important (P) than the collective racial self but of much less worth (E) and activation (A).

In the context of interethnic relations, the Black culture's high Activity rating for White Race, in contrast with the low ratings for Black Race and I-Myself, suggests the feeling of *alienation* under racial dominance by the White. The selective endorsement of personal and collective selves on the Evaluation component suggests the *separatistic* tendency to reject White values. The extremely negative rating for White Race on Potency, as opposed to positive ratings for the self concepts, seems to demonstrate the *favoritism* tendency to emphasize personal and collective significance. Perhaps such biased behavioral dispositions might be the the necessary mechanism for the Black to maintain affective harmony between self (personal and collective) esteems and motivations when the presence of the White becomes a threat to the indigenous value, significance, and role of the Black in interracial interactions.

On the other hand, the White seems to consider both personal and collective selves better (E), stronger (P), and more active (A) than the Black collective self. In addition, the White culture has congruent judgment in personal and collective self-esteems (E) but incongruent perceptions on intensity (P) and frequency (A). That is, the collective self is more important than the personal self, although the personal self is much more active than the collective self. These results suggest the existence of racial superiority over the Black by the White and the tendency for Whites as individuals to actively pursue the goodness of the collective self. In interacting with the Black in social/organizational institutions, the White might easily internalize White cultural superiority (separatism), ignore the interests of the Black (alienation), and take actions that will maximally contribute to the benefit of the White collective self-esteem (favoritism).

Our findings further show that Blacks have lower self-esteem than Whites and have negative attitudes toward Whites and foreigners. The lower self-esteem scores for the Black culture in this study may have been influenced by the *socioeconomic status* of the sample. Research has suggested that socioeconomic status frequently moderates the level of self-esteem (Hare, 1977). An examination of the social backgrounds of the Black sample indicates that it consists of predominantly middle- or lower-class teenagers.

Another interesting finding concerns *racial hostility*. Both cultures revealed within-group favoritism and between-group hostility by associating racial interaction with volatile process. Although hostility may not be apparent in daily interracial contacts, the hostility dimensions derived in Table 4.2 suggest that the two cultures harbor their hostility in the form of antagonistic social perceptions. Further, the between-group hostility appears to be associated with the within-group favoritism, feelings of alienation, and separatism.

In addition, both cultures showed a strong difference in perception of *social environment*. While the Black youth displayed social alienation (i.e., low Activity for Friend and I-Myself, as well as the alienation dimension in Table 4.2), the White youth portrayed social interaction and integration. These characteristics tend to reflect the greater self confidence among the dominant White youth, with fewer threatening elements to contend, when compared to their Black counterparts.

The interrelationships among the scores on E, P, and A components also reflected a distinct between-group difference in patterns of *affective attribution*. For example, the Black youth felt friends are good (+E) and important to have (+P); yet their behavioral activity seemed to be low (−A). This suggests a contradiction between attitudes and life experiences. This incoherence between articulation of attitudes and actual manifestation of behavior appears to be a frequent, if not consistent, factor in Black affective attribution (Wolfstetter-Kausch & Gaier, 1981). The incoherence factor further suggests discrepancies between hopes and actual attainment of goals in real-life situations for the Black youth. In addition, the results from the present study suggest that the Black subjective culture features both a strong identification with the values of the White society, and the reality-tempered conception that actual attainment of popularly achieved roles is difficult to realize.

Even though the present analysis has been based on the data from high school male respondents, its results may be generalizable to other populations to the extent that ethnicity is shared among its members. Specifically, we argue that findings of the present study can be generalized to the Black and White adult populations since the characteristics reflected in the minds of the youths are largely the products of socialization by adults within the respective cultural groups.

All in all, the present research has shown the clear phenomena of intergroup distances between the Black and White teenagers. The nature and dynamics of such distances can be delineated in terms of bicultural differences in the affective attributions to the concepts that represent the issues of personal and group esteems and the concerns in four aspects of social institutions: disparity in socioeconomics, the status of racial hostility, competence in social environment, and attribution of implicit affective systems. The present illustration of intercultural differences in these specific concepts clearly encourages similar and more comprehensive research in broader social contexts. Also, the future research needs to focus directly on the adult populations.

It should be noted that the *Atlas* data have at least apparent limitations. The unavailability of rating scores and demographic information from individual subjects makes it impossible to depict subjective cultural profiles for within-race subgroups and consequently prohibits the possibility of identifying between-race homogeneity (similarity) across different subgroups of both races. Also, the possible incomparability in socioeconomic status between the Black and White samples might confound with the ethnic factor in group comparisons on social issues. This ethnic factor might, in fact, be determined by socioeconomic tension. Overcoming these limitations is crucial to detailed delineation of the nature and dynamics of interethnic communication at the individual level.

REFERENCES

Allen, W. R. (1982). Black and blue: Black students at the University of Michigan. *Literature, Sciences and Arts, 6*(1), 13-17.

Brown, D. K., Nordlie, P. G., & Thomas, J. A. (1977). *Changes in Black and White perception of the army's race relations/equal opportunity program 1972-74* (ARI Technical Report 77-83). Alexandria, VA: U.S. Army Research Institute for the Behavioral and Social Sciences.

Campbell, A. (1971). *White attitudes toward Black people.* Ann Arbor, MI: Institute of Social Research.

Clark, K. B., & Clark, M. P. (1947). Racial identification and preferences in Negro children. In T. M. Newcomb & E. L. Hartley (Eds.), *Readings in social psychology.* New York: Holt, Rinehart & Winston.

Coopersmith, S. (1967). *The antecendents of self-esteem.* San Franciso: Freeman.

Deutsch, M., Katz, B., & Jensen, A. (1968). *Social class, race and psychological development.* New York: Holt, Rinehart & Winston.

Hare, B. R. (1977). Racial and socioeconomic variations in preadolescent area-specific and general self-esteem. *International Journal of Intercultural Relations, 1*(3), 31-51.

Jarmon, C. (1980). Racial beliefs among Blacks and Whites. *Journal of Black Studies, 11,* 235-247.

Landis, D., McGrew, P., Day, H., Savage, J., & Saral, T. (1976). Word meanings in Black and White. In H. C. Triandis (Ed.), *Variations in Black and White perceptions of the social environment.* Urbana: University of Illinois Press.

Longshore, D. (1979). Color connotations and racial attitudes. *Journal of Black Studies, 10,* 183-197.

McCombs, H. G. (1985). Black self-concept: An individual/collective analysis. *International Journal of Intercultural Relations, 9,* 1-18.

Natanson, M. (1972). The nature of social man. In H. Y. Jung (Ed.), *Existential phenomenology and political theory.* Chicago: Henry Regnery.

O'Gorman, H. J. (1979). White and Black perception of racial values. *Public Opinion Quarterly, 43,* 48-59.

Osgood, C. E., Miron, M. S., & May, W. H. (1975). *Cross-cultural universals of affective meaning.* Urbana: University of Illinois Press.

Schuman, H., & Hatchett, S. (1974). *Black racial attitudes: Trends and complexities.* Ann Arbor, MI: Institute for Social Research.

Scontrino, M. P., Larson, J. A., & Fiedler, F. E. (1977). Racial similarity as a moderator variable in the perception of leader behavior and control. *International Journal of Intercultural Relations, 1,* 111-117.

Shingles, R. D. (1979). College as a source of Black alienation. *Journal of Black Studies, 9,* 267-290.

Suen, H. K. (1983). Alienation and attrition of Black college students on a predominantly White campus. *Journal of College Student Personnel, 24,* 117-121.

Szalay, L. B., & Deese, J. (1978). *Subjective meaning and culture.* Hillsdale, NJ: Lawrence Erlbaum.

Triandis, H. C. (1972). *The analysis of subjective culture.* New York: Wiley-Interscience.

Turner, C. B., & Wilson, W. J. (1976). Dimensions of racial ideology: A study of urban Black attitudes. *Journal of Social Issues, 32,* 139-152.

Tzeng, O.C.S. (1983). The use of the *Atlas of Affective Meaning* in intercultural training. In D. Landis & R. W. Brislin (Eds.), *Handbook of intercultural training* (Vol. 1, pp. 224-252). New York: Pergamon Press.

Tzeng, O.C.S., & Osgood, C. E. (1976). Validity tests for componential analyses of conceptual domains: A cross-cultural study in methodology. *Behavioral Science, 21,* 69-85.

Wolfstetter-Kausch, H., & Gaier, E. L. (1981). Alienation among Black adolescents. *Adolescence, 16,* 471-485.

Wright, B. H. (1985). The effects of racial self-esteem on the personal self-esteem of Black youth. *International Journal of Intercultural Relations, 9,* 19-30.

5

Conflict Communication Styles in Black and White Subjective Cultures

STELLA TING-TOOMEY   ●   *Rutgers University*

This study explores conflict communication style differences in Black and White subjective cultures. A survey method was used to tap such differences. Results indicated that (1) males, regardless of ethnicity, tend to engage in significantly more indirect nonconfrontational strategies than the females; (2) Black females, overall, tend to engage in slightly more direct controlling conflict strategies than the White females; and (3) White females, overall, tend to engage in significantly more active solution-orientation conflict strategies than the Black females. Implications of the study are discussed in terms of developing a sense of rhetorical sensitivity toward gender-related ethnic communication style differences.

Conflict is a pervasive phenomenon penetrating all kinds of relationships in diverse contexts of human interaction. Conflict may serve either positive or negative ends, depending on how one manages conflict in an interpersonal situation. The conflict styles employed in managing the conflict episode will have a profound impact on the maintenance of the relationship that follows.

While conflict is an important communication construct, few intercultural researchers have paid systematic attention to this critical communication process. In the context of interethnic communication studies in North America, there is a dearth of research that systematically compares and contrasts conflict interaction styles across either ethnic group boundaries or within individual ethnic group systems. In the setting of Black and White communication, in particular, studies have been limited to investigating the use of Black English (for example,

AUTHOR'S NOTE: *This study was partially supported by a University Research Council Grant, Rutgers University.*

Baratz, 1973; Dillard, 1972; Kochman, 1972; Labov, 1972; Rich, 1974; Stanback & Pearce, 1981; Weber, 1985), the use of different nonverbal styles (Blubaugh & Pennington, 1976; Ickes, 1984; Johnson, 1976; Mayo & LaFrance, 1976; Pennington, 1979; Smith, 1973; Smith, 1983), the use of pain expression (Shuter, 1982), and more recently on the process of interracial mediation (Donohue, 1985). Few empirical studies have addressed the differences and similarities of Blacks' and Whites' use of communication styles in handling relational conflicts. We also have relatively little research information concerning gender-related ethnic styles in managing Black and White relational conflicts. Hence, the objective of this study is to fill part of the void in these areas. Conflict, in this chapter, is conceptually defined as the perceived and/or actual antagonisms and disagreements between two (or more) interdependent parties due to incompatible goals, needs, resources, values, beliefs, or attitudes.

LITERATURE REVIEW

Subjective culture is conceptually defined as "a cultural group's characteristic way of viewing the man-made part of the environment. It is the reaction of a homogeneous group of people to the social environment" (Triandis, 1976, p. 11). According to Triandis (1972, 1976), some of the major determinants of subjective culture are derived mainly from historical events. In Black and White intergroup contact, these historical events (such as slave trade, servitude, discriminatory treatment, and status group difference) severely affect how Blacks and Whites perceive and interpret their social environment. Their differential sets of social expectations, social perceptions, and social interpretations in turn affect the development of different norms of social interaction and distinctive patterns of Black and White communication styles.

Beyond historical reasoning, the rich linguistic heritage of the Black-African culture also asserts great influence in shaping the unique styles of Black-American communication. Arguing from a value orientation standpoint, Jahn (1961) observes that one of the primary values of pan-African culture is that everything in the universe exists for a purpose or a specific function. For all living creatures, there is always a reason for being, for existence. This principle is manifested through the four fundamental elements of mankind (Muntu), things (Kintu), place and time (Hantu), and modality (Kuntu). In order to be distinguished from the other three elements, mankind possessed a special magic, called "Nommo," or the "magical power of the word." Under this specific value-orientation, human beings master nature through the magical incantations of words. As leaders of the Black people, they must be able to "articulate the needs of the people in a most eloquent manner .... The speaker must generate and create movement and power within his listeners. One of the ways that is done is through the use of imaginative and vivid language" (Weber, 1985, p. 246). In the African culture, words mean power; words represent the life force of being.

Echoing the writings of Jahn (1961) on the relationship between Muntu and Nommo, Weber (1985) proposes three reasons why most Black-Americans continue to carry on the tradition of Black language in their daily interaction with others: (1) Black language articulates the unique historical-cultural experience of Black-Americans; (2) it fosters a sense of community and identity for Black-Americans; and (3) it acts as a political statement that "Black people are African people who have not given up a vital part of themselves in slavery: their language. They have retained their cultural link that allows them to think and to express themselves in a non-European form" (Weber, 1985, p. 249).

Thus, on both historical and cultural grounds, Blacks retain a distinctive subjective culture of values and norms of interaction in the context of a dominant White culture's influence. In terms of specific communication behavior differences, Shuter (1982) reports that Blacks tend to direct more questions and converse significantly much longer to females in the context of initial interactions than do Whites. Donohue (1985) observes that, in the context of interracial mediation, Blacks tend to engage in loud interaction and intense language interaction to display their emotion, while Whites tend to engage in overly solicitous and friendly communication strategies in negotiating differences. Williams (1968) reports that Blacks usually interpret Whites' politeness markers in interviewing sessions as gestures of concealing true intentions. Kochman (1974), in examining Black and White confrontation strategies, advances a cultural explanation for the value of loudness in Black subjective culture. He contends that loudness holds a positive value in Black culture as a true expression of sincerity and conviction of action (the Nommo value). To Blacks, avoidance style or compromise style in a confrontation connotes defeat and a win-lose situation. While Whites tend to view loudness as the onset of aggression and hostility, Blacks tend to interpret Whites' overly solicitous or friendly style of communication in conflict as a mask of hypocrisy and weakness.

Following up on his early work on Black and White confrontation, Kochman (1981), in his seminal work on *Black and White Styles in Conflict*, expands on his notion of "Black mode" and "White mode" of conflict style in negotiation. Based on ethnographic materials and participant-observation method, Kochman (1981) observes that Blacks and Whites, in a conflict situation, are divided not only over content but also over the conflict process—how disagreement on the issue is to be appropriately handled. According to Kochman (1981), the "Black mode" of conflict style is "high-keyed: animated, interpersonal, and confrontational" and the "White mode" of conflict style is "relatively low-keyed: dispassionate, impersonal, and non-challenging" (p. 18). While Blacks tend to use more emotionally expressive and involving modes of conflict management strategies, Whites tend to engage in more emotionally self-restrained discussions and attempt to understate and diffuse the unpleasant, intense situation. While Blacks are more affectively direct in confronting the conflict, Whites prefer to assume a cool, logical stance in seeking for an active closure to the episode.

In brief, Kochman (1981) argues that the Black subjective culture values the qualities of emotional expressiveness and intense involvement in any sociocultural activities. For Blacks, in an argumentative situation, full participation entails a "mind/body involvement of considerable depth, what blacks call *getting down into* the mode through which emotional release and spiritual rejuvenation are effected" (p. 108). Conversely, the White subjective culture treasures emotional self-restraint and self-discipline in a heated debate situation, and White members are guided by their cultural norms of "*good taste,* which have set ceilings on how intense expressive behavior may appropriately become" (pp. 114-115). Hence, the values and the normative expectations that Blacks and Whites have concerning how to handle conflict episodes appropriately, vary quite significantly. It is important to note, however, that Kochman's analysis of Black and White styles in conflict is based primarily on the differences between "black community" people (ghetto Blacks, inner-city Blacks, or lower-class Blacks) and mainstream, white, middle-class Americans. Additional studies that control for social class difference are needed to validate the numerous observations of Kochman's ethnographic study on the theme of Black and White conflict styles.

This study is an empirical update of Kochman's observation of "Black mode" versus "White mode" conflict communication styles, especially in managing relational conflicts in Black and White subjective cultures. The primary research question is: What are the distinctive communication style differences between Blacks and Whites in their managing of relational conflicts? The following three hypotheses are tested:

> H_1: Blacks are more likely to use direct control style (confrontation communication strategies) of conflict than Whites;
>
> H_2: Blacks are less likely to use indirect nonconfrontational style (avoidance and withdrawal communication strategies) of conflict than Whites;
>
> H_3: Blacks are less likely to use solution-orientation style (compromising communication strategies) of conflict than Whites.

Along with ethnic differences, the present study investigates the possible influence of gender on conflict communication styles. In past gender-related studies (Bernard, 1972; Haas, 1979; Henley, 1977; Key, 1975; Kramer, 1974; Lakoff, 1973, 1975; Pei, 1969), distinctive male and female communication differences have been found between the sexes. For example, Bernard (1972) found that while males tend to engage in a direct, instrumental style of lecturing, argument, and debate; females; tend to engage in a more tactful, indirect style of interaction. Lakoff (1973, 1975) found that the form of women's language is definitely more tentative and more polite than the men's. Other studies (McMillan, Clifton, McGrath, & Gale, 1977; Siegler & Siegler, 1977) also uncovered that females tend to employ more tag questions and verbal qualifiers than males. Finally, Nadler and Nadler (1984) concluded that in organizational negotiation settings, women typically project more low position commitment, uncertainty, politeness, and nonassertiveness in expressing their opinions than their male counterparts.

Overall, past gender-related studies suggest that in everyday negotiation situations, males typically engage in more direct, "up-front" strategies than females in dealing with differences. Females typically engage in either indirect, "smoothing" communication strategies to diffuse the conflict topic, or engage in avoidance or withdrawal strategies from the conflict situations. Finally, females are more likely than their male counterparts to employ active, compromising strategies to press for early closure for any interpersonal differences and hostilities. Thus, the following hypotheses are tested:

> H_4: Males are more likely than females to engage in a direct control style of conflict;

H_5: Males are less likely than females to engage in an indirect, nonconfrontational style of conflict;

H_6: Males are less likely than females to engage in a solution-orientation style of conflict.

In addition, the gender-related communication style differences will be examined in the context of Black and White subjective cultures. Based on previous observation concerning Black-White conflict style distinctions, and the relative communication differences between males and females, the following hypotheses are tested:

H_7: Black males are more likely than Black females to use direct, control style of conflict;

H_8: Black males are less likely than Black females to use indirect, nonconfrontational style of conflict;

H_9: Black males are less likely than Black females to use solution-orientation style of conflict;

H_{10}: White males are more likely than White females to use direct, control style of conflict;

H_{11}: White males are less likely than White females to use indirect, nonconfrontational style of conflict;

H_{12}: White males are less likely than White females to use solution-orientation style of conflict.

METHOD

A total of 318 volunteers participated in the present study. They were contacted through communication classes, engineering classes, and Black studies classes in an eastern university. Of the sample, 39% of the respondents were Blacks (n = 123) and 57% were Whites (n = 180). A total sample of 303 participants were used in this particular analysis. The mean age of the sample was 20 years, and there were 16% freshmen, 26% sophomores, 27% juniors, and 31% seniors.

In the Black sample, 33% (n = 40) were males, and 67% (n = 83) were females. In the White sample, 36% (n = 64) were males, and 64% (n = 116) were females. For both samples, the top three father's occupations were "manager/administrative," "professional," and "sales" (the third category for the Black sample was "service"). The top three mother's occupations were "clerical," "housewife," and "managerial/administrative" (the third category for the Black sample was "educational/professional"). Overall, the participants in this study came from white-collar occupation, middle-class families. For the Black sample, respondents indicated (through open-ended questions) that their typical relational conflicts with their close friends were "general relationship issues," "controversial topics," and "sex-love-dating." For the White sample, respondents indicated that their top three relational conflicts with their close friends were "relationship togetherness problems," "specific issues outside the relationships," and "general relationship issues."

Data were collected through Putnam and Wilson's (1982) Organizational Communication Conflict Instrument (OCCI). The instrument is a 30-item scale that measures the three conflict communication styles of control dimension, nonconfrontation dimension, and solution-orientation dimension in interpersonal conflict situations. The OCCI is a communication-based questionnaire that taps the multidimensional nature of conflict styles, rather than measuring one characteristic mode of conflict strategies. The instrument had been assessed to have strong construct validity and predictive validity in three previous conflict studies.

The "control" style of conflict was conceptually defined as "direct control about the disagreement; arguing persistently for one's position, taking control of the interaction, and advocating one's position." For example, two control items were (1) I raise my voice when I'm trying to get this person to accept my position, and (2) I dominate arguments until this person understands my position. An alpha of .82 was obtained when all 7 control items were combined.

The "nonconfrontational" style of conflict was conceptually defined as "indirect strategies for handling a conflict; choices to avoid or withdraw from a disagreement; such communicative behaviors as silence, glossing over differences, and concealing ill feelings." For example, two nonconfrontational items were (1) I keep quiet about my views in order to avoid disagreements, and (2) I try to smooth over disagreements by making them appear unimportant. An alpha of .93 was obtained when all 12 nonconfrontational items were combined.

The "solution-orientation" style of conflict was conceptually defined as "direct communication about the conflict; behaviors that aim to find a solution, to integrate the needs of both parties, and to give in or compromise on issues." For example, two solution-orientation items were (1) I offer creative solutions in discussions of disagreements; (2) I try to use this person's ideas to generate solutions to disagreements. An alpha of .88 was obtained when all 11 solution-orientation items were combined. A 7-point rating (1 = always, 2 = very often, 3 = often, 4 = sometimes, 5 = seldom, 6 = very seldom, and 7 = never) was used following each OCCI item. Hence, low scores represent frequent use of certain conflict communication strategies, and high scores represent infrequent use of certain conflict interaction behaviors.

The OCCI survey was administered to the participants with the following written instructions: "Think of disagreements you have encountered in situations with a person in a close relationship. Then indicate on the scale below how frequently you engage in each of the following described behaviors. Do not respond to items with a particular disagreement in mind. Instead, keep in mind your experiences when disagreeing with this person in general." The reasons for picking a "close relationship" conflict situation were twofold: First, conflict is particularly inevitable in close relationships because the situation involves two interdependent parties who are mutually attached to each other for exchange needs and resources; second, the respondents can assess more accurately their typical mode of conflict styles in a day-to-day familiar interpersonal, close relationship situation than in an impersonal, social context. The instrument was pretested with a random sample of 15 undergraduate students, and the instructions were perceived as clearly worded and easily understood. At the end of the survey the respondents were asked to identify the type of close relationship with their conflict partners. Both Blacks and Whites (52%, 48%) picked the label "lover," followed by the labels of "friend" (22%, 22%), "best friend" (12%, 17%), "relative" (8%, 9%), then others. A majority of the participants (89% Blacks, 92% Whites) indicated that their conflict partners were from the same ethnic background.

RESULTS

A two-factor (ethnicity $\times$ gender) multivariate analysis of variance (MANOVA) design was used to analyze the data. Control style, nonconfrontation style, and solution-orientation style were used as the dependent variables. Bartlett's test spericity was computed to ascertain the degree of interrelatedness among three dependent variables. A value of 11.28 (3 df, $p < .01$, determinent = .96) indicated correlations among the dependent variables were high enough to warrant multivariate analysis.

The analysis yielded significant main effects for ethnicity (Hotelling's trace = .08, Wilks' lambda = .92, F = 8.04, 3/297 df, p < .001) and gender (Hotelling's trace = .06, Wilks' lambda = .95, F = 5.57, 3/297 df, p < .001). However, no significant interaction effects were uncovered between ethnicity and gender.

Univariate Analyses

The univariate analyses revealed significant effects by ethnicity on two of the three conflict styles: control style (F(1, 299) = 7.70, p < .01, eta^2 = .03) and solution-orientation style (F(1, 299) = 18.02, p < .001, eta^2 = .06). No significant effect was found for nonconfrontational style. When the sample means of Blacks and Whites in the use of control style and solution-orientation style were examined, Blacks used significantly more controlling strategies than Whites (B: $\overline{X}$ = 26, SD = 8.3; W: $\overline{X}$ = 29, SD = 6.8). Conversely, Whites used significantly more solution-orientation strategies than Blacks (B: $\overline{X}$ = 39, SD = 9.2; W: $\overline{X}$ = 35, SD = 6.9).

In terms of gender-related conflict communication styles, univariate analyses indicated significant main effects by gender on two of the three conflict styles: nonconfrontational style (F(1, 299) = 10.53, p < .001, eta^2 = .04) and solution-orientation style (F(1, 299) = 3.64, p < .05, eta^2 = .01). No significant main effect was found for control style. In examining the group means of males and females in the use of nonconfrontational style and solution-orientation style, it was uncovered that males tend to use more nonconfrontational style of conflict than females (M: $\overline{X}$ = 53, SD = 11.7; F; $\overline{X}$ = 58, SD = 11.1). Conversely, females tended to use slightly more solution-orientation style than males (M: $\overline{X}$ = 38, SD = 7.5; F: $\overline{X}$ = 36, SD = 8.4).

t-Test Analyses

A series of t-test analyses were employed to compare the conflict style differences between Black males and Black females, and between White males and White females. While no differences were found between Black males and Black females in the use of either control style or solution-orientation conflict style, a significant difference was found between Black males and Black females in the use of nonconfrontational style (t(121) = 2.08, p < .05), with Black males using surprisingly more nonconfrontational strategies than Black females (BM: $\overline{X}$ = 53, SD = 15.1: BF: $\overline{X}$ = 59, SD = 10.9). While no differences were uncovered between White males and White females in the use of control conflict style, significant differences were found between the two groups in the use of nonconfrontational style ($t(178) = -2.42$, $p < .01$) and the solution-orientation style ($t(178) = 3.31$, $p < .001$). Contrary to expectation, it was the White males who employed more indirect nonconfrontational strategies than the White females (WM: $\overline{X} = 53$, SD = 9.1; WF: $\overline{X} = 57$, SD = 11.2). However, as hypothesized the White females did tend to use more solution-orientation strategies than the White males (WM: $\overline{X} = 37$, SD = 5.7; WF: $\overline{X} = 34$, SD = 7.3).

Finally, in cross-comparing the individual cell means between the Black males and the White males, and between the Black females and the White females, the following observations were made: (1) Black males and White males differed significantly in the use of all three conflict styles in managing close relationships conflicts; (2) Black females and White females differed significantly in the use of control style ($t(197) = 2.30$, $p < .05$), with Black females using more control strategies than White females (BF: $\overline{X} = 27$, SD = 7.7; WF: $\overline{X} = 29$, SD = 6.7); (3) Black females and White females differed significantly in the use of solution-orientation style ($t(197) = -4.32$, $p < .001$), with White females employing significantly more solution-orientation strategies than Black females (BF: $\overline{X} = 39$, SD = 9.0; WF: $\overline{X} = 34$, SD = 7.3)

DISCUSSION

In summary, the multivariate analysis indicated that both ethnicity and gender independently influenced the set of conflict variables. In the univariate tests, two of the three hypotheses were confirmed. Overall, Blacks tend to use more controlling strategies than Whites (H_1 was supported). Whites, on the other hand, tended to engage in more compromising or solution-orientation strategies in handling relational disagreements than Blacks (H_3 was supported). No significant difference, however, was uncovered between the two groups in nonconfrontational conflict style (H_2 was not supported).

In gender-related differences, there were some surprising findings. A significant difference was found between males' and females' use of nonconfrontational conflict strategies. Contrary to the results of previous gender-related studies, males tended to use more indirect nonconfrontational strategies (such as avoidance or silence) to resolve conflicts than the females (H_5 was not supported). Females, overall, tend to use more active, solution-orientation strategies to deal with relational conflicts than the males (H_6 was supported). No significant difference was uncovered, however, between the two groups in control communication style (H_4 was not supported).

In testing for hypotheses 7 through 12, no significant differences were found between Black males and Black females, and between White males and White females, in the use of direct control style of conflict (H_7 and H_{10} were not supported). Surprisingly, both Black males and White males tended to use more nonconfrontational tactics (for example, avoidance, silence, and withdrawal) to deal with relational conflicts than Black females and White females respectively (H_8 and H_{11} were not supported). While no significant difference was uncovered between Black males and Black females in the use of solution-orientation tactics (H_9 was not supported), a significant difference was revealed between White males and White females in the use of solution-related tactics (H_{12} was supported).

Contrary to expectations, both Black males and White males in this study tended to prefer avoidance strategies as the best means to deal with relational issues and antagonisms. In the Black subjective culture, Black females tended to use slightly more direct confrontational tactics to manage relational tensions. In the White subjective culture, White females tended to use significantly more compromising strategies to dispel tensions and diffuse disagreements.

It seems that the value-orientation of "Nommo" ("the magical power of the word") and the positive virtue of emotional loudness to express sincerity and conviction of action in argumentations are alive in the communication styles of Black females but not necessarily in those of Black males. Contrary to expectations, both the Black males and the White males in this study engaged in significantly more passive nonconfrontational strategies to deal with relational conflict issues than their female counterparts. Also, Black females in this study have been found to be slightly more verbose and emotionally expressive than White females in their use of intense, confrontational style of conflict. White females have been found to engage in significantly more compromising conflict strategies in dealing with relational problems.

In comparing this study with Kochman's (1981) ethnographic study on Black and White styles in conflict, the following four possible reasons for differences between the two studies may be put forward. First, both Black and White samples in this study were drawn from white-collar, middle-class families, whereas Kochman's study was based on a comparison of an inner-city Black sample and a middle-class White sample. Second, the sample size of Black males in this sample was relatively small and, hence, this study may not tap the conflict characteristics of the Black male accurately. Third, as the study asked for perceived self-report data, it may not have adequately captured the behavioral richness of Black and White conflict style and strategies. Fourth, the setting of close relationship conflicts may call for different kinds of communication repertoires from both groups than the setting of public social conflicts (Kochman's study was partially based on his observations of classroom Black and White conflicts). In the context of close relationship conflicts, males, regardless of ethnicity, may still adhere to a traditional, normative sex-role model in which emotional self-expressiveness is strongly discouraged. In the public setting, on the other hand, "upfront" confrontational strategies in the males are likely to be employed.

Future studies should take into consideration the plausible influence of relational contexts on conflict communication. Further, they should move beyond relying on perceived self-report data and systematically investigate the actual behaviors that Blacks and Whites, and males and females, use in conflict situations. Future studies should also pay close attention to the effects of dyadic compositions (ethnicity × gender) on conflict communication styles in relation to other relevant communication variables (such as self-monitoring, communicator styles, and communication competence). Finally, "triangulated methods" (using, for example, controlled time-series interaction analysis, discourse analysis, and metaphor analysis) are recommended for studies designed to delineate the specific verbal and nonverbal moves and counter-moves that Blacks and Whites make in negotiating conflict differences and eventually arriving at relational convergence.

The results of this study provide partial support for distinctive conflict communication style differences between Black and White subjective cultures. Beyond the fact that one should develop a sense of rhetorical sensitivity toward such communication differences, one should also develop appreciation and awareness of gender-related ethnic style divergences. This study has revealed some of the underlying values and distinctive conflict communication norms of the Black and White subjective cultures, and conjointly, of the male and female subjective cultures.

REFERENCES

Baratz, J. (1973). Language abilities of Black Americans. In K. Miller & R. Dreger (Eds.), *Comparative studies of Blacks and Whites in the United States.* New York: Seminar Press.

Bernard, J. (1972). *The sex game.* Englewood Cliffs, NJ: Prentice-Hall.

Blubaugh, J., & Pennington, D. (1976). *Crossing differences: Interracial communication.* Columbus, OH: Merrill.

Dillard, J. (1972). *Black English.* New York: Vintage Books.

Donohue, W. (1985). Ethnicity and mediation. In W. Gudykunst, L. Stewart, & S. Ting-Toomey (Eds.), *Communication, culture and organizational processes.* Beverly Hills, CA: Sage.

Haas, A. (1979). Male and female spoken language differences: Stereotypes and evidence. *Psychological Bulletin, 86,* 616-626.

Henley, N. (1977). *Body politics: Power, sex, and nonverbal communication.* Englewood Cliffs, NJ: Prentice-Hall.

Ickes, W. (1984). Compositions in Black and White: Determinants of interaction in interracial dyads. *Journal of Personality and Social Psychology, 47,* 330-341.

Jahn, J. (1961). *Muntu.* New York: Grove Press.

Johnson, (1976). Black kinesics: Some nonverbal communication patterns in the black culture. In L. Samovar & R. Porter (Eds.), *Intercultural communication: A reader* (2nd ed.). Belmont, CA: Wadsworth.

Key, M. (1975). *Male/female language.* Metuchen, NJ: Scarecrow Press.

Kochman, T. (1972). *Rappin' and stylin' out: Communication in urban Black America.* Urbana: University of Illinois Press.

Kochman, T. (1974). Orality and literacy as factors of "Black" and "White" communication behavior. *Linguistics: An International Review, 136,* 91-117.

Kochman, T. (1981). *Black and White styles in conflict.* Chicago: University of Chicago Press.

Kramer, C. (1974). Women's speech: Separate but unequal. *Quarterly Journal of Speech, 60,* 14-24.

Labov, W. (1972). *Language in the inner city: Studies in the Black English vernacular.* Philadelphia: University of Pennsylvania Press.

Lakoff, R. (1973). Language and women's place. *Language in Society, 2,* 45-80.

Lakoff, R. (1975). *Language and women's place.* New York: Colophon/Harper & Row.

Mayo, C., & LaFrance, M. (1976). *Moving bodies: Nonverbal communication in social relationships.* Monterey, CA: Brooks/Cole.

McMillan, L., Clifton, A., McGrath, D., & Gale, W. (1977). Women's language: Uncertainty or interpersonal sensitivity and emotionality? *Sex Roles, 3,* 545-559.

Nadler, L., & Nadler, M. (1984, May). *Communication, gender, and negotiations: Theory and finding.* Paper presented at the Eastern Communication Association Philadelphia.

Pei, M. (1969). *Words in sheep's clothing.* New York: Hawthorne Books.

Pennington, D. (1979). Black-White communication: An assessment of research. In M. Asante, E. Newmark, & C. Blake (Eds.), *Handbook of intercultural communication.* Beverly Hills, CA: Sage.

Putnam, L., & Wilson, C. (1982). Communication strategies in organizational conflicts: Reliability and validity of a measurement. In M. Burgoon (Ed.), *Communication yearbook 6.* Beverly Hills, CA: Sage.

Rich, A. (1974). *Interracial communication.* New York: Harper & Row.

Shuter, R. (1982). Initial interaction of American blacks and whites in interracial and intraracial dyads. *Journal of Social Psychology, 117,* 45-52.

Siegler, D., & Siegler, R. (1977). Stereotypes of males and females' speech. *Language in Society, 6,* 313-322.

Smith, A. (1973). *Transracial communication*. Englewood Cliffs, NJ: Prentice-Hall.

Smith, A. (1983). Nonverbal communication among Black female dyads: An assessment of intimacy, gender, and race. *Journal of Social Issues, 39,* 55-67.

Stanback, M., & Pearce, W. B. (1981). Talking to "the man": Some communication strategies used by members of "subordinate" social groups. *Quarterly Journal of Speech, 67,* 21-30.

Triandis, H. (Ed.). (1972). *The analysis of subjective culture.* New York: John Wiley.

Triandis, H. (Ed.). (1976). *Variations in Black and White perceptions of the social environment*. Urbana: University of Illinois Press.

Weber, S. (1985). The need to be: The socio-cultural significance of Black language. In L. Samovar & R. Porter (Eds.), *Intercultural communication: A reader* (4th ed.). Belmont, CA: Wadsworth.

Williams, J. (1968). Interviewer role performance: A further note on bias in the information interview. *Public Opinion Quarterly, 32,* 287-294.

II

LANGUAGE AND VERBAL/NONVERBAL BEHAVIOR IN INTERETHNIC INTERACTION

6

Perceived Threat, Ethnic Commitment, and Interethnic Language Behavior

HOWARD GILES • PATRICIA JOHNSON • *Bristol University*

This chapter explores the social psychological climate conducive for individuals to accentuate their ethnic speech markers and determines the effects of message content on listeners' language attitudes. From two studies, it was found that when Welshpersons were exposed to a threat to their ethnolinguistic ideals by a taped speaker in English, they anticipated diverging from him by an accentuated use of the Welsh language for reasons of ethnic solidarity even though societal norms for English prevailed. Such differentiation was evident, however, only when subjects were highy committed to their group and the threat was very direct, and expressedly greater when the threat derived from an outgroup speaker after group discussion about the issue. In contrast to the literature stressing the potency of accent as a cue to impression formation, the present studies showed that ethnically threatening message content could override this phenomenon completely. The theoretical implications of these findings are discussed.

For many ethnic groups, language or nonstandard dialect is an important dimension of social identity and symbolizes their distinctiveness from other ethnic groups (Giles & Johnson, 1981). Accordingly, perceived threats to valued ethnicity may be met by accentuations of the ethnic speech style in many situations (see Dube-Simard, 1983). This chapter provides a brief outline of some of our developing theoretical ideas about ethnolinguistic behavior on the one hand and ethnic language attitudes on the other; it also reports on two investigations designed to explore them.

AUTHOR'S NOTE: *We would like to express our gratitude to the staff and pupils of a mid-Wales comprehensive school and to Jane Byrne-Giles, Penny Chandler, Sanjoy Das, Sue Evans, Gerald Morgan, and Beth Thomas for their invaluable assistance at different levels of the execution of the studies reported herein.*

A consideration of "speech accommodation theory" (see, for example, Street & Giles, 1982), a model concerned with the motivations underlying consequences arising from individuals' shifts in speech styles, suggests that there are a number of factors that must be taken into account for understanding when and why speakers "converge" toward and "diverge" away from the speech styles of others. For instance, in contexts where ethnic in- and outgroup members wish to cooperate and facilitate interaction (perhaps in pursuit of superordinate goals), an *attenuation* of interlingual differences is predicted. Such convergence, or at least "speech maintenance" (Bourhis, 1979), is also likely when ethnic identity is less salient or when an outgroup member is perceived to be sympathetic to ingroup aims (Bourhis & Giles, 1977).

A study examining these issues was conducted in Quebec by Taylor and Royer (1980) where language has been central to the conflict between French and English Canadians (FCs & ECs). The authors twice examined the responses FC students anticipated making to an EC whom they expected later to meet: once initially, and the second time after a group discussion of the matter at hand. The EC ethnic outgroup member was presented as having either sympathetic or antagonistic attitudes toward the linguistic aims of FCs. FC subjects anticipated responding with more English to the former and more French to the latter, with small group discussion resulting in subsequent polarization of the initial responses. Thus, support was provided for the notion that linguistic convergence and divergence are more likely in cooperative and conflictual ethnic contexts respectively. While only behavioral expectations were forthcoming in this study, it can be argued that these reflect participants' motivations and evaluations and hence the likely direction of their actual behavioral responses in similar situations (see Bourhis, 1984).

In Taylor and Royer's study only an ethnic *out*group image was presented to subjects. It seems not unreasonable to suggest that ethnically committed subjects would react more strongly by accentuation/attenuation of ethnic speech markers in response to perceived threat/support from an outgroup rather than ingroup member. However, if the latter is perceived to break solid ingroup norms and act as a "cultural traitor" (Khleif, 1979), then listeners might react more vehemently under threat than when the target was an outgroup person. The present study examines this issue by an extended replication of Taylor and Royer's study in another ethnic context by including speakers who could be defined as in- or outgroup members on the basis of linguistic and other cues. Furthermore, the dependent, as well as the independent, variables were also extended, as the Quebec study only included measures relating to anticipated language responses and the motivations underlying them. It could be expected that *social evaluations* of ethnic ingroup and outgroup speakers would be judgmental complements. Much research in the "language attitudes" paradigm (e.g., Giles & Edwards, 1983; Giles, Ryan, Hewstone, & Johnson, in press) has shown across the world that representative speakers of a dominant ethnic group's language variety are upgraded on traits relating to socioeconomic success (e.g., intelligence, confidence, ambition) even by listener-judges from subordinate ethnic groups. Far less consistently, however, has been the not infrequent finding that subordinate power group speech styles are often upgraded by speakers of them on traits relating to solidarity (e.g., sociability, generosity, likability). The present study attempts to extend the scope of language attitudes research in intergroup contexts (see Ryan, Hewstone, & Giles, 1984) and to underline potential malleability of social evaluations to speech.

In appraising the language attitudes that (subordinate) ethnic group members would be likely to hold in situations defined as ethnically threatening/supportive (see Gallois, Callan, & Johnstone, 1984; Taylor et al., 1982), it seems useful to refer to Giles and Ryan's (1982) two-dimensional model of speaker evaluations. Therein linguistic judgments were considered in terms of group- versus person-centered and status-versus solidarity-stressing. It is suggested that situations that are perceived in terms of ethnic threat/support may be characterized as emphasizing solidarity-stressing and group-centered dimensions. Thus it is expected that a speaker perceived to be ethnically supportive would be upgraded, particularly on solidarity traits, in comparison with another who was ethnically threatening. Again, evaluations of the speaker may be exaggerated when the speaker is perceived to be an out- rather than an ingroup member.

The Giles and Ryan distinction between status- and solidarity-stressing dimensions in the perception of intercultural interactions raises a further consideration in the context of the present studies. It may be expected that the more a situation is perceived in terms of the former dimension, the greater the influence of societal rather than ingroup norms on the behavior (anticipated or otherwise) of respondents (see Ball et al., 1984; Genesee & Bourhis, 1982). In the Welsh-English context of these studies there are powerful societal norms favoring the use of English over Welsh as the language of status and prestige, thus mitigating against the accentuation of ethnic speech markers by Welsh speakers in interaction with their English counterparts. In addition, the studies are run in schools, and the speaker is presented as an unknown academic figure, both of which are liable to reinforce emphasis on status- rather than solidarity-stressing dimensions in the perception of the situation. Thus there are a number of factors inhibiting linguistic differentiation in the anticipated responses of subjects. Yet it is expected that for Welsh speakers attending a bilingual school in a strongly Welsh-speaking area, identification with the ethnic group and language will be sufficiently strong to overcome the influence of social norms favoring the use of English over Welsh. Accordingly, the school in which the study was run was carefully chosen on the basis of previous research (e.g., Williams, 1978; Williams, 1979) as being an area where the Welsh group and language were valued highly.

In sum, the hypotheses proposed that the subjects will

(1) anticipate greater accentuation of their ethnic speech markers in response to a speaker perceived as ethnically threatening rather than supportive;

(2) anticipate greater accentuation/attenuation of their ethnic speech markers to a speaker perceived as ethnically threatening/supportive when he is also perceived to be a member of the outgroup rather than the ingroup;

(3) anticipate accentuating/attenuating their ethnic speech markers for reasons associated with assertion of their ethnic identity/desire for communicational efficiency and affiliation with the speaker;

(4) upgrade the speaker perceived as ethnically supportive compared with the speaker perceived as ethnically threatening, particularly on traits relating to the solidarity dimension:

(5) accentuate their upgrading of the speaker perceived as ethnically supportive rather than threatening when he is perceived to be an outgroup rather than an ingroup member;

(6) accentuate their anticipated linguistic responses to the speaker and their attitudes toward him following group discussion of their responses.

STUDY 1

Method

Subjects

Forty Welsh-speaking adolescents aged between 14 and 15 years from a bilingual comprehensive school in mid-Wales (Aberystwyth) participated in the experiment. The group included five "learners," that is, children from English-speaking homes who had Welsh as their second language but spoke it fluently. An examination of these subjects' (Ss') responses to 10 items of Lewis's (1975) "Attitudes toward Welsh" scale revealed that they held generally favorable attitudes toward the language.

Materials

Anticipated Linguistic Strategy Scales. These consisted of three 10cm. lines labeled bipolarly as "Welsh accented-BBC (English) accented"; "Welsh language 100%-English language 100%"; "Many Welsh words and sayings-few Welsh words and sayings."

Motivations for Anticipated Strategy Scales. These consisted of a 10 cm. line labeled at either end "definitely-definitely not" next to each of 11 possible reasons for a particular linguistic response. The test sheet was headed, "I will speak to the researcher in the way I indicated . . . " and each of the 11 reasons began " . . . because." Thus an example would be " . . . because I want to show I can speak like a Welshman," Three of the reasons related to the individual's sense of Welsh identity, three to his or her sense of British identity, one to the ethnicity of the researcher, and the remaining four to social constraints and ease of communication.

Attitudes Toward the Speaker Scales. These consisted of ten 10 cm. lines labeled at either end "extremely-not all." On the basis of previous language attitude research, three scales each were selected to represent status-stressing (that is, "intelligent," "confident," and "ambitious") and solidarity-stressing (that is, "kind," "sincere," and "sociable") dimensions. A further three scales were chosen so as to reflect cooperation and supportiveness (that is, "cooperative," "ingratiating," and "full of empathy") with a final scale tapping perceived accentedness ("Welsh accented-BBC [English]").

Stimulus Audiotape. A one-minute passage was recorded in a standard English (RP) accent and in a South Welsh accent by the same speaker using the matched-guise technique (Lambert, 1967); this (male) speaker had previously been validated by a dialectologist as having authentic RP and South Welsh accents (Bourhis et al., 1973). The recordings were of the same length with the same emphases and inflections of voice. The recorded passage was carefully prepared so as to contain six clear statements of similar import, three supporting and three critical of bilingual education, in order that the same passage could authentically be used in both "supportive" and "threatening" experimental conditions. The passage appears to be the beginning of a talk by the researcher on bilingual education in Wales where the speaker began by examining the effects of bilingual education in Quebec and the U.S.A.

Design

The study had a three factorial design with two levels in each factor and repeated measures on one of these (pre- or postdiscussion ratings) as seen in Table 6.1.

Procedure

Ss were assigned randomly to one of the four experimental conditions. The 10 Ss in each condition were then introduced to the experimenter (E) by the headmaster in Welsh and told they were at liberty to leave at any time if they did not want to participate in the investigation. The headmaster left for the duration of the experiment, and it was clear to Ss that E did not speak Welsh. The experiment was conducted in four phases:

Phase 1. Ss were led to believe that E was interested in how we form impressions of people. It was further commented that our voices tend to change in different situations (e.g., when talking to the headmaster rather than chatting with friends at breaktime). Ss were then asked to mark on the accent and language scales how they thought they sounded when talking to their teacher in that classroom; this measure formed the baseline scales. Ss were then told that E was mostly concerned with the impressions people would form of a certain researcher who they would be meeting later that afternoon to discuss bilingual education. If Ss were those 20 assigned to the SU condition, they were told the researcher was giving a series of talks on the benefits and rewards of bilingual education in Wales, and as a result of his work he had generally positive attitudes about bilingual education in the principality. This was reiterated in different terms a few minutes later. If Ss were those 20 assigned to the TH condition, they were told the researcher was giving a series of talks on the difficulties and problems of bilingual education in Wales, and as a result of his work he had generally *negative* attitudes about bilingual education in Wales. This was also reiterated a few minutes later.

In the WE condition, the researcher was introduced as Mr. Glyn Edwards from Cardiff (Wales). In the EN condition, he was introduced as Mr. Peter Fletcher from Reading (England). (Note that the researcher

TABLE 6.1
Study Design

		Pregroup Discussion	Postgroup Discussion
Welsh-accented speaker	Threat	10 Ss	10 Ss
	Support	10 Ss	10 Ss
English-accented speaker	Threat	10 Ss	10 Ss
	Support	10 Ss	10 Ss

was actually not present in either condition although Ss were led to believe that they would meet him later and have a chance to put their views to him.) In both conditions, Ss were told that although the researcher spoke a number of European languages, he did not speak Welsh. Ss were also told that he was not used to giving public talks and was concerned about how he could convey his message more effectively, what sort of impression he was giving, and therefore how people were likely to react to him. E then introduced the idea of group discussion, saying that we generally form impressions of other people *with* other people and are influenced by their ideas too. Ss were told that they would hear a short tape of the researcher speaking and would discuss in small groups of five their ideas about him and how they thought they would react to him. Initially, however, they would have the chance for a practice run-through in order to get used to the scales and tape; the use of the anticipated linguistic strategy *and* the attitudes toward speaker scales were then explained to Ss.

Phase 2. Ss listened to one of the recorded passages (corresponding to the WE/EN conditions) and then completed individually the two sets of rating scales just mentioned.

Phase 3. Ss then discussed their responses on the questionnaire for two minutes in mixed-sex groups of five.

Phase 4. It was then remarked that Ss may or may not have changed their ideas, but they would now hear the tape again and they were asked to fill in a second questionnaire of exactly the same scales, now that they supposedly had a firmer idea of their impression of Mr. Fletcher/ Edwards. Ss then heard the same tape again and completed a second set of the scales as used in Phase 2. Finally, Ss were provided with the motivations for their anticipated linguistic strategies scale, and after these had been explained, they completed them. At the end of the session, Ss were briefed and engaged in discussion; none of the Ss appeared to be upset by the deception of the speaker's reported attitudes.

Results

Preliminary analysis of variance on the baseline linguistic measures indicated that there were initial differences apparent between the four experimental groups. These necessitated separate and appropriate $2 \times 2 \times 2$ analyses of covariance on each of the three anticipated linguistic strategy scales. Three main effects of stimulus speaker's accent emerged with Ss anticipating using more of a Welsh accent ($F = 5.22$, df = 1,35; $p < 0.05$), the Welsh language ($F = 5.67$; $p < 0.05$), and Welsh words and phrases ($F = 9.04$; $p < 0.01$) to the WE than the EN speaker, irrespective of his ethnolinguistic orientation or the fact that group discussion had occurred.

Separate $2 \times 2 \times 2$ ANOVAs were carried out on each of the 11 "motivation" scales with five main effects emerging for the accent of speaker variable. Ss who expected to meet WE rated their reasons for their anticipated responses more highly on "to show I can speak like a Welshman" ($F = 8.52$, df = 1,36; $p < 0.01$), "to show I am proud of being Welsh" ($F = 14.09$; $p < 0.001$), and "because the discussion will be here in a Welsh school in Wales" ($F = 6.17$; $p < 0.025$) than did Ss who expected to meet EN. The latter on the other hand rated "to show how British I am" ($F = 8.36$; $p < 0.01$) and "to show I am proud of being British" ($F = 6.95$; $p < 0.25$) more highly than the former.

Separate $2 \times 2 \times 2$ ANOVAs were computed for each of the 10 attitudes toward speaker scales. A couple of main effects emerged for speaker's accent in that, and of course, the WE speaker was perceived to sound less "standard" ($F = 158.3$; $p < 0.001$) than the EN counterpart but also viewed as more "cooperative" ($F = 4.66$; $p < 0.05$). Three main effects emerged for speaker's viewpoint in that the SU target was rated as significantly more "ambitious" ($F = 6.47$; $p < 0.025$), "confident" ($F = 5.59$; $p < 0.025$) and "sincere" ($F = 7.89$; $p < 0.01$) than the TH person. Furthermore, interactions indicated that speakers in the SU condition were rated as more "ambitious" ($F = 5.32$; $p < 0.05$) and "confident" ($F = 7.87$; $p < 0.01$) after group discussion, while those in the TH condition were rated as *less* of these qualities after group discussion. There was another interaction between accent of speaker and speaker's attitude for the trait "ingratiating" ($F = 6.46$; $p < 0.025$). The SU/WE speaker and the TU/EN speaker were rated as more ingratiating than TU/WE and SU/EN speakers. Interestingly, all speakers were rated as less "kind" following group discussion (F = 5.44; p < 0.05). Finally, there was a three-way interaction on ratings of the trait "intelligence" (F = 6.41; p < 0.025). Newman-Keuls analysis of these data revealed that the source of the difference was essentially between the ratings of EN after group discussion and the other speakers. Under these circumstances, he was rated as significantly more intelligent than all the other speakers in any condition; the former was also perceived as more intelligent after group discussion than before it.

Discussion

The results of the study contrast with both the hypotheses generated and with the results of Taylor and Royer's (1980) study. Overall, they suggest that Ss' anticipated linguistic strategies were more of a function of the speaker's accentedness and perceived status than his known attitudes toward bilingual education. More specifically, Ss anticipated responding with greater attenuation of their ethnic speech markers (particularly in the use of Welsh words and phrases) to the EN than WE speaker and no support whatsoever was derived for Hypotheses 1 to 3. Moreover, Ss did not differentiate between the ethnically supportive/ threatening speakers in either their anticipated linguistic responses or in their reasons for these. Nevertheless, there was evidence from a number of interactions that they *were* aware of both of the stimulus independent variables.

In this regard, Ss differentiated on some traits between speakers with SU and TH attitudes as well as between the WE and EN conditions. However, overall they appear to have evaluated the SU/EN speaker most favorably, notably on the trait "intelligent." Furthermore, the SE speaker with SU views was evaluated differently from the WE speaker with TH attitudes. Although the WE speaker was perceived as more cooperative than the EN one, the WE/SU speaker was also perceived as more ingratiating, and it therefore seems that "cooperativeness" did not have favorable connotations, at least with respect to WE. In sum, contrary to Hypotheses 4 and 5, Ss appeared to have generally upgraded EN relative to WE, particularly when he was ethically supportive and on dimensions relating to status (e.g., intelligence) rather than solidarity. The results therefore reflect the overall pattern of traditional matched-guise studies (see Ryan & Giles, 1982).

It is suggested that Ss were influenced to a greater extent than had been anticipated by the status-related dimensions of the experimental situation and therefore emphasized the status-related rather than solidarity traits in their evaluations of speakers. In this study, a number of factors could have contributed to this interpretation. First, the speaker was presented as being an unfamiliar, older person with high academic status. Second, E was an unfamiliar English person with academic status. Third, the context of the study was formal with experimental procedures and topic of debate carried out in the school setting. All of these factors may be seen as contributing to an emphasis on status- rather than solidarity-stressing dimensions of the situation (Day, 1982). Insofar as English is the language of the dominant, high status group, such an emphasis may highlight societal norms favoring its use and inhibit conformity to ingroup linguistic norms prescribing use of Welsh, at least toward English speakers in the context of this study.

Hypothesis 6 also received very little support, although admittedly several significant differences in pre- and postgroup discussion indicated a move toward more *neutral* rather than extreme positions. These effects may be examined in light of the two preconditions for group polarization suggested by Wetherell and Turner (1979) as (1) identification as a common group and (2) a nonneutral initial response. First, while Ss were chosen who were expected to identify strongly with the Welsh group, following the experiment it emerged that five of the admittedly bilingual Ss were actually from English-speaking homes. Such individuals might represent marginal group members and respond either in terms of being "more Welsh than the Welsh" or by dissociating from this group. The inclusion of such Ss of course increases heterogeneity to an unknown degree and mitigates against common group identification and group polarization. Second, examination of the data indicates that in many instances the initial responses were not sufficiently marked for significant polarization to be expected.

A number of explanations have been offered as to the incongruity between the hypotheses and the results obtained. However, a final thorny issue revolves around the perceived strength of the ethnic *threat*. For instance, the topic of the taped passage has been chosen so as not to arouse too much antipathy in Ss to the experimental situation and centered on the advantages and disadvantages of bilingual education in Quebec and the United States. However, it may have been too far removed from the Ss' personal experiences to have been of sufficient relevance to involve them. Thus, although the attitudes of the speaker were presented in terms of general favorability-unfavorability toward bilingual education in Wales, the topic of the taped message only indirectly reflected his attitudes toward Welsh. In addition, in order to provide comparability between the experimental conditions, the same message was used and therefore contained arguments both for and against bilingual education. Of relevance to the present findings is

Cacioppo and Petty's (1982) notion that where there is high involvement in an issue Ss actively process and elaborate on message arguments. However, when listeners are not highly involved in a persuasive communication (in their paradigm) they are more likely to respond to noncontent cues than to aspects of verbal message itself. Relatedly, Bond and Yang (1981) have suggested that compromise (e.g., cultural accommodation) is possible on less important issues that are more peripheral to one's cultural self-concept whereas ethnic affirmation (e.g., perhaps linguistic differentiations) occurs on issues *central* to one's sense of ethnic identity in order to buttress cultural distinctiveness from other groups.

In conclusion, it is suggested that as a result of these factors together with the elements that contributed to the status-stressing dimension of the experimental situation discussed above, the Ss were less assertive of their ethnic identity than older Ss might have been. These points also indicate differences between the present study and that carried out by Taylor and Royer (1980) and may account for the discrepancies in the results of the studies. It is suggested that a stronger manipulation of the ethnic threat variable by focusing directly on the advantages and disadvantages of bilingual education *in Wales itself* might overcome these factors. This would reinforce Ss' perceptions of the solidarity-stressing dimensions of the situation and facilitate an assertion of ethnic identity in their anticipated linguistic responses to the threatening speaker. Indeed, such experimental modifications would also be expected to lead to more extreme nonneutral initial responses by Ss and greater common group identification and therefore judgmental polarization after group discussion. Following on from this interpretation of Study 1, a modified replication was conducted incorporating the above mentioned changes so as to assess again the merits of the six hypotheses rendered earlier in exactly the same comprehensive school and experimental design.

STUDY 2

Method

Subjects

Fifty-eight (29 males and 29 females) bilingual, first-language Welsh speakers, aged 17 and 18 years, participated in this study. While Lewis's

(1975) language attitudes study suggests that pro-Welsh attitudes decline with age, it is expected that these Ss attending a bilingual school in a strongly Welsh-speaking area will retain relatively strong identification with their ethnic group and language. Moreover, the fact that Ss have attended this school for six or seven years suggests that they will be more highly involved in and committed to an attitude position on bilingualism in Wales. This was confirmed by means of a preexperimental questionnaire designed to assess their degree of enthnolinguistic identification. Not only did all Ss utilize the self-referent "Welsh" rather than "British" or "English" when asked to make a choice between them, but their scores on scales tapping their Welsh identity, value attached to the Welsh language, and desire for their offspring to learn that language were 9.59, 9.31, and 9.35, respectively (on 10-point scales where 10 was the most pro-Welsh rating available). Interestingly, the female Ss rated a sense of Welsh identity stronger than their male counterparts ($p < 0.05$). Finally, on the same 10-item "Attitudes toward Welsh" scale (Lewis, 1975) adopted in Study 1, examination of the mean ratings for each statement indicated that Ss were highly pro-Welsh in all cases.

Materials

Anticipated Linguistic Strategy Scales. The same three scales as used in Study 1 were again adopted here.

Attitudes Toward Speaker Scales. In total, 13 scales were used on this occasion. The same six scales adopted in Study 1 to represent "status" and "solidarity" were used again together with an item measuring Ss' perceptions of the speaker's accent. However, different items were included under the rubric "supportiveness/cooperation" given their apparent ineffectuality previously; these were "understanding," "very similar in his views and goals to myself," and "trying to make people like him." In addition, the traits "likable" and "hostile" were included to tap more directly Ss' feelings toward the speaker, and the trait "reserved and cautious" was included so as to assess listeners' perceptions of the speaker's outspokenness.

Motivations for Anticipated Linguistic Strategies. These were an elaborated version of the comparable set utilized in Study 1. Three of the reasons related to individuals' sense of Welsh identity, three to British identity, and one to ease of communication. Two other reasons related to liking or disliking what the speaker says and thinks. One reason related to the effort of the speaker in coming to talk to the Ss later, and the other related to social constraints; that is, one concerned the status of the speaker and the formal nature of the meeting with him, while the other concerned the fact that the topic of discussion would be Welsh education taking place with Welsh people in a Welsh school in Wales. Finally, one reason tapped directly the social norm that Welsh people should not speak Welsh in the presence of English people and Ss were asked on completion of these 14 scales to provide two further reasons of their own.

Stimulus Audiotape. A one-minute passage (RP) was recorded in a standard English accent and a South Welsh accent by the same speaker as in Study 1. The recordings were of the same length holding again perceived personality and paralinguistic features constant. The recorded passage was carefully prepared to contain a number of clear statements of similar impact, with an equal number supportive and critical of bilingual education and the position of the Welsh language in Wales. The passage appeared to be the beginning of a talk on bilingual education in Wales where the speaker prefaced his own views on the subject by presenting "both sides of the debate."

Procedure

Ss were randomly assigned to one of the four experimental conditions and the procedure followed the same four-phase format as in Study 1. All that is necessary here is to outline some special and distinctive procedural modifications in Study 2. In Phase 1, Ss were afforded the following background information about Mr. Glyn Edwards/Peter Fletcher from an education college in Cardiff/Reading. In the SU conditions:

> He's *very* keen on bilingual education in Wales and he sees a strong need for bilingualism in Wales. Basically, and I quote, he feels there is a need for *positive* discrimination to encourage the survival of the minority language. He feels bilingual education gives the Welsh a chance to use their own language, gives the language itself more economic and social power, and means that Welsh is more widely used. On top of this, he is fairly firm in his views and he believes there is now a secure future for Welsh in modern society.

In the TU conditions:

> He's *not* very keen on bilingual education in Wales and really he questions the need for bilingualism in Wales at all. Basically, and I quote, he doesn't

see *any* point in encouraging a minority language which relatively few people speak and which is gradually dying out anyway. He feels Welsh has little economic or social power and is rarely used outside of local affairs in Wales. On top of this, he is fairly firm in his views and doesn't see much future for Welsh in modern society.

Then to all groups:

Well, I'm sure you'll have something to say about this yourselves and what I'll be interested in today is firstly your impression of Mr. Edwards/ Fletcher, secondly how you think you would actually respond to him if he was here now, and thirdly what you think of what he is saying given your experience of being in a Welsh comprehensive.

In order to maximize the perception of SU and TU throughout the procedure, the views of the speaker toward Welsh bilingual education were again reiterated after group discussion in Phase 4.

This procedure, then, contrasts with the previous study where the speaker's attitudes were presented only with reference to his generally favorable or unfavorable attitudes to the issue. It is expected that these changes strengthen the effect of ethnic threat or support offered by the speaker and override the demand characteristics of the status-stressing dimensions of the experimental situation (described earlier). Thus, these changes are expected to lead to a clearer definition of the situation in interethnic terms and facilitate the assertion of ethnic identity in response to the threatening speaker. In accord with this, it is expected that Ss' response will follow a pattern of differentiation based primarily on content rather than noncontent cues and emphasize solidarity-stressing dimensions in evaluations of the speaker. In addition, the changes described are expected to lead to more extreme nonneutral initial responses by Ss and greater common group identification in the situation. Thus greater group polarization is expected to follow group discussion of Ss' responses than emerged in Study 1. To facilitate the emergence of this process, the group discussion in Phase 3 of the procedure is slightly longer—that is, five minutes—than previously.

Results

Preliminary ANOVAs were computed on the baseline linguistic measures and exhibited a number of between-group differences. In order to take into account this variation, separate $2 \times 2 \times 2 \times 2$ analyses of covariance were performed on each of three anticipated linguistic strategies with the factors of attitude of speaker (TH versus SU), ethnoaccentedness of speaker (EN versus WE), sex of listener (M versus F), and repeated measures on nature of rating (pre- versus postgroup discussion). While two significant effects for sex of listener were apparent with males anticipating using more of the Welsh language (F = 6.54, df = 1,45; p < 0.025) and more Welsh words and phrases (F = 9.70; p < 0.01) than females, the most important result emerging was a three-way interaction between attitude of speaker, accentedness of speaker, and nature of rating (F = 4.47, df = 1,47; p < 0.05) on the Welsh language measure. Newman-Keuls analyses of these data revealed that, before group discussion, those in the TU conditions anticipated using more Welsh to the speaker than did those in the SU conditions, whereas *following* group discussion, the ethnoaccent as well as the attitudes of the speaker more clearly affected Ss' reactions. In this instance, those who heard the SU/EN speaker anticipated using more Welsh than did those who heard either of the WE speakers (TH or EN), and those who heard the SU/EN anticipated using least Welsh.

With respect to Ss' expressed motivations for their anticipated linguistic responses, $2 \times 2 \times 2 \times 2$ ANOVAs were computed on each of the 14 scales separately. Overall, all Ss rated the reasons associated with Welsh identity as very important and those associated with British identity as not very important. However, those who heard the TU speaker emphasized the reasons with Welsh identity even more strongly ("...to show I am proud of being Welsh"[F = 4.94; p < 0.05], "...to show how Welsh I am"[F = 13.03; p < 0.001], "...to show I can speak like a Welshman"[F = 12.5; p < 0.001]), and also that they did not like what he said and thought (F = 53.74; p < 0.001). Those who heard the SU speaker emphasized the effort of the speaker in coming (F = 11.56; p < 0.01) and liked what he said and thought (F = 62.52; p < 0.001) more than the contrastive conditions. Finally, females rated as more important than males "...to help us understand each other easily" (p < 0.025) and also all three reasons associated with British identity (p_s = 0.05 – 0.025).

Separate $2 \times 2 \times 2 \times 2$ ANOVAs were performed on each of the 13 attitudes toward speaker traits. A number of significant main and interaction effects emerged. Ss rated SU as more "intelligent" (F = 22.87, df = 1, 46; p < 0.001), "reserved and cautious" (F = 17.46; p < 0.001), "kind" (F = 88.9; p < 0.001), "sincere" (F = 18.66; p < 0.01), "very similar to their own views and attitudes to themselves" (F = 120.65; p < 0.001), "trying to make people like him" (F = 5.22; p < 0.05) than TH, and as less "confident" (F = 4.44; p < 0.05) and "hostile" (F = 22.62; p < 0.001). There were significant interactions between attitude and ethnoaccent of speaker for the traits "ambitious" (F = 9.34, df = 1,47; p < 0.01), "sociable" (F = 5.26; p < 0.05), and "understanding" (F = 11.63; p < 0.01), and a three-way interaction between these two variables and pre- versus postgroup discussion for the trait "likable" (F = 4.20; p < 0.025). Newman-Keuls analyses for these interactions revealed the following trends.

For the trait "ambitious," there were no significant differences between the four experimental groups. However, examination of the means showed that SU/EN was rated more favorably than TH/WE, who was rated more favorably than SU/WE, who in turn was rated more positively than TH/SE. In addition, in all conditions, the speaker was rated as more "ambitious" following group discussion than before it. For the trait "sociable," the SU/EN was rated as significantly more so than both of the WE speakers, who were rated as more "sociable" than the TH/EN speaker. For the trait "likable," in both pre- and postgroup discussion conditions, the EN and WE, SU speakers were rated as significantly more likable than the TH/WE speaker who was rated more so than the TH/EN speaker; the Newman-Keuls revealed no significant differences for nature of rating. The same evaluative trend emerged also for the trait "understanding."

Overall, then, Ss' ratings were most favorable toward the SU/EN speaker and least favorable toward the TH/EN speaker with ratings for both WE speakers (SU and TH) falling between these two. Finally, WE was seen to have more of a Welsh accent than EN (F = 207.33; p < 0.001) and the SU speakers as having less standard accents than TH (F = 7.52; p < 0.01), with female Ss rating speakers as more "ambitious," "intelligent," "confident," "sociable," and "sincere" but less "cautious and reserved" than did males (p_s = 0.05 – 0.001).

DISCUSSION

The results of Study 2 support Hypotheses 1 through 6 and contrast with those obtained in Study 1. They are in accord with the findings of Taylor and Royer (1980) insofar as Ss' anticipated converging toward/diverging away from ethnically supportive/threatening speakers. Moreover, the present results extend those of Taylor and Royer in that they suggest that responses to the speaker are based less on his or her group membership as defined by linguistic attributes and more on perceived group membership in terms of attitudes toward the ethnic group and language.

Ethnolinguistic divergence was evidenced only on the Welsh language measure and not on the other two anticipated linguistic strategies. It seems that for Welsh-speaking Ss, use of the language is more important than accent in English (see Price et al., 1983). Further, given language divergence from TH speakers, *accent* divergence is redundant. Support for this comes from Ss' free comments and further reasons for their anticipated responses. For example, one informant stated, "it isn't necessary to speak in a Welsh accent to prove that you are Welsh. The ability to speak the language is more important." The results for Ss' anticipated responses to the speaker therefore confirmed Hypothesis 1 that in reaction to a perceived threat from the speakers, Ss will anticipate accentuating their ethnic speech style and attenuating it in the face of perceived support for their ethnic identity. The coherent pattern of these results provides some support for the use of the "anticipated" linguistic response measure. As indicated earlier, there may well be discrepancies between reported and actual linguistic behavior. Needless to say, in future research of this nature, it would be useful to examine Ss' actual responses to a speaker as well as explore the influence of demand characteristics of the experimental situation, such as the experimenter's perceived ethnolinguistic identity. Obviously, the expression of support, particularly from outgroup members, has to be perceived as genuine and non-Machiavellian for it to induce linguistic attenuation. Whether this phenomenon will be confirmed cross-culturally is a moot issue. Undoubtedly situations exist where conflictual relations between groups have been historically so intense (e.g., in South Africa) that individual outgroup support would be construed with suspicion if not downright ignored.

The predominant emphasis on the attitudes of the speaker rather than on his accent was borne out in Ss' ratings of their reasons for their strategies. All Ss rated as extremely important to them all three of the reasons associated with their Welsh identity and rated as unimportant to them those associated with their British identity. There were no differences in the ratings of reasons for the WE and EN speaker groups. However, those in the TH conditions particularly emphasized reasons associated with their former identity and that they did not like what the speaker had to say. Those in the SU conditions emphasized the effort of the speaker in coming to talk to them (as they anticipated meeting him) and that they did like what he said and thought. These results therefore support Hypothesis 3.

In their ratings of the speaker, Ss again differentiated primarily between the ethnically threatening and supportive speakers, rating the latter overall more favorably. However, on a number of traits the SU/EN speaker was upgraded further than the WE speakers. Thus, for example, the SU/EN speaker was rated as more sociable than the WE speakers, who were rated as more sociable than the TH/EN speaker. Similarly, the SU speaker (EN and WE) was rated as more likable and understanding than the TH/WE speaker, while the TH/EN speaker was downgraded even further.

There is some evidence that favorable responses toward the SU/EN speaker may have been due in part at least to attributions made internally to the speaker (see, for example, Hewstone, 1983). For example, the SU/EN speaker would likely have been seen to support a cause that would not really affect *himself*. This perception would be expected to contribute to the upgrading of the SU/EN speaker relative to other speakers on the trait "sociable," as well as to the upgrading of both WE/ and EN/SU speakers on the traits "likable" and "understanding." In contrast, the TH speaker, and in particular the TH/EN one, would likely be dismissed as not understanding the situation the Welsh people and language face.

It was predicted in Hypothesis 4 that the SU speakers would be upgraded particularly on traits relating to the solidarity dimension. The only discrepancy from this trend was for the trait "sociable." However, given the interpretation for ratings on this trait, it seems that this hypothesis was confirmed by the results obtained.

While the SU speakers were rated as being more similar in their attitudes and views to the Ss than the TH speakers, they were also rated as more "reserved and cautious" and less "confident." The SU speakers may have been seen as more confident through their ability to present such dissimilar views without apparent hesitation. Alternatively, it is possible that while Ss perceived the SU speakers' attitudes as similar to their own, they may hold more extreme views than were presented by the SU speakers.

Attitudes toward the speaker also likely affected Ss' perceptions of their accent. Thus although WE were perceived as having more Welsh accents than the EN counterparts, there was also a bias toward perceiving SU as having less standard accents than TH. That is, the content of the speaker's message affected the perception of his accent (see Nisbett & Wilson, 1977). Besides this effect, speech style can act as a salient cue for categorization, and once assigned to a category the individual assumes the evaluative content of that category. It is possible that in the case of the TH/EN speaker, the views ascribed to him may have served to reinforce the stereotype of the English held by Welsh bilinguals. Thus, this speaker was downgraded on the traits "understanding," "likable," and "sociable" and evoked comments from the Ss that he did not understand the situation of the Welsh people and their language.

There were also a number of sex differences in Ss' ratings of speakers. These seem generally consistent with research into sex stereotypes and may be attributed to the sex of the speaker (Smith, 1984). Thus, females rated the speaker as being more "ambitious," "intelligent," "confident," "sociable," and "sincere," and less "reserved and cautious" than did the males. The first five traits (with the possible exception of "sincere") may be regarded as generally closer to the male than the female stereotype. This may be why female Ss emphasized these traits with respect to the male speaker more strongly than did the male Ss, differentiating from the speaker in terms of gender and maintaining their preconceptions of how a male speaker ought to or does talk.

The stronger disagreement by males than females to the statement "Welsh people should not speak Welsh in the presence of English people" may be linked to the sexes' differences in anticipated linguistic responses and reasons for these. The males' disinclination with this social norm is consonant with their greater anticipated use of Welsh to the speaker. Furthermore, males were less concerned with the reason " . . . to help us understand each other easily," as well as with the reason associated with British identity. It seems from these responses that male Ss were more willing than females to assert their Welsh identity and counter norms for "polite" behavior. These findings accord with language attitude research suggesting that females are more concerned with correctness and status than males (e.g., Trudgill, 1974). An alternative interpretation, however, is that the female Ss were more concerned with ease of communication, and this is consonant with their greater emphasis on this reason in their motivational responses.

It can be argued that greater involvement in both the message and the evaluation task (since they anticipated meeting the speaker) yielded contrasting results to those obtained in Study 1 and in traditional matched-guise studies. The information provided about the speaker's attitudes as well as other information about him appeared to decrease the influence of the association between low status ethnic speech styles and the social class variable (see Stewart et al., 1985). Thus in the present study, Ss did not simply upgrade the higher status speaker, or given the emphasis on solidarity, the ingroup ethnic speech style. Rather, more differentiated constructs were used in the appraisal of speakers, revealing underlying processes of attribution and social comparison. As such, the results herein suggest some crucial limiting conditions of speech style evaluations as obtained in traditional evaluation research (see also Giles & Ryan, 1982).

A further perspective on these results is provided by the more general notions of balance theory (Heider, 1964) and cognitive consistency (Festinger, 1957). According to these positions, it would be hypothesized that if the speaker is negative about issues relating to Welsh identity and the listener values the Welsh identity highly, then the listener will be negative toward the speaker and diverge linguistically and psychologically from the speaker; the results of Study 2 accord with these notions. Consistent with these interpretations is the notion of reactance. Brehm's (1972) reactance model suggests that when freedom is threatened, the threatened alternative is chosen and more favorable attitudes toward it ensue. Clearly this related closely to research on the "boomerang" effect (see Bond & Yang, 1981) and reactance will only occur when the threatened alternative is sufficiently valued for the loss of freedom to be salient, as in the present case. Thus, Study 2 provides evidence of accentuated favorability toward an ethnic language in the face of perceived threat to it by a speaker (see Gallois et al., 1984).

In both studies reported herein, even in a strongly Welsh-speaking area and a bilingual school in the context of a formal discussion with a non-Welsh-speaking stranger, social norms would prescribe polite (English) sociolinguistic behavior. In other words, there were significant costs associated with the use of Welsh. That Ss perceived the social norms in this way was evidenced by some of their comments at the end of Study 2. The clearest example was: "Some questions asked whether we would be polite to Mr. Edwards by talking to him in his own language, the fact that we did was then made to look as if we were not proud of being Welsh"; note that this was the S's interpretation of what was asked. Some said it would be rude not to "respect someone who has spent time to come and discuss problems of this sort."

There was further evidence of awareness of these social norms in that a number of Ss thought that a standard accent would be more readily accepted and listened to: "I don't want my opinions to be dismissed because of the accent I use." Furthermore, some Ss appeared to wish to counteract the negative stereotyping of the Welsh which they saw as following from use of the Welsh accent: "I don't want to be labeled with the usual image of Wales, i.e., booze and rugby. I wish to try to convey to people outside of Wales that there is more to my country than that alone." To this extent, Ss showed an awareness of the definition of their group by the dominant group and of the prescribed norms for acceptable behavior (see McKirnan & Hamayan, 1983). It may also seem from comments that some of the Ss still accepted this definition and were not fully aware of the implications of cognitive alternatives to the social structure of the Welsh and English groups (see Turner & Brown, 1978). Yet there were also indications that some of the Ss were reassessing the definition of normative behavior in their tendency to disagree with the statement "Welsh people should not speak Welsh in the presence of English people" (particularly when this was presented as a reason for their anticipated linguistic strategies) in contrast with the neutral response to the statement in Study 1. Furthermore, several Ss commented directly on such norms for interaction with outgroup members, for example: "I belive that if you must live in Wales and in a Welsh community then you should accept the fact and learn to speak the language because Welsh people should not change just for the sake of foreigners." Or again: "I believe it is every person's right to express their own feelings in their own language."

Two further factors are worthy of airing in examining the strength of differentiation demonstrated by Ss in response to TH speakers. The first of these is pragmatic in that if Ss wished to continue the discussion with the speaker and put forward their own views as a counterpoint to his own, they would have to talk in English as they were told that the speaker did not understand Welsh. A number of Ss (n = 6) commented on this as well as their strong desire to give him the "Welsh people's" views since he "did not understand the situation." The second is that the stimulus passage was balanced in presenting the pros and cons of Welsh bilingual education. This was necessary given the design of the experiment in order that the same passage would be heard in all experimental conditions. Thus the passage presented an apparently reasoned and balanced attitude to the issue, in stark contrast to the information Ss were afforded of the speaker's own attitudes in either the SU or TH conditions. In line with this apparent anomaly, several Ss commented that they would have liked to have heard more of the taped talk in order to find out "what Mr. Edwards/Flecther really thought himself." Thus, the balanced nature of the passage counteracted to some extent the reinforced "quoting" of the speaker's views. Furthermore, research on persuasion indicates that where Ss are highly involved in an issue, a rhetorical type of communication detracts from rather than adds to its impact (Cacioppo & Petty, 1982). Thus, overall there were a number of factors mitigating *against* differentiation from or convergence toward a speaker and the fact that these phenomena occurred in spite of them indicates a strong underlying process. Hypotheses 1, 3, 4 (and 6) were therefore confirmed by the result of Study 2.

Hypotheses 2 and 5 predicted that Ss would make more extreme responses (in either direction) to the speaker when he was perceived to be a member of the out- rather than ingroup. These were supported in Ss' anticipated use of Welsh following group discussion when they anticipated greater convergence toward and divergence away from the ethnically supportive/threatening SE speaker than to the WE speakers. Similarly, their evaluations of the SU/EN speaker were most favorable and those of the TH/EN speaker least favorable with evaluations of the WE speakers falling between. Thus, the results may be interpreted as suggesting that Ss reacted more strongly to the outgroup than the ingroup member on the basis of external cues. However, this is probably too simplistic a view of the attribution of in- or outgroup membership to a speaker. First, Ss' responses suggest that they took more account of "group membership" in terms of attitudes toward Welshness and the Welsh language than in terms of external criteria such as accent. Second, while they labeled the Welsh-accented speaker (Mr. Edwards) a Welshman, it is likely that he was not perceived to be a member of their "own group" since he did not speak Welsh. Indeed, Ss emphasized the link between Welsh identity and speaking the Welsh language in their free comments (see also, Giles et al., 1977). The impact of the antagonistic attitudes of the Welsh speaker were therefore less likely to invoke the notion of "cultural traitor" than if this speaker had been Welsh-speaking.

Hypothesis 6 predicted that Ss' responses would be polarized following group discussion of their responses. Overall, however, there were fewer effects than had been expected. In a number of cases this is attributable to the extreme pregroup discussion responses suggesting ceiling effects accounted for the lack of further polarization following discussion. Ideally, the data should have been analyzed for each discussion group individually in order to identify patterns between them as well as within the subject group as a whole, but there were too few Ss for this to be performed with reliability. Nevertheless, the group polarization effects that did occur were consonant with the hypothesis.

CONCLUSION

The results of Studies 1 and 2 together confirm the importance of the perceived centrality of an ethnic threat in leading to a definition of an encounter in interethnic terms. They suggest that an ethnic threat on an issue in which subordinate ethnic group members feel involved and highly committed in their attitudes is more likely to result in the assertion of ethnic identity in evaluative reactions and anticipated linguistic responses to the other interactant.

Where individuals are not strongly committed to an attitude position on which an outgroup member opposes them or where they do not perceive the issue to be central to their sense of ethnic identity, they are likely to conform to societal, rather than ingroup, linguistic norms defining appropriate behavior, such as use of the higher status group's ethnic speech style (see also Genesee & Bourhis, 1982). In this type of situation, individuals are likely to respond primarily to noncontent (e.g., vocal) cues of ethnic group membership and to attenuate their ethnic speech style in response to an ingroup member. Their reasons for these responses will be associated with ease of communication and the perceived effort and involvement of the other interactant. That is, the individuals will demonstrate both linguistic and cognitive convergence (see Beebe & Giles, 1984).

Where individuals are strongly committed to an attitude position on which an outgroup member opposes them and perceives the issue to be central to their sense of ethnic identity, they are likely to define the interaction and act primarily in terms of their ethnic identity rather than in terms of societal norms. That is, they are likely to redefine the social norms for appropriate behavior that would prescribe use of the higher status group's speech style. In this type of situation, individuals are likely to respond primarily in terms of content cues to ethnic group membership (and presumably often assess the authenticity of their perceived sincerity) and to actively process and elaborate upon the other's message. They are likely to accentuate their ethnic speech markers in response to a perceived threat from an outgroup member (even when this outgroup is of a higher status in the broader social structure). Their reasons for this response will be associated with pride in their group identity and speech style and a wish to dissociate from the other interactant. That is, individuals will demonstrate both linguistic and cognitive divergence.

In addition, in the former type of situation individuals are likely to upgrade the higher status group member, particularly on the dimension of status/competence. In the latter type, individuals are likely to downgrade the speaker who is perceived to threaten their sense of ethnic identity, particularly on the dimension of solidarity. This effect may be further accentuated when the threatening individual is defined as an outgroup member on the basis of noncontent as well as content cues.

In summary, this chapter has elucidated some of the ways in which *situational* variables can affect anticipated linguistic divergence/convergence and ethnic language attitudes. These findings necessitate modest, but important, modifications to speech accommodation and ethnolinguistic identity theories (see Beebe & Giles, 1984) as well as to the intergroup model of ethnic language attitudes (Ryan et al., 1984) and will be forthcoming elsewhere in due course. Finally, Studies 1 and 2 do underline the need for future language attitude studies to include not only radical variations in message content within our experimental designs but to do so on issues to which listener-judges are committed in one way or another; future research in this direction is likely to dismember many of the golden "rules" of this research tradition.

REFERENCES

Ball, P., Giles, H., Byrne, J., & Berechree, P. (1984). Situational constraints on the evaluative significance of speech accommodation: Some Australian data. *International Journal of the Sociology of Language, 46*, 131-146.

Beebe, L., & Giles, H. (1984). Speech accommodation theories: A discussion in terms of second language acquisition. *International Journal of the Sociology of Language, 46*, 5-32.

Bond, M., & Yang, K. (1982). Ethnic affirmation versus cross-cultural accommodation: The variable impact of questionnaire language. *Journal of Cross-Cultural Psychology, 13*, 169-185.

Bourhis, R. Y. (1979). Language in inter-ethnic interaction: A social psychological approach. In H. Giles (Ed.), *Language and ethnic relations* (pp. 117-142). Oxford: Pergamon.

Bourhis, R. Y. (1984). Cross-cultural communication in Montreal: Two field studies since Bill 101. *International Journal of the Sociology of Language, 46*, 33-48.

Bourhis, R. Y., & Giles, H. (1977). The language of intergroup distinctiveness. In H. Giles (Ed.), *Language, ethnicity and intergroup relations* (pp. 119-136). London: Academic Press.

Bourhis, R. Y., Giles H., & Tajfel, H. (1973). Language as a determinant of Welsh identity. *European Journal of Social Psychology, 3*, 447-460.

Brehm, J. W. (1972). *Responses to loss of freedom: A theory of psychological reactance.* Morristown, NJ: General Learning Press.

Cacioppo, J. R., & Petty, R. E. (1982). Language variables, attitudes and persuasion. In E. B. Ryan & H. Giles (Eds.), *Attitudes toward language variation* (pp. 189-207). Baltimore: Edward Arnold.

Day, R. (1984). Children's attitudes toward language. In E. B. Ryan & H. Giles (Eds.), *Attitudes toward language variation* (pp. 116-131). Baltimore: Edward Arnold.

Dube-Simard, L. (1983). Genesis of social categorization, threat to identity and perception of social injustice: Their role in intergroup communication. *Journal of Language & Social Psychology, 2*, 183-206.

Festinger, L. (1957). *A theory of cognitive dissonance.* Stanford: Stanford University Press.

Gallois, C., Callan, V., & Johnstone, M. (1984). Personality judgments of Australian Aborigine and White speakers: Ethnicity, sex and context. *Journal of Language & Social Psychology, 3*, 39-57.

Genesee, F., & Bourhis, R. Y. (1982). The social psychological significance of code-switching. *Journal of Language & Social Psychology, 1*, 1-27.

Giles, H., Bourhis, R. Y., & Taylor, D. M. (1977). Dimensions of Welsh identity. *European Journal of Social Psychology, 7*, 29-39.

Giles, H., & Edwards, J. R. (Eds.). (1983). Language attitudes in multicultural settings. *Journal of Multilingual & Multicultural Development, 4*(2/3).

Giles, H., & Johnson, P. (1981). The role of language in ethnic group relations. In J. C. Turner & H. Giles (Eds.), *Intergroup behavior* (pp. 199-243). Chicago: Unversity of Chicago Press

Giles, H., & Ryan, E. B. (1982). Prolegomena for developing a social psychological theory for language attitudes. In E. B. Ryan & H. Giles (Eds.), *Attitudes toward language variation* (pp. 208-232). Baltimore: Edward Arnold.

Giles, H., Ryan, E. B., Hewstone, M., & Johnson, P. (in press). Language attitudes: A review, priorities, and a model. In U. Ammon et al. (Eds.), *Sociolinguistics: An international handbook of the science of language and society.* The Hague: Mouton.

Heider, F. (1958). *The psychology of interpersonal relations.* New York: John Wiley.

Hewstone, M. (1983). The role of language in attribution processes. In J. Jaspars, F. Fincham, & M. Hewstone (Eds), *Attribution theory and research: Conceptual development and social dimensions* (pp. 241-260). London: Academic.

Khleif, B. (1979). Insiders, outsiders and renegades: Towards a classification of ethnolinguistic labels. In H. Giles & B. Saint-Jacques (Eds.), *Language and ethnic relations* (pp. 159-172). Oxford: Pergamon.

Lambert, W. E. (1967). The social psychology of bilingualism. *Journal of Social Issues, 23*, 91-109.

Lewis, E. G. (1975). Attitudes to language among bilingual children and adults in Wales. *International Journal of the Sociology of Language, 4*, 103-125.

McKirnan, D., & Hamayan, E. (1983). Speech norms and intergroup perceptions: A test of model in a bicultural context. *Journal of Language & Social Psychology, 3*, 21-38.

Nisbett, R. E., & Wilson, T. D. (1977). Telling more than we know: Verbal reports on thought processes. *Psychological Review, 84,* 231-259.

Price, S., Fluck, M., & Giles, H. (1983). The effects of language of testing on bilingual preadolescents' attitudes towards Welsh and varieties of English. *Journal of Multilingual & Multicultural Development, 4,* 149-161.

Ryan, E. B., Hewstone, M., & Giles, H. (1984). Language and intergroup attitudes. In J. R. Eiser (Ed.), *Attitudinal judgment* (pp, 135-158). New York: Springer-Verlag.

Smith, P. M. (1984). *Language, the sexes, and society.* Oxford: Blackwell.

Stewart, M., Ryan, E. B., & Giles, H. (1985). Accent and social class effects on status and solidarity dimensions. *Personality & Social Psychology Bulletin, 11,* 98-105.

Street, R. L., Jr., & Giles, H. (1982). Speech accommodation theory: A social cognitive model of speech behavior. In M. Roloff & C. R. Berger (Eds.), *Social cognition and communication* (pp. 193-226). Beverly Hills; CA: Sage.

Taylor, D. M., & Royer, L. (1980). Group processes affecting anticipated language choice in intergroup relations. In H. Giles et al. (Eds.), *Language: Social psychological perspectives* (pp. 185-192). Oxford: Pergamon.

Taylor, D. M., Wong-Reiger, D., McKirnan, D. J., & Bercussion, T. (1982). Interpreting and coping with threat in the context of intergroup relations. *Journal of Social Psychology, 117,* 1257-1269.

Trudgill, P. (1974). *Sociolinguistics.* Harmondsworth: Penguin.

Turner, J. C., & Brown, R. J. (1978). Social status, cognitive alternatives and intergroup relations. In H. Tajfel (Ed.), *Differentiation between social groups* (pp. 201-234). New York: Academic Press.

Wetherell, M., & Turner, J. C. (1980, September). *Group polarization and social identification.* Paper presented at the annual conference of the Social Psychology Section of the British Psychological Society, Guildford.

Williams, C. (1979). An ecological and behavioral analysis of ethnolinguistic change in Wales. In H. Giles & B. Saint-Jacques (Eds.), *Language and ethnic relations* (pp. 27-56). Oxford: Pergamon.

Williams, G. (Ed.) (1978). *Social and cultural change in contemporary Wales.* London: Routledge & Kegan Paul.

7

Jesse Jackson's "Hymietown" Apology
A Case Study of Interethnic Rhetorical Analysis

WILLIAM J. STAROSTA • LARRY COLEMAN •
Howard University

The analysis describes Black-Jewish relations in the United States as a context to understand Jesse Jackson's apology for his characterization of New York Jews as "Hymies" and of New York as "Hymietown" during the presidential election campaign in 1984. After examining how Jackson exemplified selected traditions of the Black church, his apology is examined from the standpoint of "interethnic healing" and of "political healing." As a political healer, Jackson attempted to overcome a gaffe by means of a "degradation ritual" in order to show himself as honoring widely accepted American values. Six stages of criticism are enumerated for interethnic criticism, and five factors common to interethnic rhetoric are employed in this analysis.

On February 26, 1984, about four months after declaring his candidacy and nearly two months after securing the release of downed Navy aviator Robert Goodman from a Syrian prison, Reverend Jesse Jackson appeared before the Jewish Temple Adeth Yeshurun to apologize for derogatory remarks he made about New York Jews. A *Washington Post* editorial of February 18 reported that Jackson had made the remarks in a private conversation that was overheard by a *Post* reporter later identified as Milton Coleman. Jackson first denied having used the terms "Hymie" and "Hymietown" but later admitted using these characterizations of New York Jewry. Such remarks undermined public confidence in the Rainbow Candidate for the Democratic Party's presidential nomination and damaged the candidate's political image. Early in the primary races, when momentum could be gained or lost that would be magnified in subsequent primary elections, Reverend Jackson moved to start a process of healing wounds to his political image. He did so with his apology to those assembled at the temple.

His overheard remarks concerning Hymie and Hymietown were interpreted also in the context of a history of ethnic relations between

Afro-American and American Jew and were issued by a candidate whose personal views of Arabs and Jews had recently been questioned in unfavorable press reports. At a separate level from the healing of Jackson's political image, the address attempted to smooth interethnic abrasions between American Black and Jew. Thus, at two levels, Jackson faced parallel problems of healing. Jackson appropriately entitled his chosen response "Binding Up the Wounds."

The present analysis traces the task of interethnic healing of bruised ethnic relations and the healing of a damaged political image through three stages: (1) historical relations between Black and Jewish Americans; (2) public and political expectations for the address; and (3) interethnic analysis.

The format adopted for the analysis of Jackson's interethnic rhetoric should be of use in examining all specimens of interethnic exchange. The framework comprises six stages: (1) the delineation of historical relations between the speaker's culture and that of the audience culture; (2) identification of those elements of a speaker's culture that normally determine the speaker's style of discourse; (3) the specification of any prior image the speaker may have among those of the audience culture; (4) the enumeration of public expectations concerning the address; (5) message analysis in light of the preceding factors; and (6) analysis at the level of interethnic rhetoric.

Message analysis requires neither the assessment of effect nor the prescriptive judgment of whether the speaker was "good" or "bad" on the basis of set rhetorical standards. The temptation is strong for a critic to see mainly what is hoped for or expected in an interethnic address. It is therefore unlikely that a single observer can gain sufficient critical distance from the analysis of a contemporary interethnic exchange to render a judgment of effect meaningful. Likewise, juridical criticism, wherein "right" and "wrong" are prescriptively mandated (Baskerville, 1971), invites ethnocentrism whereby the standards of one culture are inappropriately applied to critique the pronouncements of another.

Instead, the present message analysis explores how the speaker consciously exercises message options to place a desired impression in the minds of members of another ethnic group. Such strategies are detailed and the ethical qualities of this attempt are discussed in light of criteria for interethnic relations offered later in the analysis.

HISTORICAL RELATIONS BETWEEN
BLACK AND JEW IN AMERICA

General Historical Relations

The history of interethnic relations between Afro-Americans and Jewish Americans contains many examples of bias, controversy, and ambivalence. The Black American stereotype image of a manipulative and tricky Jewish merchant, who chiefly aims to make money from his Black patrons while protecting and developing his business at the expense of Blacks, has contributed to the damaging of interethnic relations. Likewise, the Jewish American stereotype image of Afro-Americans as carefree, happy-go-lucky people whose condition of servitude and oppression is to some extent deserved and largely outside the control of the Jewish community (Cohen, 1969; Cruse, 1967; Drake & Cayton, 1962; Weisbond & Stein, 1972) also serves to illustrate the historical mutual mistrust, denial, anger, and frustration that has dominated relations between the two groups.

The causes for such distance and such intense wounds between the two communities can be traced to the early American history of Black-Jewish relations. During the period of American slavery the Jewish immigrant found ethnic background and immigrant status to be liabilities in the southern United States. Therefore, most Jewish merchants did not "rock the boat" of slavery out of fear of calling greater attention to themselves and of alienating their slave-holding patrons. Tacit acceptance of slavery made good economic sense (Weisbond & Stein, 1972). As a race living and working in the northern and southern states during the nineteenth century, American Jewry seldom spoke out against slavery (Weisbond & Stein, 1972, p. 33). While certain Jewish abolitionists such as Rabbi David Einhorn of Baltimore did speak out against slavery, American Jewry was largely mute on the issue.

This silence on issues of American racism and slavery left a bitter taste in the mouths of twentieth-century Blacks. Black intellectuals such as Harold Cruse (1967) praised the support of Jewish individuals in the 1920s and 1930s. However, Cruse also voiced the resentment and contempt that Black intellectuals and artists of the twentieth century hold for what he called "paternalistic" Jewish thinkers who often take on the role of "interpreter" of Black problems and experiences (Cruse, 1967, p. 260).

Another illustration of the origin of injured relations between Blacks and Jews springs from the famous court case of the Scottsboro Boys.

Carter (1969) reports that a rabbi named Goldstein in Montgomery, Alabama, tried to help in the defense of nine Black youths who were sentenced to death for allegedly raping two white girls. In 1933, however, the Montgomery Jewish community eschewed involvement in the case, persuaded Rabbi Goldstein to resign his position in the local temple, and ushered him off to New York.

Situations such as the Montgomery Jewish community's reaction to the Scottsboro case, general Jewish American silence on issues of Black civil and human rights, and Black-Jewish conflict over the interpretation of the Black experience provide a historical frame of reference for examining specific events such as the Hymietown reference by Reverend Jackson and the subsequent apology to American Jews.

Specific Relations

The specific relationship between Jesse Jackson and the Jewish community must be examined relative to several important issues. These issues include Jackson's views on Arab-Israeli relations; his delay in accepting responsibility for referring to Jews as Hymies and to New York as Hymietown; his alleged statement that he was tired of hearing about the Holocaust; reported threats by the Jewish Defense League to harm Jackson and to sabotage his campaign; and Jackson's past association with Minister Louis Farrakhan, leader of the Black Muslim Nation of Islam (Berman, 1984; Gold, 1984).

Because of his views on the Arab-Israeli conflict in the Middle East, Jackson's image for the Jewish community has declined over the last two decades. Political analyst Paul Berman (1984), writing in *The Nation*, quotes a Chicago reporter who says that Jackson raised money from Arab organizations with the caveat, "If you don't support me, I won't support you." Berman's point is that Jackson's verbal and organizational support went to political and ethnic groups who offered support for his campaign. By this view, when Jewish support waned for Jackson's Operation PUSH (People United to Save Humanity), Jackson switched his allegiance to the Arabs, the historic foes of Israeli Jews.

In Berman's article, "The Other Side of the Rainbow," several other alleged anti-Jewish, anti-Israeli remarks were enumerated. Jackson was alleged to have said that Jews were a "bigger obstacle" for Blacks "than the Ku Klux Klan"; that Israel was founded "illegitimately"; and that Zionism is "a philosophy based on race." While the authenticity of these reported remarks or their meaning bears further analysis, the rumored statements served to alienate Jackson further from American Jewry.

One of the most significant factors affecting Jackson's public image (persona) and his alienation from American Jewry was his close association with Minister Farrakhan, leader of the Nation of Islam, a group of Black Muslims with a deeply separatist philosophy. Farrakhan had been inspired by Jackson's involvement in the campaign. While well over 50 years of age, Farrakhan chose 1984 as the year he first registered to vote and encouraged his Muslim following to do the same. He offered to Jackson the support of his paramilitary Fruit of Islam as bodyguards to protect his life until U.S. government security officers undertook this task.

It was Farrakhan's powerful and sometimes inflammatory rhetoric that added fuel to the smoldering embers on which rested Jackson-Jewish relations. The April 3, 1984 edition of the *New York Times* reported that Farrakhan had said he would make an example of *Washington Post* reporter Milton Coleman for leaking the Hymietown remark to another reporter. Farrakhan's speech reportedly called Coleman "a traitor" and proclaimed that "one day soon we will punish you with death." An April 13, 1984 *New York Times* report quoted Farrakhan's warning to the Jewish people, saying that "If you harm this brother, he will be the last one." (Farrakhan later explained that he was addressing the militant Jewish Defense League and the Jews Against Jackson.)

The spring of 1984 yielded repeated reports on Farrakhan's caustic, often symbolic references to Judaism as "a dirty religion" and to Hitler as having been a "great man." Despite attempts by Farrakhan and Jackson to defend their image against what Farrakhan called "wicked and malicious tampering with his remarks," Jackson's image among the Jewish people was continually being weakened. In June 1984, press reports announced that Jackson had disassociated himself from Farrakhan.

Jackson's image among Jews during the campaign suffered greatly as a result of his Hymietown remarks, his delay in admitting the remarks, other comments attributed to him by the press, and his association with Minister Farrakhan. A March 12, 1984 article in *Time* declared that some of the "luster" had been "lost from Jackson's moral crusade on behalf of the nation's have-nots." The article referred to Jackson's New Hampshire speech of apology. A Jews Against Jackson advertisement in the November 11, 1983 *New York Times* illustrated the disenchantment between Jackson and some Jews:

We believe that Jesse Jackson is far more powerful than most think. We believe that he is successfully building a coalition of malcontents who will be a disaster for Jews, for Israel, for America, for the Free World. We believe that he is successfully moving to a position of power within the Democratic Party. We are afraid and we intend to act. Jesse Jackson is no good for Jews, Israel, or for America. Stop him. Ruin Jesse, now.

Message Analysis

Since the death by assassination of Martin Luther King and Malcolm X, Jesse Jackson occupies the foremost national position among Black charismatic communicators. Barbara Reynolds (1975) examined at length Jackson's ability to communicate to his audiences and to those in positions of power during Operation Breadbasket and within Jackson's PUSH operation. Jackson received acclaim as a speaker from news commentators along the entire political spectrum during the presidential debates, being designated among America's most talented speakers by Dan Rather, Ted Koppel, and George Will.

An appreciation of Jackson's style and effectiveness cannot be gained without placing Jackson's speechmaking into the context of the Black church. Jackson exemplifies the style historically developed by the Black preacher (Atwater, 1984), which finds its roots from within the environment of the Black community.

The Black preacher holds a profoundly upright and solid image within the Black American community. The Negro church reigns as the most respected institution within the community. Henry Mitchell (1970) notes that "the Black preacher has always enjoyed the status of being the national leader of the Black community." Jackson the preacher and Jackson the man emerge from this legacy as the person of moral stature who speaks with dynamic delivery, with emotive force, and with an eye that detects the will of God in matters mundane.

Jackson chooses language and stylistic structure that spring from the Black church tradition. According to Mitchell (1970, p. 173),

> The Black congregation responds to beauty of language—the well-turned phrase. This does not mean complexity of structure. In fact, Black culture preachers often use short, easily remembered sentences. But they use rhetorical flair.

In Jackson's case, this "flair" stems in part from the use of poetic devices of style. Brown (1984) enumerates Jackson's penchant for symbolism, assonance, alliteration, rhyme, and antithesis. Not only is Jackson remembered for his call-and-response chant "I am somebody," his poetic devices also appear in the statements "It's not the bus but it's us [Black people]," "Don't make a baby until you can raise a baby," and "We are going from the outhouse to the courthouse to the Statehouse to the White House."

Mitchell also explains how the traditional Black preacher masters storytelling and how he places himself into the sermon as a character out of the scriptures. Bible stories merge logically with present-day needs in narratives based on the story of Job, the parable of the sower and the seeds, David and Goliath, and the crucifixion of Christ.

Jackson honors this tradition in his speeches by regularly turning to Bible stories and to stories about great men and women. An example comes from a speech before Shiloh Baptist Church in Washington, D.C. Jackson alludes to the Biblical account of Saul, who is converted from disbeliever to believer while on the road to Damascus. He is "turned" from persecutor of Christians to promoter of Christianity. In Jackson's eye, this is also the story of his own successful negotiation for the release of downed U.S. Navy pilot Lt. Robert O. Goodman, performed while Jackson too "walked the road to Damascus." Ironically and symbolically, Jackson "turned" Syrian President Assad from a persecutor of U.S. interests to a person who makes a gesture of cooperation toward the United States.

Thus it is not surprising on the occasion of the address by Jackson to those at Temple Adeth Yushurun to hear Jackson begin with the story of Jacob, who wrestled with an angel. Jacob and Jackson faced a crisis where they are torn by spiritual needs on the one hand and "outer" needs on the other:

> Like Jacob, for a week, my inner and outer self has wrestled. I have been confronted by conflicting moral challenges. When confronted by the charge I hesitated, for to say "Yes, I had said that" I feared would have thrown up an insurmountable obstacle to my efforts to keep open the much needed path to dialogue. To have said "No" would have compromised my essence, my moral integrity and authority. (From text supplied by Jackson campaign staff).

Within the Black church, it is not uncommon to seek the forgiveness of the congregation in a public appeal for sins that have been committed. The novelty of the occasion is that Jackson attempted to seek forgiveness across the lines of ethnicity and religion.

With characteristic use of antithesis, Jackson then states the major problem to be addressed by his remarks:

We can take the low road of continued antagonism and mistrust, or we can turn aside all hatred and find another way. . . . This is not the Middle East, this is America. . . . We can begin to talk to each other at home and transport our peace across the world.

Drawing from his image as Black preacher, Jackson centers his address on mutually familiar references to Old Testament stories. Jackson hopes to draw credibility, respect, and authority by establishing himself symbolically as a "lowly prophet" like Nathan, who stands up to King David to tell him of his error. He says that his task now is to "be prophetic," at whatever cost.

Jackson accepts blame for his delay in coming forth and for making the remarks in the first place. Then he quickly shifts from self-criticism to restrained defense, telling that his remarks were made "not in a spirit of meanness." As a moral leader, Jackson seeks forgiveness, while simultaneously extending his forgiveness for any misdeed directed at him or his campaign by members of the Jewish community. "We must forgive each other, redeem each other, regroup, and move on." This attempt to transcend differences refers in part to Mier Kahane's Jewish Defense League and the Jews Against Jackson, including "Ruin Jesse Ruin." Members of the JDL reportedly threatened Jackson's life and were considered "a dangerous group" who "should be carefully watched" (Berman, 1984).

Jackson appeals for sympathy by volunteering that his own family has been threatened and that his children have suffered interethnic strain. Jackson explains that his daughter was asked at an admissions interview at Harvard to differentiate her position on Israel from her father's. He refers likewise to a JDL 19-page memorandum to reporters as an attempt to "discredit, disrupt, and destroy my campaign." Jackson has by now ceased to refer again to the apology for his own remarks, broadening his remarks to address issues of mutual concern. Jackson turns to Old Testament religious symbolism as a "binder of wounds" while seeking sympathy and empathy by mentioning his family and the misquotations of his positions.

In a broader sense, Jackson's ethos derived as a Black preacher trying his best to be prophetic helps to bolster his defense against appearing anti-Semitic. Serrin (1972) described Jackson as perhaps the finest preacher of his day, "better than . . . Dr. Leon Sullivan, as good as, perhaps better than Malcolm or Martin." Berman (1984), writing in *The Nation*, then notes that Jackson's overall good character helps to deflect charges of anti-Semitism from Jackson:

> H. Carl McCall, the Commissioner for human rights in New York State . . . has stressed to me that Jackson's good character is his best defense. McCall observes that while Jackson has said some foolish and insensitive things his sensitivity is improving as the campaign progresses.

Berman proceeds to report that Jackson has been looking for a chance to speak out on the oppression of Jews in other countries as a means of mending hurts.

Jackson's campaign can be described as reformist and based on a grassroots effort in support of America's underrepresented. These impressions support Jackson's desired image, while his Hymietown characterization and his delay in apologizing damage this persona. Jackson's speech before Temple Adeth Yushurun is at the same moment an interethnic and a political apology, the subject of analysis in the next section. Jackson adopts a defense and transcendence format in the effort to ameliorate damage and to heal wounds in relations with Jewish Americans. Jackson stresses Biblical and spiritual commonality, forgiveness, and reconciliation between peoples as the balm for mutually suffered wounds.

Jackson makes other attempts to establish his commonality and history as a man sympathetic to Jewish causes. He reminds the audience of the time when he "spoke out against American Nazi atrocity against Jews in Skokie, Illinois." This shared ground is important: While Blacks may not have been as direct victims of Hitler's theory of Aryan supremacy as were Jews, both groups were subjected to Nazi hatred.

Jackson also articulates the religious common ground that all Jewish people share with him with his references to King David, Nathan, and Jacob. Jackson seeks to extend God's Old Testament covenant with the Jews to create a "new covenant" of "harmony among Christians, Jews, and Muslims." He appeals for continued dialogue between Blacks and Jews and Arabs as a matter of "being prophetic," initiating a temporal shift of focus from a broken past to a mended future. Jackson attempts to place behind him the possibility that he could be either anti-Israeli or anti-Jewish.

In his 1984 article Philip Green defines an anti-Semite as one who intends derogation toward the Jewish people and who offers no apology for that effort. Jackson's Hymietown apology does much to dismiss the label of anti-Semite from his campaign and his person. It strategically attempts to shift focus from historic and recent differences to prospective areas of agreement, common cause, and dialogue.

PUBLIC AND POLITICAL EXPECTATIONS FOR THE ADDRESS

General Expectations

A candidate for president of the United States must respond to the expectations of the electorate. Apart from the urgings of any given moment, a candidate must appear to be worthy of election, to be an appropriate leader, and to represent suitably America and that which is most American (Doyle, 1984; Edelman, 1967; Fisher, 1980). The president must embody values held by the American public, among which Steele and Redding (1962) number a belief in equality in principle between all Americans and a tolerance of those of other religious faiths.

The presidential candidate creates an "image" that represents this person to the public as a "doer" or "person of morals" with "leadership qualities." The created image then "fans out" among potential supporters, creating an attractive "vision" (Bormann, 1972, 1973, 1982a, 1982b; Cragan & Shields, 1977; Gronbeck, 1980; Mohrmann, 1982) that invites public participation. A voter participates in the ritual drama of election by offering an endorsement of the persona.

Reverend Jackson's persona powerfully symbolizes the Black presence in American politics. He is the condensation symbol (Edelman, 1967) through which Black voters are drawn into a sense of identification with the mainstream political process, as evidenced by increased Black voter registration. Jackson symbolizes a new scene in international politics where the Arab world holds greater sway, with a possible Arab-Black alliance. Jackson stands for a newly articulated interest by Black Americans in foreign affairs. Jackson is viewed as a friend of Minister Louis Farrakhan, who himself represents a powerful symbol for White Americans. Jackson's efforts to deal directly with Cuban and Nicaraguan leaders, and his success in gaining the release of a downed American aviator from a radical Arab leader, render him a symbol of independence, a capricious force loose in the political arena, a force identified somehow with Black America.

Seen as a dramatic character or persona (Gronbeck, 1980), Jackson is a character from a drama that he scripts himself, not a player in the drama of another. His presence invites group fantasizing by Black voters and by other members of the Rainbow Coalition in a vision centered on political participation and power after years of perceived neglect. The fantasy starts to fan out with primary election successes and with increased minority voter registration. As noted by Bormann (1973), each candidate who builds a persona faces a choice between stressing scene, acts, or persona. Scene is not a useful uniter except for minority members of the Rainbow Coalition, who in common may feel overlooked within the political scene, and who do not themselves approach an electoral majority. Acts usually are the province of the incumbent, who has an established administrative record. What is left for Jackson is to stress persona, that is, his qualities as a person of character.

Bormann describes an earlier attempt by George McGovern to build a coalition behind the "pragmatic" strategy of stressing persona in the 1972 presidential campaign. McGovern and Jackson alike call for faith in a messianic personality. That is why a wound is felt all the more deeply when his persona is undermined and brought into question. The view of Jackson as a man of the cloth, a civil rights activist, an outspoken critic of racial injustice and human deprivation, is shaken if Jackson is shown to be insensitive to the Holocaust, to Jewish sensibilities, and to acts of political terrorism in the Middle East.

As with the case of Senator Eagleton 12 years earlier, the news media happened onto a story that might injure a presidential candidate's persona, the candidate's chief means of garnering political support. In 1984 as in 1972, "the media went to work to create a good news story," one with "the ability to hold the interest of the audience." Bormann (1973) noted:

> A drama to be compelling requires plausibility, action, suspense, and sympathetic characters. . . . Because of the shortage of time on the evening news the skillful media professional goes for conflict and suspense. (p. 152)

In Jackson's words, "I watched as the word (Hymie) expanded into paragraphs, and then into chapters. At first I was astonished by the press's interest in this ethnic characterization made in private conversations." Jackson seems bewildered that "something so small has become so large." The "drama" is found in the unfolding of facets of a candidate's moral character over time in response to the stresses of the campaign. The charge is made "plausible" due to the strain between Jackson and the Jewish community that has been detailed above. "Sympathy" comes from the urge to want to support an emergent Black leader of national or international stature. "Action" is furnished by the chase, with repeated denials and repeated renewals of the attack. "Suspense" results from the playing out of the script in Watergate fashion.

Specific Expectations

What happens to the political persona of a candidate who tries to establish an image as coalition builder between persons of varying ethnicity after the candidate is reported to have used the ethnically offensive references "Hymie" and "Hymietown" in private conversation? Since these remarks call into question the moral worthiness of the candidate, and cast doubt on the candidate as a man who truly embodies professed American values, a degradation ritual is called into play to reinstate the candidate in the good graces of the electorate.

Degradation rituals, notes Bennett (1981), "occur in almost any setting in which new members are socialized, status is conferred, and character is tested." The campaign for president of the United States by a Black American who is accused of ethnic slurs fits each of these criteria. First, Bennett's analysis itself centers on gaffes by candidates for public office, since the campaign represents to Bennett a time of initiation in the public eye into the American political arena. Second, the elevation of a person from that of private citizen to national figurehead indisputably introduces a change of status. The case of Reverend Jackson is unique in American political history, as voters watch to seek to understand how a Black American might manage to symbolize majority White America. Third, a public can do little but assess a candidate's carefully managed image as moral leader during a brief political campaign. The public therefore demands from Jackson a statement that reaffirms his moral commitment to professed American ideals.

Message Analysis

When a public persona faces the accusation of moral wrongdoing, an apology follows. Ware and Linkugel (1973) explain that a speaker may choose from among four "postures" or "stances" to resolve the public's "belief dilemma":

(1) *Absolution*: The speaker says the act was not what was understood, and that it did not occur as charged anyway.

(2) *Vindication*: The speaker steps beyond the charge to appear morally superior to his or her accusors.

(3) *Explanation*: The speaker assumes a defensive posture that the person who condemns does not correctly understand the charge.

(4) *Justification*: The speaker suggests that the person who properly understands the charge would have been led to do the same thing, in the name of one or another greater good.

Reverend Jackson first seeks to deny *Washington Post* reporter Coleman's charge when asked by reporters. His repeated denials should be viewed as an absolutive strategy in which the facts themselves are disputed, with Jackson denying any trace of wrongdoing. When the absolutive strategy does not squelch the accusations against his persona, Jackson is forced to shift strategies and to admit political guilt before those assembled at the New Hampshire synagogue.

Within Jackson's text, each of the remaining three strategies is used singly or in combination. First Jackson turns to transcendence of "politics" in favor of "personal morality" and a cleansed soul:

> There are temptations before us to do that which is popular or expedient because our humanity yearns for acceptance in the face of so much rejection. There is temptation to be political, because in the face of competition we want to win. (from recording)

But the honorable course, instead, is to be "prophetic," which is to do that which is moral and right even if it is politically inexpedient, "and even if you lose." There is scant benefit in gaining the world "but losing our souls."

Jackson next intensifies and broadens the scope of his vindication strategy in two ways. First, he minimizes the significance of his act, noting with surprise and dismay that his use of the word "Hymie" in a "private conversation, apparently overheard by a reporter," would prove offensive. After all, "the context and spirit of the remark must be appreciated. In private talks we sometimes let our guard down." Jackson denies any "spirit of meanness" with his "off-color remark having no bearing on religion or politics." He stresses his past appearance in Skokie and with prominent Jewish leaders to bolster his tarnished persona. Second, Jackson turns the tables on his accusor. He claims that his privacy has been violated, summoning one widely shared American value to answer another, and that Coleman exercised poor judgment, "the propriety of which has been questioned even by the newspaper's own ombudsman." Jackson returns again to transcendence to call himself a "healer," hoping that the characterization of himself as an anti-Semite has been transformed through vindication: "The healing within this Rainbow Coalition must take place, because the world is at stake." The earlier reference to Jackson as "prophet" is thus reaffirmed.

Explanation, Jackson's chief strategy of apology, is viewed by Ware and Linkugel to be primarily a "defensive" strategy. Jackson denies any personal anti-Semitism. He says the remark, even if "innocent and unintended," is "insensitive and wrong." He quotes the aphorism "To err is human, to forgive is divine," and searches the Old Testament for common ground between himself and the Jewish community. He says his offense is minor next to the importance of his attempt to promote new "dialogue and relationships" between Blacks, Jews, and Arabs.

Finally, Jackson steps from the defensive to state his political position on matters of concern to American Jewry and to Israel. In a justification effort, he says he seeks dialogue and neutrality between Jews and Arabs and wants a U.S. policy that will foster these ends. He claims remarks about the Holocaust reported from his visit to the Vad Yashem museum in Israel to be falsified by Blazer. He reviews his comparison of the PLO and Israel's military arm alike as "terrorists" and says he was dealing only with the respective perceptions of the parties to the immediate conflict. He says his political posture is clearcut and is a matter of "substance," not merely "trite and rhetorical." What is important is "to share our point of view and air our differences."

It becomes clear from the comparative study of Jackson's apology as a means of repairing interethnic wounds and the apology to repair a tarnished political image that both sides of the apology carry the listener through stages of prostration in guilt, bolstering defense, and renewal at a higher plane of attention. The candidate leaves the disavowed past behind in favor of the future.

ON RHETORICAL ANALYSIS
OF INTERETHNIC DISCOURSE

Interethnic rhetoric is necessarily a process of mutual enlightenment. Philipsen (1975, p. 22) argues:

> Americans from diverse communities—or with diverse regional, class, or ethnic backgrounds—bring to the communication encounter differing underlying values about what is appropriate and proper communicative conduct. This suggests the importance of understanding the diversity of cultural outlooks . . . in contemporary America.

Reverend Jackson, in detailing how he has interacted over the years with American and Israeli Jews, carries out this goal of cultural enlightenment and sharing of cognitions.

The interethnic speaker is viewed as a person who shows greater or lesser awareness of and sensitivity to ethnic differences between self and audience. By extension, the speaker uses or fails to make use of available cultural commonalities between self and audience. The level of cultural awareness between Reverend Jackson and his Jewish audience is quite high, a point that Jackson does not hesitate to stress for his listeners through references to common scripture, convenants, and social circumstance.

The interethnic speaker soothes or exacerbates standing interethnic differences. Beyond the level of the feeling of an ethnic audience toward a particular person of differing ethnicity, the audience forms impressions about that speaker's culture, its goodwill, its interest in future relations, and its sense of common cause or solidarity in the face of common challenges. Jackson's stress on "healing" and "binding up wounds" opts to stress commonality and transcendence of past differences between communities.

Interethnic rhetoric opens the avenue to construction of mutual new meanings between those of disparate cultures. A recently kindled interest in "cultural criticism" within the speech communication community (Gronbeck, 1983, p. iii) centers on the idea that

> one's culture at any given moment represents a society's fundamental commitments in such areas as collective beliefs, modes of thought, means of access to others, interpretative rules, rationalizations and justifications, mythic accounts of past/present/future, formal expectations, institutional and personal practices.

By sharing impressions between those of different cultures rather than choosing separatism and isolation, the chance for misunderstanding is lessened, and the opportunity to discover meanings in common is enhanced. Such new meanings include the idea of a Black-Hispanic-Arab-Jewish "New Covenant" as members alike of a "Rainbow Coalition."

The interethnic communicator chooses whether to view self and audience as members of distinctive cultural traditions and ethnicity or whether to downplay extant cultural differences. Jackson, in this instance, starts with words that view self and audience as persons with separate communities but then moves to gloss these differences through words at a higher level of generality.

It can be argued that these options confront interethnic communicators at every level of discourse, from interpersonal to mass media. At every level from cultural exchange to media stereotype, then, change transpires at the level of cognition.

Similarly, each transaction is marked by impressions concerning whether the other communicator is sensitive to and appreciative of that which renders one's own culture distinctive. A media portrayal or speech can give the impression that the interpreter sought to convey a true understanding of the culture in question or that the understanding was muddled and biased. At the interpersonal level, failure to appreciate the other's worth as a cultural entity calls up impressions of racism or ethnocentrism.

Each communique between ethnically distinct communicators, at whatever level, affects the psychological distance between the communities, however greatly or slightly. The message that does not draw the other community closer through the affective impressions that are conveyed will tend to increase isolation of the two communities from each other.

Meanings constantly change for a people. The rhetorical critic should be alert to meanings that are in flux (Brummett, 1984, p. 115):

> People use patterns of meaning to order and explicate the world. The critic's primary function is to explicate those patterns of meanings, to show how those meanings guide the apprehension of the world and how those meanings are manipulated rhetorically.

Part of the process of building a sense of inclusivity or exclusivity rests upon the choice of characterizations, god-terms, broader identifications to replace smaller ones, by the speaker. If these characterizations are rendered plausible, change should follow in perceptions and interethnic relations.

Finally, each choice of message, each nonverbal signal or emblem, each speech makes a statement about whether the communicator feels distinct from the members of the other community and about whether that distinctiveness is positive (we are all unique, but we make our own important contributions) or negative (we are unique, and I am better). In certain cases, the communicator may also convey that the differences that may be meaningful to the audience of another culture are of no importance personally (you only think you are different—why won't you assimilate?). The intentional or unintentional offering of the impression that the other person is different and inferior, different and ridiculous, or identical but falsely pretending to be different, destroys interethnic closeness.

All in all, it is clear that at least two parallel tasks are being dispatched by means of Jackson's single apology. While content diverges, the two lines ultimately follow the same format: admission of wrongdoing, seeking forgiveness and understanding, minimization of the offense, transcendence of the impasse, and the indication of a new and more harmonious future.

Whether political persona or interethnic image is more at stake, and whether the healing is of a secular or religious sort, Jackson rises to the occasion in the best country preacher tradition and shows himself a worthy contender for the office of president. Jackson moves quickly from a news item on the thirty-seventh line of a *Washington Post* report to the need to "be prophetic," to forge a "new covenant," and "to bind up wounds." He measures his success by determining the degree to which the two communities put some of their past differences behind them to embrace an urgent moral common imperative, and the degree to which the voting public at large decides that Jackson does indeed subscribe to cherished American values.

At the level of interethnic address, Jackson stresses that distinctive cultural communities can learn to work for greater mutual understanding, find common meanings, join with each other to deal with mutual problems, and feel more positive toward each other, if the members of those communities will allow wounds to heal. That they succeed or not in capturing the presidency can be viewed as secondary, at this level, to whether interpersonal distances between American Black and Jew are lessened.

REFERENCES

Atwater, D. F. (1984). Jesse Jackson: Issues and image—the country preacher in action. Paper presented at the Eastern Communication Association, Providence, RI.

Baskerville, B. (1971). Rhetorical criticism, 1971: Retrospect, prospect, introspect. *Southern Speech Communication Journal, 37,* 113-124.

Belatedly Jackson comes clean. (1984, March 12). *Time,* p. 27.

Bennett, W. L. (1981). Assessing presidential character: Degradation rituals in presidential campaigns. *Quarterly Journal of Speech, 67* (August), 310-321.

Berman, P. (1984, April 7). The other side of the rainbow. *Nation,* pp. 407-410.

Bormann, E. G. (1972). Fantasy and rhetorical vision: The rhetorical criticism of social reality. *Quarterly Journal of Speech, 58,* 398.

Bormann, E. G. (1973). The Eagleton affair: A fantasy theme analysis. *Quarterly Journal of Speech, 59,* 143-159.

Bormann, E. G. (1982a). Fantasy theme analysis of television coverage of the hostage release and the Reagan inaugural. *Quarterly Journal of Speech, 68,* 133-145.

Bormann, E. G. (1982b). Fantasy and rhetorical vision: Ten years later. *Quarterly Journal of Speech, 68,* 288-305.

Brown, D. (1984). *Style and delivery: The impact of Reverend Jackson's use of antithesis.* Paper presented at the Eastern Communication Association, Providence, RI.

Brummett, B. (1984). Consensus criticism. *Southern Journal of Speech Communication, 49,* 111-124.

Carter, D. T. (1969). *Scottsboro: A tragedy of the American South.* Baton Rouge: Louisiana State University Press.

Cohen, H. (1969). *Justice: A Jewish view of the Black revolution.* New York: Union of American Hebrew Rabbis.

Cragan, J. F., & Shields, D. C. (1977). Foreign policy communication dramas: How mediated rhetoric played in Peoria. *Quarterly Journal of Speech, 63,* 274-289.

Cruse, H. (1967). *The crisis of the Negro intellectual.* New York: William Morrow.

Doyle, T. A. (1984). *"Sermons on amount": Secular religious images in presidential broadcast economic policy messages, 1923-1983.* Unpublished doctoral dissertation, Howard University.

Drake, S., & Cayton, H. R. (1962). *Black metropolis: A study of Negro life in a northern city.* New York: Harper & Row.

Edelman, M. (1967). *Symbolic uses of politics.* Urbana: University of Illinois Press.

Fisher, W. R. (1980). Rhetorical fiction and the presidency. *Quarterly Journal of Speech, 66,* 119-126.

Gold, V. (1984, May 18). From Hymie's son. *National Review,* pp. 28-29.

Green, P. (1984, March 12). The reality beneath the rainbow. *Nation,* pp. 305-306.

Gronbeck, B. E. (1980). Dramaturgical theory and criticism: The state of the art (or science?). *Western Journal of Speech Communication, 44,* 315-330.

Gronbeck, B. E. (1983). The "scholar's anthology": An introduction. *Central States Speech Journal, 34,* iii.

Jackson, J. (1984)."Apology." Delivered before the Temple Adeth Yushurun, New York. Washington, DC: Rainbow Coalition.

Mitchell, H. (1970). *Black preaching.* Philadelphia: J.B. Lippincott.

Mohrmann, G. P. (1982). An essay on fantasy theme criticism. *Quarterly Journal of Speech, 68,* 109-132.

Philipsen, G. (1975). Speaking "like a man" in Teamsterville: Culture patterns of role enactment in an urban neighborhood. *Quarterly Journal of Speech, 59,* 273-283.

Reynolds, B. (1975). *Jesse Jackson: The man, the myth and the movement.* Chicago: Nelson-Hall.

Serrin, W. (1972, July 9). Jesse Jackson: I am, audience: I am, Jesse: Somebody, audience: Somebody. *New York Times Magazine,* p. 16.

Steele, E. D., & Redding, W. C. (1962). The American value system: Premises for persuasion. *Western Speech, 26,* 83-91.

Ware, B. L., & Linkugel, W. A. (1973). They spoke in defense of themselves: On the general criticism of apologia. *Quarterly Journal of Speech, 59,* 273-283.

Weisbond, R. T., & Stein, A. B. (1972). *The bittersweet encounter of the Afro-American and the American Jew.* New York: Schocken Books.

8

Black Verbal Dueling Strategies in Interethnic Communication

THOMAS KOCHMAN • *University of Illinois at Chicago*

The present chapter takes a close look at the structure governing Black verbal dueling in order to investigate the boundary between play and nonplay within this black cultural activity and the general capacities and strategies that Black culture promotes and develops stemming from that placement. This study also compares the corresponding White cultural patterns of the play and nonplay boundary. It then shows how these differences contribute to Black and White communicative conflict, particularly in verbal aggression. Finally, it shows how social interaction between Blacks and Whites can continue to benefit from comparative cultural analyses and offers specific examples thereof.

There are many problems affecting Black and White communication. At the general level, the main social problem is how to combat the nefarious social practice of racial discrimination. Some inroads have been made in this regard through equal employment opportunity legislation and affirmative action programs in the workplace. But the number of Blacks and other minorities reached by these programs has been limited.

Moreover, the effectiveness of these programs is measured almost exclusively in terms of numbers: *how many* Blacks and members of other minority groups (vis-à-vis White males) are represented within various levels of an institution or organization. It hardly considers the quality or effectiveness of Black/White *communication*, which, practically speaking, begins when present and past desegregation programs such as affirmative action and busing, respectively, end. For when Blacks and Whites engage each other face to face, often for the first time, as social equals, in this context, Blacks and Whites begin to experience the communication problems that arise as a result of differences in their cultural attitudes and styles.

Up to the present these differences have been a barrier to effective communication, not so much because of the irreconcilable nature of the

AUTHOR'S NOTE: *This chapter is based on Kochman (1983).*

differences themselves as the absence of any individual or organizational incentive to address them directly. Black and White social networks are still by and large racially segregated even in so-called integrated social settings (such as high schools, colleges, and the workplace). Most people would still rather avoid difficult situations than spend the time and energy needed to learn to deal with them effectively.

The outlook is not altogether bleak, however. Many organizations have come to realize that such avoidance is unprofitable not only because of the amount of time spent on managing tension and conflict in the workplace, but because of the loss of many valued Black employees who leave an organization in the absence of ethnic role models in upper levels of management. These individuals—and they are growing in number—have rejected the premise that one needs to "move out" (deethnicize) to "move up," a pattern that until now has been the historic one for minorities wishing to advance in American society. By rejecting the prerequisite of deethnicization, members of minority groups are, in effect, repudiating unilateral social accommodation to dominant White mainstream cultural norms and values. This challenge has led organizations to develop a more respectful attitude toward Black cultural norms and values leading to a more reciprocal pattern of accommodation. This pattern has already happened in commercially profitable sports such as basketball and football. And, if this pattern continues, cross-cultural communication based on reciprocity (rather than unilateral accommodation) will ultimately emerge as the social pattern of choice. Individuals will be likely to consider, even more than at present, the ways in which cultural differences influence such things as interpersonal communication, leadership style, and work and play attitudes and strategies.

This study works within this newly emerging sociopolitical framework. As such it builds on past work (e.g., Kochman, 1972, 1981) in further seeking to explore and clarify the ways in which Black and White communicative styles are different. As with past work, it also considers how such differences contribute to Black and White interpersonal conflict.

THEORETICAL FRAMEWORK

The present study can be said to fit within the disciplinary framework of present-day sociolinguistics, most specifically, within that area of sociolinguistics known as *ethnography of communication* or *ethnogra-*

phy of speaking. This framework, as two of its most notable proponents, Gumperz and Hymes, have established, focuses upon the interaction between language and social life, especially the various nonidiosyncratic social constraints that act upon and guide language choice. As Gumperz and Hymes have said (1972, p. vi):

> Language usage—i.e., what is said on a particular occasion, how it is phrased, and how it is coordinated with non-verbal signs—cannot simply be a matter of free individual choice. It must be affected by subconsciously internalized constraints similar to grammatical constraints.

Taking from the study of grammar the notion of linguistic competence—the knowledge that enables native speakers of a language to produce well-formed (acceptable) sentences (that linguists work to organize and represent in the form of rules)— ethnography of communication operates with the notion of communicative competence. Communicative competence can be best understood as what a speaker needs to know to communicate effectively or appropriately in culturally significant settings (Gumperz & Hymes, 1972, p. vii). Alternatively, one can consider ethnography as a descriptive theory—the knowledge that would enable an outsider to a culture to generate and interpret behavior in ways that native members of the culture would regard as authentic (Frake, 1964, p. 112). Spradley's (1979) definition of culture as "the acquired knowledge that people use to interpret experience and generate social behavior" (p. 5) is, except for its more generalized focus, akin to the notion of communicative competence that sociolinguists use. This again shows that it is from the plane where the disciplines of linguistics and anthropology intersect that ethnographers of communication draw their methodological presuppositions and practices.

Because communicative competence and culture refer to subjective knowledge that members of a particular group share, one can also relate the present study to phenomenological studies in psychology and sociology, starting perhaps with James's (1869/1950) "Perception of Reality"; Husserl (1952); Gurwitsch (1964); Schutz (1945/1962); and, more recently, Garfinkel (1967); Berger and Luckmann (1966); Cicourel (1973); and Goffman (1974); see Goffman's excellent discussion of this development pp. 1-20.

It was Schutz (1970, p. 125) who, as Goffman (1974, p. 4) notes, redefined the earlier phenomenological notion of "reality" as being constituted by the "meaning of our experience" and not the "ontological structure of the objects." From such studies emerged a notion of "cognitive style," a way of looking at the world, which could formally be represented by a kind of cognitive map. This map would reflect the meanings that members of a group attach to behavior and events that occur in their everyday social experiences. Ultimately, ethnographers could hope to be able to represent this cognitive map formally and generate it in a finite set of rules. Were this constitutive feat to be accomplished, it would become what Goffman called "the sociologist's alchemy" (1974, p. 5).

Linguists looking at discourse have taken the text (rather than the sentence) or the dialogue (rather than the monologue) as the unit of analysis. Others, operating within the same general scheme, have worked to develop explicit models of the relationship between discourse production and comprehension (Freedle, 1977, p. xvi). Still others, operating within this latter construct—I would include parts of the present study within it—explore the relationship between the sociocultural realm and its effect on discourse in a naturalistic setting (see, for example, Gumperz, 1982b; Kochman, 1981; Tannen, 1982). In this latter operation, analysts interested in discourse production and comprehension might well concern themselves with the strategies that speakers from various cultural backgrounds bring to bear in comprehension, which Freedle (1977) defines as the "likelihood judgments" that come from one's social interactions and experiences in the naturalistic world. They suggest bases or schemata that one would need to know to determine which presuppositions are likely to be correct in comprehending the covert intentions of a speaker (Freedle, 1977, p. xvi; see also Gumperz, 1982a; and Hymes, 1980). Part of the present study, which examines the placement of the boundary line between play, nonplay, and ambiguity in Black verbal dueling, deals precisely with the schemata that Blacks bring to this speech event.

What is going on? From whose point of view? And what are the organizing schemes within any particular point of view that give rise to the productions and understandings that individuals from various sociocultural realms generate in their everyday social interactions? These are the basic questions that ethnographers generally grapple with whether the larger disciplinary frames of reference are in ethnographic and/or cognitive sociology, cognitive anthropology, interactional sociolinguistics, ethnography of communication, or discourse analysis. These are also the questions that have generated the methodological assumptions and practices of the present study.

THE PRESENT STUDY

William Labov, in his "Rules for Ritual Insults" (1972b) and "The Art of Sounding and Signifying" (1974), formulated rules for *sounding* (Black verbal dueling) that saw ritual insults, but not personal insults, as properly falling within the framework of Black verbal play.

In my review of these chapters (in Kochman, 1975, 1977, respectively), it was argued that Labov's decision to place personal insults outside of the framework of the sounding was incorrect. It was contended that personal insults, like ritual insults, also functioned as part of the game, as data showed (Kochman, 1970, pp. 160ff.), and as Blacks, with whom this matter was discussed over the years, uniformly insisted to be the case.

The reason for bringing the matter up again here is that researchers interested in contrasting play- and fact-oriented dispute genres, such as Goffman (1974, pp. 40-123) and Danet (1980, passim), have taken Labov's analysis of the role and function of personal insults in sounding to represent the true state of affairs in Black culture. Consequently, they have ended up misrepresenting the actual boundary between "play" and "the serious," at least as that boundary manifests itself in the context of Black verbal dueling.

The objective here is to establish what can be considered the proper Black cultural perspective on the role and function of personal insults in sounding and the boundary between play and nonplay within the context of that activity. This will be done by recapitulating the relevant aspects of Labov's formulation of the rules for sounding and my own disagreement with it. Next, it will be shown how these different views bear upon the determination of the boundary between play and nonplay in the context of sounding. Then, the significance of the proper placement of the boundary between play and nonplay in sounding will be discussed by considering the different cultural consequences that would arise from regarding personal insults to be part of verbal play or not. Afterwards, the use of personal insults in sounding in terms of more broadly based Black cultural patterns will also be considered. Finally, how these Black cultural patterns differ from White cultural schemes of production and interpretation will be shown, and how, as a result, problems arise when Blacks and Whites communicate with one another at the interpersonal level.

SOUNDING AND RITUAL SOUNDING

Sounding is the term that Blacks in Harlem, New York, use to describe Black verbal dueling. Blacks in different communities use other terms for the activity, such as *basing, chopping, cracking, cutting, hoorawing, joning, ranking, screaming, signifying, snapping,* and *woofing,* to name just the terms that have been cited in the literature (Abrahams, 1974; Folb, 1980; Kochman, 1970; Labov, 1972b). The reader is referred to these sources for a further discussion of these terms and a more complete description of the genre itself. The term *sounding* will be used here to keep it consistent with Labov's usage, to which I will have frequent occasion to refer below.

As indicated above, the basic question that Labov's analysis raises is over the evaluation and placement of personal insults within the context of verbal dueling. Are they to be regarded as part of sounding or not? Labov's contention is that only ritual insults qualify as sounds in Black verbal dueling, the key criterion for ritual insults being that they are known to be untrue. On that basis, Labov contends that personal insults would not qualify as sounds because: (1) they are true, and (2) they are answered by a denial, excuse, or mitigation, or, rather, they are answered by a denial, excuse, or mitigation because they are true. Moreover, one comes to know that they are true *because* they are answered by a denial, excuse, or mitigation. Labov's exact words on this point are: "A personal insult is answered by a denial, excuse, or mitigation whereas a sound or ritual insult is answered by another sound" (1972b, p. 298).

In support of this analysis, Labov offers the following exchange between Boot and David (1972b, pp. 296ff):

A DAVID: So your . . . So then I say, "Your father got brick teeth."

B BOOT: Aw your father got teeth growing out his behind!

C DAVID: Yeah, your father, y-got, your father grow, uh, uh, grow hair from, between his, y'know.

D BOOT: Your father got calluses growin' up through his ass and commin' through his mouth.

E BOOT: Your father look like a grown pig.

F DAVID: Least my—at least my father don't be up there talking uh-uh-uh-uh-uh-uh!

G BOOT: Uh-so my father talk stutter talk what it mean?

H BOOT: At least my father ain't got a gray head! His father got a big bald spot with a gray head right down there, and one long string. . . .

I DAVID: Because he' old, he's old, that's why! He's old, that's why!

That F and H are personal insults rather than ritual insults is shown, according to Labov, by the fact that they are denied (at points G and I by Boot and David, respectively). Moreover, *because* they are denied, Labov sees personal insults as ending the sounding contest and themselves not qualifying as sounds. Thus, in his definition of sounding, Labov insists that both contestants must believe that the verbal insults are not true for them to be considered sounds.

If A makes an utterance S in the presence of B and an audience C, which includes reference to a target related to B, T(B), in a proposition P, and

(a) B believes that A believes that P is not true, and
(b) B believes that A believes that B knows that P is not true...

then S is a *sound,* heard as T(B) *is so X that P* where X is a pejorative attribute, and A is said to have *sounded on* B. (Labov, 1972b, p. 302)

Now it is certainly possible to accept Labov's contention, as I do, that denial, excuse, and mitigation (as represented by Boot and David at points G and I) qualify the insults F and H as personal (i.e., true) without also having to accept Labov's other (implicit) claim that insults are not personal (i.e., are ritual and untrue) because they are not denied. That is, insults may still be personal (true) even though they are not denied. Labov does not consider this last possibility, because he lets the determination of the truth of an insult be dependent entirely upon whether it is denied or not. Thus, he would consider verbal insults that have the *appearance* of being personal, such as "Your mother's on Fifth Avenue" (i.e., a prostitute), to be ritual insults (untrue) rather than personal ones (true) so long as they are not denied. And it is on this point that (it is contended here) Labov's analysis is seen to have gone wrong. In sounding, insults can be personal (true), not be denied, and still qualify as sounds. My own data have clearly shown this (1970, pp. 160ff.), as said earlier. Furthermore, it can readily be shown using Labov's own illustration of the verbal exchange between Boot and David given above. If the denials G and I did not occur and could be deleted from the sequence, then the remaining entire exchange would qualify as sounding, notwithstanding the occurrence and use of personal insults F and H. That would make Labov's formulation of the rules for sounding to be true only for the special case of *ritual* sounding, but not for sounding as a whole.[1]

Implications for the Placement of the Play/Nonplay Boundary

What, then, does this difference make with regard to the boundary between play and nonplay? Labov's contention (following the Boot/David exchange, with increasing denials by David) is that "What follows now is no longer the controlled counterpoint of sounding, of the form A e B e, but an excited *argument*" (1972b, p. 297, emphasis added). Labov's assertion is correct. Sounding has ended or been interrupted, that is, play has also ended or been interrupted, and serious argument has begun. But the critical question is, at what point? Labov contends that the shift from sounding to argument begins *at the point that a personal insult*—one known to be true—*has been uttered*. In the Boot/David exchange, that would be at points F and H. But the actual point at which play becomes serious is *at the point of denial*. It is the denials of G and I in the above exchange that do not qualify as sounds and redefine the activity as something other than sounding (i.e., argument), not the personal insults F and H. Labov's formulation misrepresents the role and importance of the factuality of the utterance in differentiating verbal insults that are play from those that are serious.

This, in turn, has led others who have used this analysis to misperceive and misplace the boundary between play and nonplay. Thus Danet (1980, p. 503) reports "the difference between ritualized and personal insults—*between playing and being serious*" (emphasis added). And Goffman (1974, pp. 49ff.) wrote:

> In the game of "dozens" played by Black urban youths, statements made about a player's parent are seen as displaying the wit of the insulter, not the features of the parent, and so can be wondrously obscene. A mild-sounding insult that happened to refer to known features of the particular parent would be given a different relevance and *cease* to be unserious. (emphasis added)

Edwards, in his discussion of Guyanese *tantalisin*, gives support for the Black view as it is represented here (originally in Kochman, 1975):

> In some cases . . . a tantalise can bear a close relationship to the truth. Its acceptance as a tantalise act in such a case depends on the recipient's

willingness not to take the insult personally. I therefore suspect that Kochman is correct in his disagreement with Labov's thesis that *sounds* are obligatorily false. In Guyana many tantalises are at least partially true. (1979, p. 22)

Some Cultural Consequences of the Different Placements of Play/Nonplay Boundaries

The different boundary that Labov's analysis and my own establishes between sounding and argument, play and nonplay, has important cultural consequences. A few of the more salient ones will be considered here.

Responsibility. In Labov's analysis, as already stated, the point at which verbal insults begin to get personal (true) is the point at which play ends. Using Danet's phrasing (1980, p. 497), it is at this point that the contestant decides not to maintain the play frame within which normal conditions of accountability are relaxed. But this means that the person who first introduces personal insults must also accept the responsibility and blame for the serious activity that follows because his or her personal insults are seen as not only provoking the defensive denial, but entailing it. That is, personal insults restrictively define the frame within which the recipient may appropriately respond to that of nonplay. Within this conception, personal insults *unequivocally* define the frame as "serious" and, consequently, entail a response that is also "serious," namely, *argument*.

But if personal insults can also be considered play, then *the responsibility for determining whether the play frame shall be maintained or not belongs with the recipient.* If the latter responds to a personal insult with his or her own counterattack in a personal or ritual insult, then his or her response will constitute a sound and indicate a decision to maintain the play frame. Thus, in the exchange between Boot and David, were Boot's personal insult H to have followed David's personal insult F directly, then the play frame (sounding activity) would have remained intact throughout the exchange. The alternative represents what actually happened. Boot and David, as recipients of personal insults, respectively *chose* to take them seriously by responding to them heatedly and defensively (points G and I). "*Chose* to take them seriously" is emphasized here to underscore the point that recipients act independently, not dependently (reactively), as Labov's analysis implies. To Blacks, personal insults in sounding are seen to be provocative but not determinative (in terms of *cause, necessary* perhaps, but not *sufficient*). Consequently, not only is it not obligatory for recipients to take personal insults seriously, but the rules of sounding require that they do not, in observance of the sequencing rule (Labov's formulation of this is correct) that a sound is to be answered by another sound.

That is why in sounding, to be able to elicit a denial from one's opponent, one wins the contest (by forfeit) as readily as would actually having outsounded him or her. From the recipient's perspective, therefore, to issue an impulsive (uncontrolled and uncalculated) heated, defensive protestation or denial to a personal insult is tantamount to losing. And this is precisely what makes the use of personal insults tactically effective as sounds within the framework of the game. Its provocative and potentially disabling character increases as sounds get more personal. Their deniability and potential for actual denial by recipients increases with the tension between contestants and the increasing risk that the activity will in fact cease to be taken as play as a result of the increasing difficulty of recipients to take their opponent's personal insults *un*seriously.

The quality of the play activity is also affected by who is seen to bear the responsibility for further play (or nonplay) action. For example, to place the burden of responsibility for the subsequent serious activity on the shoulders of individuals who first introduce personal insults would make them accountable not only for their own behavior but for the behavioral response of the recipients. That, in turn, would have an inhibiting effect on those contestants who would/might initiate personal insults. However, to place the burden of responsibility on the shoulders of recipients for the way they choose to respond gives contestants greater freedom to introduce personal insults themselves; they are not seen thereby to have automatically defined the activity as serious, that is, as having restricted the response of recipients to the nonplay frame. Their personal insults can still be play. Whether they count as play or not depends upon how the recipient ultimately takes them.

Safety. If only ritual insults—those insults known to be untrue—were sounds, the boundaries for play in sounding would be safer than they actually are.[2] This is not to say that players do not protect themselves through the use of ritual insults. They do, especially younger contestants whose own sensibilities are still relatively susceptible. These and other contestants know that ritual insults, especially those that are obviously untrue, provide players with a measure of safety that they would lose were they to get personal. But other players, such as the older teenagers reported by James Maryland (in Kochman, 1970), and the still older players Maryland portrayed in his own chapter (1972), use personal insults considerably more often than they do ritual ones. Moreover, personal insults realize one function of Black verbal dueling precisely *because* they further decrease the measure of safety for the contestants. The ability to manage the tension that comes from increasing the risk of players to the point where they can almost no longer take personal verbal assaults *un*seriously is at least one contribution that verbal dueling makes directly to Black psychosocial development. It is a process that works to raise thresholds of tolerance and endurance by learning to take what is normally serious *as* play, until it can, more comfortably, *become* play.

Other Cultural Effects. It has been said elsewhere (Kochman, 1981) that Black culture generally is a high-stimulus culture. And for Black culture to maintain itself as a high-stimulus culture, it is important to develop capacities among its members to manage the impulses that potent stimuli produce without becoming overwhelmed by them. Sounding as a play activity works to develop just such capacities, which then enable Blacks to manage more effectively their responses to accusations and vilifications in nonplay contexts as well. Conversely, increasing the capacity of Blacks to manage potent stimuli as recipients also gives them greater freedom to produce such stimuli in their role as assertors, activators, or agitators. Individuals can be more powerful in their assertions if they know that others can receive them without becoming overwhelmed by them.

By way of contrast, White mainstream culture generally is a low-stimulus culture. As noted earlier, making individuals initiating potent stimuli (such as personal insults) entirely responsible for the serious way they might be taken works to inhibit the production of potent stimuli. This inhibition also works to ensure that the capacity of recipients to manage powerful stimuli will remain low. It withholds from them the powerful stimuli that they would need to be exposed to on a more regular basis if they were ever to learn to manage them better. Unlike Black verbal dueling, White verbal contests do not push the contestants to the limits of their endurance for the purpose of expanding their capacity to endure (see Labov, 1972b, pp. 287ff). This accounts for the greater sensitivity of White sensibilities and overall lower thresholds of tolerance in these matters. Reciprocally, the realization that recipients have relatively low thresholds of tolerance for potent stimuli, and will invariably be overwhelmed by them, works to further inhibit forceful self-assertion. In my view, the placement of the boundary between play and nonplay that logically derives from Labov's treatment of personal insults within the context of sounding defines a structural pattern (psychological reality) that is more representative of White mainstream culture than Black culture.

Ambiguity

The argument that personal insults can still function as part of the game of sounding, that is, as play, should not be construed as meaning that there is no significant difference between the use of ritual insults and personal insults within sounding. There is, insofar as the shift from ritual to personal insults within sounding moves the activity into the area of ambiguity, a state of potentiality for *becoming* nonplay; or returning to play, but itself indeterminate or inconclusive until such time as nonplay (or play) areas are more definitively reached. In placing the burden of interpretation of whether personal insults are play on recipients, the culture also places upon them the responsibility for determining its final character (meaning). More specifically, Black culture gives the recipient three options here. The person can:

(1) Resolve the ambiguity once again in favor of play (such as in sounding, returning a personal insult with a ritual one). Thus, in a situation Maryland describes (1972, p. 213), when the confrontation between Sweet Red and Black Power got especially tense at one point in their series of verbal exchanges, Black Power relieved much of the tension by offering a ritual insult: moreover, one which was as much directed to the crowd as to Sweet Red, his opponent ("Don't worry, baby; before this devil-lover leaves here that lye in his hair is either gonna eat the sickness outta this nigger's head or eat up his damn brains").

(2) Resolve the ambiguity in the direction of the serious (such as by making a provocative *movement*). An example of this is Joe Frazier getting out of his seat and moving to stand directly in front of Muhammad Ali after Muhammed Ali called Frazier *ignant* ("grossly stupid"). This was shown on television's *Wide World of Sports*. Both fighters were being interviewed after their first fight, which Ali lost (see Kochman, 1981, pp. 43-62).

(3) Maintain the ambiguity of "Is this play or nonplay" by returning an adversary's personal insult with one of your own (see several of the exchanges between Sweet Red and Black Power in Maryland, 1972). This last move returns the favor, so to speak, by placing your opponent in the recipient's role, thus in the position of having to assume the responsibility for determining the meaning of the activity (i.e., main-

taining or changing its character). Consequently, maintaining ambiguity here is often seen not as *escalating* matters toward the serious but as demonstrating an unwillingness to move the activity in the direction of the serious (as well as perhaps also indicating a refusal to return it to safer realms of play).

In fact, the reciprocal maintenance of ambiguity by adversaries through several exchanges or personal insults is precisely what occurs in nonritual sounding, the goal of which (as Abrahams has said with regard to the more aggressive kind of joking behavior generally found on the street) is to "keep even the other participants wondering whether one is still playing" (1974, p. 41). This is especially indicated when the tempo of the sounding increases, or, in other speech events such as *woofing*, where insult is accompanied by threats and other forms of intimidating behavior.

Notwithstanding the personal nature of the insults in sounding or the accompanying threats and other forms of verbal intimidation in woofing, Black culture still sees sounding and woofing as falling conceptually within the general realm of *talking* (here contrasted with *fighting*). Thus, an often-used expression in the Black community goes, "So long as I'm talking, you got nothing to worry about. But when I *stop* talking, *then* you might have something to worry about." This view holds even where play (ritual insult or joking) is not an option, that is, where the options are essentially between *woofing* and *fighting*, as between rival gang members (Keiser, 1969, p. 44). Even in this last context, woofing is seen to fall within the realm of *talking,* not *fighting.* For *fighting* to begin, one of the adversaries within the context of woofing (or quarreling) would have to make a provocative move (option two)—one that is not part of their customary way of talking (Kochman, 1981, pp. 45-48), as Figure 8.1 shows.

Given the general cultural distinction between talking and fighting, the use of personal insults in sounding can now be regarded as safer on two counts than might otherwise be the case. Personal insults could still be play (as already noted); but even were they to become nonplay, they would become *argument* (quarreling) or *woofing*, but not *fighting.* Compare that to White mainstream culture, where personal insults and threats are already seen as a form of *fighting* (e.g., *starting* a fight): thus, neither play nor an activity in which adversaries are seen to be still "only talking."

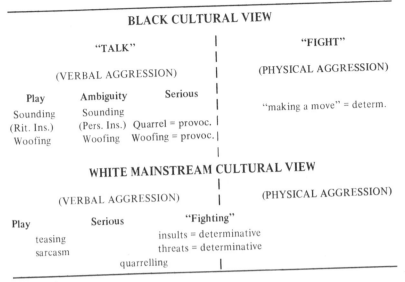

Figure 8.1

IMPLICATIONS FOR BLACK/WHITE INTERGROUP COMMUNICATION

The account of the role and use of personal insults in sounding defines a pattern that has its parallel in real-life accusations and denials. There, though more so with general than specific accusations, the Black rule is "If the shoe fits, wear it." Here again, the determination of the truth of the accusation principally falls on the recipient, not the accuser. The latter may be seen as directing the general flight of the arrow, opening a field as it were, but the target (recipient) is the one seen to guide the arrow home, to determine whether it applies specifically. This perspective is broadly Afro-American. It is captured in the Black American proverb, "If you throw a stone in a pack of dogs, the one that yelps is the one that got hit." In Jamaica, it is, "If you throw a stone in a pig an de one that say 'quee, quee,' is him de stone hit." In Barbados, the same idea is expressed by "Whoever de cap fit, pull de string" (Fisher, 1976, p. 234).

Because heated defensive denials in Black culture are taken as evidence that the effect of the remark has been felt, and that it must therefore be true, the strategy for those who might consider themselves accused is to pretend that they have *not* been touched. With such a noncommittal response, they imply that the accusation did not apply to (or include) them. Fisher describes the same strategy with respect to the Barbadian speech pattern *dropping remarks,* which occurs when an accusation is ostensibly made to a second party but is really intended for a third who is within earshot. The strategy for the party for whom the remark was intended, however, is *not* to respond. To assume a defensive posture would be tantamount to an admission that the remark had been felt and that it, therefore, must also be true by implication (Fisher, 1976, p. 231).

Black *signifying* follows the same pattern, keeping accusations general and letting those of whom they are true apply them to themselves. Mitchell-Kernan (1972, pp. 95-96) gives an example of a third-party recipient (Mary) who took seriously a remark that ostensibly was not directed at her but at Mitchell-Kernan ("Or are you one of those Negroes who don't eat chitlins?"). According to the accuser, Barbara, she did not have Mary in mind at all when she made the remark. Rather, Mary was seen to implicate herself by responding heatedly and defensively to it. As Barbara said to Mitchell-Kernan afterward, "Well, I wasn't signifying at her, but like I always say, if the shoe fits, wear it."

In summation of this point, the strategies of the accusers and recipients in nonplay contexts find their parallel in the Black play activity, sounding. Personal insults in sounding are comparable to general accusations in nonplay situations. The strategy of the accuser in nonplay situations and of the instigator of personal insults in sounding is to provoke an admission that the accusations are true. This strategy works if the accusations are defensively denied, excused, or mitigated. The strategy of those accused in each situation is to resist the temptation to react impulsively and defensively in denial of the accusation. To do otherwise in such contests, power struggles, or disputes is to implicate oneself, which in Black social circles is generally taken as self-incrimination.

Purposeful Ambiguity

Mitchell-Kernan, in her discussion of *signifying,* talks about the speaker's use of purposeful ambiguity as giving the speaker control of the situation at the receiver's expense (1972, p. 103). Mitchell-Kernan gives as an example a secretary saying to a boss whose hand occasionally brushed her knee as he talked, "Oh, excuse me Mr. Smith, I didn't mean to get my knee in your way." Note that, by not herself assigning any meaning to that act, the secretary strategically avoided assuming responsibility for determining conclusively what the boss's hand brushing against her knee "meant" (that gesture itself being ambiguous). This is especially so, since, if she did, she could well be placed in the "wrong" position however he interpreted it. As Mitchell-Kernan notes (p. 104), even if guilty, he could always *feign* innocence, for example, and make it appear that *she* was the one that had the "dirty" mind, not he. Consequently, the secretary responded to the ambiguity of the boss touching her knee with a noncommittal remark of her own which had the effect of placing the boss rather than herself in the position of having to decide what his gesture "meant." In effect, her handling of the situation was in line with the option of maintaining ambiguity (in this case, being noncommital).

The speech event, sounding (or woofing), orients Blacks also to take advantage of the opportunity to utilize ambiguity in other strategic ways. For example, it enables a speaker to test a person by placing them in a position where options are present, such as the three options noted above, and then letting them show the kind of person they are through the option they choose. A nice example of this was provided by Wicker (1975). The setting is a troop train that was to take Wicker, two other White sailors (like Wicker, also from the South), and 27 Black sailors (from Seattle, Washington) to Virginia to be discharged, a trip that would take about two weeks. The time is 1944. Wicker, as the "tall redhead," was placed in charge. As soon as all of the men were alone, Wicker was confronted by a tall Black sailor as follows: "Hey you, Red!"

According to Wicker, at that point, "Silence fell on the car like soot from a steam engine." After Wicker replied, "Yeah," the Black sailor said "Suck my Black dick." Wicker said half the Blacks laughed, a little uncertainly, and one or two eyed him stonily. He said he could not tell whether he was being teased or challenged. Nonetheless, he was "astonished . . . that the tall black man thought there was any reason to be hostile, even more astonished that a black man would dare to speak so to a white." He had to respond, but how? He could deal with this Black youth as a "Southern white man would deal with a colored person, whether nigger, nigruh, or Negro, and back it up, or else he would have to deal with him as one human with another and live with the consequences." Wicker decided on the latter course of action. An old joke flickered in his memory.

"Why, your buddy there told me you didn't even have one. Said a dog bit it off." The Black sailor grinned, and the other Blacks laughed. He replied, "Shee-it. You git home, man, you ask your girl friend, see if I ain't broke it off in her pussy." Wicker responded, "After mine, I reckon she wouldn't even *feel* that old biddy toothpick of yours." There was more laughter and backslapping, according to Wicker, at which point, another Black man called amiably, "Hey, Red. You the head man, when we gone chow down?" (1975, pp. 157-159).

Wicker had "passed" the test insofar as he resolved the ambiguous remark of the Black sailor in favor of the nonserious, thus showing that he was willing to deal with the Black sailor, as he put it, as "one human with another and live with the consequences." Of course, the Black sailor's aggressive remark could function as a test only because it was ambiguous; that is, it contained, within its scheme, the option to move the action in the direction of play, and not the option to treat it as serious, as would be the case in White male mainstream culture.

In light of this episode one might ask how Wicker, a White man, recognized that he had an option to define the Black sailor's taunt as play. The answer may be that as a *Southern* White man, Wicker had acquired an understanding of Black cultural patterns through informal social contacts with Blacks. This is Raven McDavid's view of Wicker's response (personal communication), which I quote from here. If correct, it would serve to explain Wicker's apparently anomalous cultural response (from the standpoint of White male mainstream culture):

> It is an historical fact that in communities where Blacks and Whites have long lived side by side, there has been a gradual breaking-down of Black-White informal contacts over the last century (it was noted in some Southern communities as far back as 1880; and I have noticed it in my own lifetime), even as formal relationships have been more or less officially equalized. The fact that Wicker knew the option suggests some familiarity through the informal contacts; but if he had come from say, Bridgeport, where such informal contacts never existed (and Bridgeport is but a symbol for the Northern urban scene), I don't think he could have made it.

Although Wicker recognized that he had an option to define the situation as one of play, his characterization of the Black sailor's remark ("Was he being teased *or* challenged?") still reflects a White mainstream cultural view in that: (1) it implies that what the sailor was doing could only be either one thing or the other, but not both, and (2) at the moment the sailor made the remark he could both be expected to know which meaning it had and be expected to know the social rule that would hold him accountable for knowing which meaning it had. These views ultimately misrepresent the true ambiguity or noncommittal nature of the Black sailor's remark as well as the critical role that Black culture places upon the receiver in such situations to determine (through their response) what the remark, in fact, "means."

Thus, from the Black cultural standpoint, the Black sailor's remark was *both* a tease *and* a challenge. Insofar as Wicker had chosen to take the sailor's remark seriously and decided to fight, the Black sailor was prepared to do that. Conversely, had Wicker chosen (as he did) to define the situation as one of play, the Black sailor was ready to deal at that level, as he showed. Moreover, the equivocal and noncommittal aspect of the sailor's remark was there at the time that he made it. Consequently, had someone asked him (trying to assess whether the sailor was being *serious or not*) what his remark "meant" at the time that he made it, the correct answer from the Black cultural perspective would be, "Nothing definite, yet." The Black sailor, along with the culture, through the strategic use of ambiguity, effectively assigned to Wicker the *authority* for determining the meaning of his remark, thus also the *responsibility for deciding* the ambiguity in favor of play or nonplay. Consequently, until Wicker responded, the sailor's remark had no definite *single* meaning. As Labov noted (personal communication) in response to Kochman (1983): "This follows the Sacks/Shegloff position that there are a great many speech events whose meaning is not determinate until they are reacted to."

The reason that Wicker was likely to view the Black sailor's remark in terms of being *either* teased *or* challenged (but not both) stems from the White male mainstream view on aggressive behavior: a male either means it or he does not. Moreover, if he does (or does not) mean it, but does not clearly show whether he does or not, then he is said to be *bluffing*. But *bluffing and exploitive fabrication* (Goffman, 1974, pp. 103-111) would be wrong characterizations of the Black sailor's remark since they imply that he did not mean to be serious at the time that he made it (given the hindsight fact that the situation ultimately was resolved in terms of play). The White mainstream cultural view sees the meaning of verbally aggressive behavior a direct outgrowth of speaker *intent.* Thus, if a person *appears* to be serious (without that proverbially disarming *smile,* then he can be taken by others to *be* serious. The speaker's initial demeanor (signifying intent) is seen to irrevocably define the key for the whole activity. There is no allowance here for the contribution that recipients might make in determining the meaning of what is going on. There is certainly no realization that the recipient might be given even a more critical (socially accountable) role than the initial speaker in determining the meaning of a particular remark or gesture, or, in this instance, key (serious *or* nonserious tone, but not both), as has been the case in the situations shown here. It is for these reasons that Whites will tend to hold speakers more accountable than Blacks will for the behavioral responses that recipients make to speakers' verbal provocations.

CONCLUSION

There are many areas of Black-White contact to which the above analysis can apply and prove useful, especially within the areas of disputation and verbal aggression. For example, one White graduate student learned from the analysis that, as a recipient, he was not obligated to respond seriously to a direct verbal attack—as in his own culture—but could exercise the option that Blacks call "playing it off" (option one), much the way Wicker did when confronted by the Black sailor. Thus, when the graduate student who worked in a hospital was verbally attacked with an opening "fuck you," by an angry Black male patient, he responded, "A simple 'Good Morning' would be sufficient." That remark completely transformed an aggressively hostile situation into a joking one, thereby eliciting laughter not only from the other patients nearby but also from the Black patient who initiated the verbal attack.

Likewise a Black woman agreed to reconsider the conclusion that she initially drew about some White women in her office upon learning about the different ways Blacks and Whites assign responsibility for determining the applicability of a general accusation. The White women started saying something about Blacks as a group and then said, "Of course, we don't mean you, Betty." Betty, however, felt that the White women had intended the statement also to apply to her, notwithstanding their disclaimer.

This is because in Black culture, generic statements are seen to be general rather than categorical. Moreover, the receiver is seen to have the responsibility for determining the applicability of a general accusation. Therefore, if the White women did not intend for their comment to include Betty in the general statement, they should (from Betty's Black cultural perspective), have said nothing, leaving it to Betty to decide whether the remark applied to her or not. By singling out Betty, even in the context of exempting her as a possible target of attack, the White women in effect preempted Betty's role in deciding whether the remark applied to her. This act led Betty to believe that they did intend the remark to apply to her, even though they stated the contrary.

Later, Betty learned of the cultural difference that, when Whites make a general accusation, the responsibility for determining the specific applicability of the accusation falls on the accuser. To avoid accusing someone falsely, therefore, the White speaker often qualifies his or her accusation at the outset by granting dispensation to those who fit the generic category but to whom the speaker feels the accusation does not apply (see Kochman, 1981, pp. 89-96, for a fuller discussion).

These situations are revealing and suggestive insofar as they show that many communication problems that Blacks and Whites experience as a result of ethnocentric interpretations can be remedied simply by members of each group enlarging their understanding to include the cultural frames of reference of members of the other group.

But not all examples of Black and White cultural conflict can be resolved this way. Other cultural differences (such as Black culture displaying and valuing highly individualized personal expression, spontaneity, intuition, and improvisation) require entirely different kinds of reciprocal accommodation before they could be considered settled (see Kochman, 1981, passim, for a more complete account). White mainstream (organizational) culture, by contrast, displays and values standardized (uniform) operating procedures, a separation of the planning and implementation stages of individual and group functioning, and generic work role models that are intolerant of any but instrumental stylistic patterns and values. It is in those contexts where White mainstream cultural values are seen as exclusive (most mainstream organizations and institutions) that Black cultural values are most inhospitably regarded and treated.

From a methodological standpoint, these examples and discussion point out the need to contextualize the areas of structural and functional nonequivalence between cognitive (cultural) systems when doing comparative analysis. They also show the importance of understanding the *variable* cultural schemes at work in cross-cultural transactions. As in these cases, the variable cultural schemes organize respectively different behavioral options for speakers and listeners, as well as contain within them different views on who is more (and less) socially accountable for determining the meaning of any particular remark or gesture. Only on gathering and assimilating that information will we, as researchers, be able to answer the large *activity* question: What is going on here—and for whom?

NOTES

1. Labov has written (as a footnote in Kochman, 1983), that he agrees with the point that the sounding session changes character with the denial, rather than with the use of personal subject matter. He adds, "This potentiality in the character of a speech activity can be determined only by looking closely at the interaction itself" (see Labov, 1982).

2. Conversely, Labov's analysis can also be taken to suggest that the use of personal insults in the context of verbal dueling is more *dangerous* than it really is, since, according to Labov's analysis, the use of personal insults automatically defines the activity as "serious."

REFERENCES

Abrahams, R. D. (1974). Black talking on the streets. In R. Bauman & J. Sherzer (Eds.), *Explorations in the ethnography of speaking* (pp. 240-262). London: Cambridge University Press.

Berger, P. L., & Luckmann, T. (1966). *The social construction of reality*. New York: Anchor.

Cicourel, A. (1973). *Cognitive sociology*. London: Penguin.

Danet, B. (1980). Language in the legal process. *Law & Society Review, 14,* 445-564.

Edwards, W. F. (1979). Speech acts in Guyana: Communicating ritual and personal insults. *Journal of Black Studies, 10*(1), 20-39.

Fisher, L. (1976). Dropping remarks and the Barbadian audience. *American Ethnologist, 3,* 227-242.

Folb, E. A. (1980). *Runnin' down some lines: The language and culture of Black teenagers.* Cambridge, MA: Harvard University Press.

Frake, C. (1964). A structural description of Subanum "religious" behavior. In W. Goodenough (Ed.), *Explorations in cultural anthropology* (pp. 111-130). New York: McGraw-Hill.

Freedle, R. (1977). Introduction. In R. O. Freedle (Ed.), *Discourse production and comprehension*. Norwood, NJ: Ablex.

Garfinkel, H. (1967). *Studies in ethnomethodology*. Englewood Cliffs, NJ: Prentice-Hall.

Goffman, E. (1974). *Frame analysis*. New York: Harper/Colophon.

Gumperz, J. (Ed.). (1982a). *Language and social identity*. London: Cambridge University Press.

Gumperz, J. (1982b). *Discourse strategies*. London: Cambridge University Press.

Gumperz, J., & Hymes, D. (Eds.). (1972). *Directions in sociolinguistics*. New York: Holt, Rinehart & Winston.

Gurwitsch, A. (1964). *The field of consciousness*. Pittsburgh: Duquesne University Press.

Husserl, E. (1952). *Ideas: General introduction to pure phenomenology*. London: George Allen & Unwin.

Hymes, D. (1980). Foreword. In S. B. Shimanoff, *Communication rules: Theory and research* (pp. 9-27). Beverly Hills, CA: Sage.

James, W. (1950). *Principles of psychology* (vol. 2). New York: Dover.

Keiser, R. L. (1969). *The vice lords: Warriors of the streets*. New York: Holt, Rinehart & Winston.

Kochman, T. (1970). Toward an ethnography of Black American speech behavior. In N. E. Whitten, Jr., & J. Szwed (Eds.), *Afro-American anthropology* (pp. 145-162). New York: Free Press.

Kochman, T. (Ed.). (1972). *Rappin' and stylin' out: Communication in urban Black America*. Urbana: University of Illinois Press.

Kochman, T. (1975). Grammar and discourse in vernacular Black English. Review of Labov (1972a), *Foundation of Language, 13*, 95-118.

Kochman, T. (1977). Review of Gage (1974). *Language in Society, 6*(1), 49-64.

Kochman, T. (1981). *Black and White styles in conflict*. Chicago: University of Chicago Press.

Kochman, T. (1983). The boundary between play and nonplay in Black verbal dueling. *Language in Society, 12*, 329-337.

Labov, W. (1972a). *Language in the inner city: Studies in the black English Vernacular*. Philadelphia: University of Pennsylvania Press.

Labov, W. (1972b). Rules for ritual insults. In T. Kochman (Ed.), *Rappin' and stylin' out: Communication in urban Black America* (pp. 265-314). Urbana: University of Illinois Press.

Labov, W. (1974). The art of sounding and signifying. In W. W. Gage (Ed.), *Language in its social setting* (pp. 84-116). Washington, DC: Anthropological Society of Washington.

Labov, W. (1982). Speech actions and reactions in personal narrative. In D. Tannen (Ed.), *Georgetown University Roundtable on Language and Linguistics* (pp. 219-247). Washington, DC: Georgetown University Press.

Maryland, J. (1972). Shoe-shine on 63rd. In T. Kochman (Ed.), *Rapping' and stylin' out: Communication in urban Black America* (pp. 209-214). Urbana: University of Illinois Press.

Mitchell-Kernan, C. (1972). Signifying, loud-talking and marking. In T. Kochman (Ed.), *Rappin' and stylin' out: Communication in urban Black America* (pp. 315-335). Urbana: University of Illinois Press.

Schutz, A. (1962 [1945]). On multiple realities. In *Collected papers* (vol. I). The Hague: Martinus Nijhoff.

Schutz, A. (1970). *Reflections on the problem of relevance* (R. M. Zaner, Ed.). New Haven, CT: Yale University Press.

Shimanoff, S. B. (1980). *Communication rules: Theory and research*. Beverly Hills, CA: Sage.

Spradley, J. (1979). *The ethnographic interview*. New York: Holt, Rinehart & Winston.

Tannen, D. (1982). Ethnic style in male-female conversation. In J. Gumperz (Ed.), *Language and social identity* (pp. 217-231). London: Cambridge University Press.

Wicker, T. (1975). *A time to die*. New York: Quadrangle/The New York Times Book Co.

9

"Nobody Play by the Rules He Know"
Ethnocentric Interference in Classroom Questioning Events

DONALD L. RUBIN • *University of Georgia*

The communicative functions of questions in classroom settings often differ markedly from their normative use in everyday discourse. This article focuses on classroom questions that function as veiled directives for regulating student behavior or as pseudo-questions that test students' achievement. Comparative ethnographies of classroom and community speech events reveal sources of potential mismatch between the schools' expectations for questioning events and the communication rules by which many students from nonmainstream ethnic cultures operate. This analysis suggests that greater educational opportunity may be offered to nonmainstream ethnic students by altering certain discrete questioning behaviors and by restructuring certain aspects of classroom interaction.

Progressive pedagogical thought advocates student-centered discovery modes of classroom instruction. Rather than mere information dispensers, teachers are regarded as engineering experiences that enable students to assimilate actively new information or accommodate new concepts. In this view, teachers ought not to dominate classroom talk, but they still must regulate it by structuring topics of discussion, facilitating student interaction, and staging and sequencing students' transitions from one inquiry to another. In all this, the teacher's stock-in-trade is the question.

But even well-intentioned teachers committed to student-centered learning are struck by the fact that these methods fail some students. One teacher remarked in a not atypical comment:

> They don't seem able to answer even the simplest questions. . . . I sometimes feel that when I look at them and ask a question, I'm starting at

AUTHOR'S NOTE: *I acknowledge the helpful suggestions of Joel Taxel on earlier drafts of this chapter.*

a wall I can't break through. There's something there; yet in spite of all the questions I ask, I'm never sure I've gotten through to what's inside that wall. (in Heath, 1982a, p. 108)

Such students are not normally reticent. They are social and talkative in other settings. In class discussion they may even display sporadic flashes of interest or amusement. In the main, however, they are nonparticipative. It is as if the discovery classroom is operating according to some set rules to which a substantial minority of students have not been made privy. This state of affairs is apparent to even lay observers:

My kid, he too scared to talk, 'cause nobody play by the rules he know. At home, I can't shut 'im up. Miss Davis, she complain 'bout Ned not answerin' back. He says she asks dumb questions she already know 'bout. (in Heath, 1982a, p. 108)

Quite often—too often—that nonparticipative minority is in fact composed of ethnic minorities. The middle-class Anglo students respond; many ethnic minority students and many working-class students do not.

The terms *mainstream* and *nonmainstream* are admittedly vague. They can probably only be defined tautologically: Mainstream cultures are those that enjoy economic, social, and educational privilege relative to nonmainstream cultures. The terms are intended to be comprehensive of ethnicity, socioeconomic class, educational attainment, and social custom. The exact parameters delineating the two types of cultures vary from region to region and from time period to time period. The term *Anglo* denotes the mainstream culture dominant in most regions of the United States. Throughout this chapter cultural designations such as *Anglo, Native American,* or *working class* are intended as generalizations about some core of observed cultural patterns. These generalizations are not intended to be applicable to any given individual. By the same token, it is recognized that considerable variation within cultures and across situations must temper any attempt at generalization.

Numerous accounts have been promulgated to explain the disparity in school achievement between mainstream and nonmainstream ethnic students. Some of these point to inequities in the allocation of educational resources (Glasman & Binimianov, 1981). Some attribute educational failure to alienating motivational factors that may be transmitted through peer group cultures (Labov, 1972) or that may arise from social realities that discourage nonmainstream ethnic youth from perceiving much pay-off in the academic enterprise (Katz, 1976; Ogbu, 1981). Still other accounts suggest that differences in cognitive style, though not in intellectual ability, create a gulf that impedes the progress of nonmainstream students (Banks, McQuatar, & Hubbard, 1978).

Without discounting the potency of any of these factors, this study explores some fairly subtle sources of cultural interference that bear quite directly on how talk is regulated in classrooms. In particular, this report examines that aspect of communicative competence that defines what is to "count" as a question and what is to count as an appropriate answer to a question. For questions are the scaffolding by means of which teachers foster new knowledge structures among students. Yet there can be considerable mismatch between the way questions are used in the speech communities of the schools, and the way questions are used in nonmainstream students' primary speech communities.

THE NATURE OF
CLASSROOM QUESTIONING EVENTS

Typical studies of classroom interaction tabulate questions according to who is doing the asking and what level of cognitive operation each question demands. Thus we know that nearly all classroom questions are posed by teachers. Of those few questions that students do ask, the great majority are procedural in nature such as "Will it be graded?" and "How wide should the margins be?" (Brophy & Good, 1974; Gall, 1970).

The cognitive demands associated with classroom questioning are typically ascertained by applying some taxonomy of educational objectives, such as Bloom and his associates' (1956). Using such an approach, students of classroom interaction have determined, for example, that teachers' questions characteristically call for literal recall and rote recitation of factual material (Gall, 1970). Most such questioning serves as formative evaluation, as an ongoing check of student learning. A major goal for teacher training is to encourage teachers to formulate questions that tap a wider range of cognitive operations, to use questions for genuine inquiry and discovery (Hunkins, 1972).

These approaches to studying the users and types of classroom questions are limited, however, in the sense that they ignore the varied communicative functions of teacher questions and ignore the social facts of classrooms viewed as speech communities. The widely accepted Flanders (1970) interaction coding scheme, for example, contains but a single category for "question" and a single category for "student response." This system and others like it cannot represent the dependencies between teacher elicitations and student responses. It is especially ill-equipped to handle smaller questioning events nested within larger, hierarchically organized units of discourse.

More recent analyses of classroom interaction that use ethnographic methodologies (e.g., Dillon & Searle, 1981; Green, 1982; Green & Wallat, 1981; Mehan, 1979; Sinclair & Coulthard, 1975; Wells, 1981; Wilkinson, 1981; Willes, 1981), on the other hand, provide for more fine-grained functional descriptions of teacher questions, and more adequately represent questioning events as part of the overall structure of conversational interaction within classrooms. Ethnographies of communication require extended and close observations of naturalistic interaction and require analytical schemes that emerge from the data rather than the imposition of categories defined a priori. It further requires that events be described in context rather than as isolates (Hymes, 1974). Ideally, classroom ethnographies would also link micro-level observations to the broader social and political climate in which they are embedded (Ogbu, 1981).

Ethnographies of classroom interaction have revealed, for example, a fundamental dissimilarity between the structure of classroom questioning sequences and the structure of questioning sequences in the home. Parent-child interaction is most often composed of two-term units of discourse: a question followed by a response (Dore, 1977). Classroom interaction, in contrast, displays a three-term structure that can be described as initiation-reply-evaluation (Mehan, 1979), opening-answering-follow-up (Sinclair & Coulthard, 1975), or solicit-give-acknowledge (Wells, 1981). Becoming a competent member of the classroom speech community entails learning these tacit rules for exchanging talk, much as acquiring linguistic competence entails learning tacit rules of language structure (Green & Wallat, 1981; Mehan, 1979).

In addition to sequencing talk, rules of classroom interaction allow members of the classroom to respond appropriately to teachers' questions. That is, students must come to recognize the various social functions that school questions can play. In ordinary conversation, a question is prototypically a request for information. The rules that constitute questioning as a speech act, that set the parameters for what is to "count" as a question, dicate that I ask you a question in order that I may become enlightened about something. Furthermore, I ask you a question only if I have a reasonable expectation that you possess the information I am seeking (Searle, 1969).

In classroom communication, however, these ordinary language rules are not operative; teacher talk includes questions that are not true requests for enlightenment. Typically, teachers ask a great many identification questions, the answers to which are more likely known by the teachers than by the students. Indeed, if the teachers could be certain that the students knew the answers to these questions, they would not bother to ask at all. Barnes (1969) calls such utterances *pseudo-questions*. With greater bluntness, Bernstein (1977) identifies the "testing" function of such questions. Thus, when a teacher asks, "What is the molecular composition of water?" the students are well aware that the teacher is not seeking new insights into molecular structures but rather checking their recall of course material. Under certain circumstances, when the teacher asks, "What did you do on your summer vacation?" the teacher is less interested in student pastimes than in eliciting an evaluable performance that will reveal weaknesses in language skills. Dillon and Searle (1981) note that such quasi-questions call for student responses that may be classified as oral copying, oral multiple-choice, oral fill-in-the-blank, or oral charades.

Utterances which are grammatically marked as questions may also function as directives, attempts to get a listener to do something for a speaker (Brown & Levinson, 1978; Ervin-Tripp, 1976). If a teacher asks, "Do you have the homework you were to turn in today?" a response of "Yes" is not wholly adequate. A response of "Here it is" addresses the directive force of the "question" more appropriately. (Notice, however, that the "Yes" response would be appropriate if the question were asked not by a teacher but by a fellow student. A question functions as a directive only when an implicit obligation is operating, as in the obligation of a subordinate to fulfill the wishes of a more powerful interlocutor.) Indeed, children face an important developmental task in learning that the form of an utterance does not unambiguously define its function (e.g., "Do you know what time it is?" is interpreted as "Get to bed this instant!" when said to a youngster who has stayed awake beyond bedtime; Western, 1974).

In general, the question form is a way of minimizing the face threatening potential of directives (Brown & Levinson, 1978). To make a direct request is to emphasize asymmetric power relations. Teachers use questions as directives most often when considerable social distance separates them from students because saving face is important in such situations. When teacher and student are less remote interpersonally, as when they are both members of the same cultural group, direct requests are more frequent (Cazden, 1979). The threat to face is intrinsically reduced when teacher and student share a common cultural reference group.

Question directives and quasi-questions are but two examples of the varied functions that questions perform in classroom interaction. Classroom questions do, of course, sometimes perform the function of true inquiry: "Who can think of a good way to explain the chemical composition of water to, say, a five-year-old?" "Why do summer vacations never work out the way we hope they will?" "Do you know anybody who kind of reminds you of Captain Ahab?" But the classroom-bound expectations for even such straightforward inquiries are fairly constrained. One expects that the answers will be topically relevant, be expository and generalizable rather than anecdotal and particularistic, and be elaborated at least to the degree that the student makes it clear how the answer addresses the intent of the question.

CULTURAL VARIATION IN QUESTIONING EVENTS

Schools are oriented toward mainstream, middle-class modes of talk. That is the kind of talk that is expected and rewarded (Bernstein, 1977; Matluck, 1978). There is twofold value, then, in describing the ways in which nonmainstream talk diverges from this model. First, the nature of the dominant culture, usually invisible to its members, becomes foregrounded by virtue of cross-cultural comparisons. More to the point of this essay, we can identify some sources of school failure by becoming aware of subtle mismatches between the communicative expectations of classroom talk and those of the nonmainstream ethnic cultures. These mismatches fall roughly into four related categories: (1) norms for loquacity, (2) norms for discourse structure and sequence, (3) norms for participant relations, and (4) ways of construing the functions of questions.

Norms of Loquacity

Certainly all human cultures depend on talk as the matrix of social structure. Hymes (1974), however, claims that cultures can be arrayed along a continuum from voluble, verbose, and elaborate to pithy, taciturn, and restrained. Verbosity in response to questions (that is, goal-directed talk) is one metric that teachers use to assess student ability. Many North American cultures including middle-class Anglo—but also inner-city Black—prize verbosity, and, in that sense, conform to the school standard. But many other cultures do not. Gay (1981) remarks that Native American and Chinese American students are typically verbally passive in classrooms. Their learning style is primarily visual, involving observation and imitation rather than verbalization (see Matluck, 1978).

Philips (1976), by way of illustration, describes informal learning among Native American Indian children in the Pacific Northwest. At home, they silently observe their elders performing such tasks as cooking or carving. They receive no didactic instruction nor do they ask questions. When alone, the children will practice the tasks until they are satisfied that they have attained mastery. Then, again without comment, they will begin performing those tasks at home in a matter-of-fact fashion. Such children cannot function well in a school setting that demands that students display their skills before they are fully mastered (e.g., working arithmetic problems at the chalkboard) or that expects children to talk about material only imperfectly learned.

Considerable controversy attends questions pertaining to the relationship between verbosity and social class. British researchers' early use of the term *restricted code* to label a working-class speech style (Bernstein, 1962) conjured an overly simplistic and erroneous depiction of working-class children as nonverbal (Rosen, 1974). Later refinements of the British theory clarified the concept as referring to ways of meaning rather than linguistic competence. In effect, children socialized in "positional" families may learn to favor more compressed, economical ways of packaging information and employ them in a broader range of situations than children socialized in families with a "personal" orientation (Bernstein, 1973). Thus, for example, Williams and Narremore (1969) found that middle-class and lower-class youngsters answered closed or yes/no questions in a similar manner, but that middle-class children produced more speech in response to open questions. Philipsen (1975) further described the reserved speech style valued in an industrial working-class community.

In short, school speech communities ask students, first of all, to talk when questioned, and beyond that, to display all the relevant knowledge they possess. Nonmainstream children may be penalized due to their cultures' divergent norms for loquacity.

Norms for Discourse Structure and Sequence

It is axiomatic to all systems of conversational analysis that talk involves turn-taking; a remark—especially a question—is paired with a response (Sacks, Schegloff, & Jefferson, 1974). But even this fundamental principle breaks down under cross-cultural comparison. Phillips (1976) observes that, among native American Indian groups, a question carries with it no obligation for an immediate response, and that any forthcoming response need not be verbal, but may very well be some behavioral act performed at some future point.

Basic tenets of conversational analysis likewise dictate that one person speaks at a time and that a question should be answered by the person to whom it is addressed (Mehan, 1979). Indeed, teachers take great pains, and inflict a good many as well, in enforcing this rule of talk. However, an ethnographic description of a native Hawaiian classroom (Boggs, 1972) suggests that children were eager to shout out answers to questions directed to other members of the class. When even the simplest questions asking for the number that follows "1" were directed to individual students, however, those students sat as if mute. It was not atypical for children to raise their hands and then call out the answer when a different child was called upon. But even if the child called upon had been waving his or her hand, the teacher's question went unanswered by the student whom the teacher designated.

Apparently these Hawaiian children regarded collective relationships as criterial in constituting contexts for talk. Dyadic interaction between unequals (i.e., between a teacher and an individual child) did not count as a context for talk. On the other hand, when an adult was perceived as truly receptive, a conversational equal, then children were most talkative (see also Day, 1981).

These examples of Native American and native Hawaiian cultures remind us that our fundamental assumptions about our interaction process are not cultural universals. The picture is further complicated by introducing considerations of situationally dependent variation within cultures. Norms of conversational sequencing and structure that hold between one set of participants (e.g., peers) may not hold when interactants stand in different role relationships (e.g., adult to child).

Norms for Participant Relations

Classroom teachers and researchers alike are persistently puzzled by students who are stonily nonparticipative in class but highly verbal in unstructured interaction among their peers. Students who exhibit no interest in speech within the walls of a classroom may display considerable skill at role-playing school talk with their friends (Gleason, 1973; Heath, 1982a). What is operating in these cases are rules that label contexts either as speech-appropriate situations or speech-inappropriate situations on the basis of participant role relations. For some cultures, typical classroom social structure simply does not count as a speech-appropriate situation.

Native American cultures again provide a useful contrast to the mainstream norm. Cherokee Indian children are described as very serious about their studies but paradoxically nonresponsive in classroom settings (Dumont, 1972). Because of their silence, their academic achievement is often depressed; they have little facility in using English as a vehicle of learning. In those few Cherokee Indian classrooms in which talk does flourish, the class answers questions and solves problems as a cooperative unit. One student's response is elaborated, refined, corrected by the others. Indeed, the answer belongs to the group, not to any individual. Silence reigns in those classes in which students are forced to dissociate themselves from the group in answering questions. The Cherokee Indian children simply do not possess a construct for interaction between a teacher and a single student. Speech that ignores the group is inconceivable.

Similarly, the Warm Springs Reservation children described by Philips (1970) have no way to cope with teacher questions that demand individual speech performance. These children come from a culture that does not recognize the sort of static roles common in mainstream culture that delineate a leader from a group of followers. Rather, leadership is a shared and dynamic *process* among Warm Springs adults. Moreover, children are given a good deal of autonomy, even to the extent of deciding for themselves in what household of extended family they will live. Young children are more often under the direct care of their siblings and younger relatives than under direct adult supervision. All of this renders the typical participant relations in mainstream classrooms especially unfathomable to Warm Springs youngsters. These children do not clearly comprehend the teacher's authority to make demands of them. They show interest more in what other students are doing than in what the teacher is enacting at the front of the classroom. They are particularly unable to understand demands for individual verbal performance.

Philips notes that successful classrooms on the reservation make adaptations to the participant relations that the children regard as speech-appropriate. While the children do not respond when questioned by the teacher, they do voluntarily approach a trusted teacher individually. Most important, they function particularly well in leaderless problem-solving groups, displaying remarkable persistence in such contexts.

A similar sort of peer culture immersion and socialization is reported among working-class black children. Beyond the "lap baby" stage, their interaction with adults is far more circumscribed than is typical among mainstream children (Gay & Abrahams, 1973; Heath, 1982a). In particular, black working-class youngsters are only infrequently exposed to adult-child questioning for either inquiry or testing. Instead, adults often use question forms in the context of behavioral control. For example, an adult accuses a child of wrongdoing by "asking," "Where have you been all afternoon?" Black working-class children, operating on their community's rules for construing adult questioning events, may interpret teachers' classroom questions as implicit accusations or threats.

Ways of Construing the Functions of Questions

As the preceding example suggests, a teacher may intend to pose one kind of question, say a true inquiry, but students socialized into nonmainstream cultures may construe the question's function altogether differently. Puerto Ricans tend to use strategies that blunt the face-threatening potential of direct requests. As a result, Puerto Rican speakers generally presume that questions are motivated by needs other than informing (Morris, 1981). Among Greeks, as well as Greek Americans, a similar tendency is apparent. Tannen (1981) recounts that she innocently asked her Greek host if the host ever prepared eggs by beating them; the question was of anthropological interest. Throughout the remainder of her visit, Tannen was invariably served scrambled eggs for breakfast, despite the fact that she has a strong dislike for the dish. Among the Gonja of Africa, questions also serve a wide range of purposes. As a result, the Gonja likewise seek out the motives for questioning. Indeed, the Gonja are extreme in this respect, for they apparently do not recognize questioning as being of any value for teaching purposes (Goody, 1978).

The use of quasi-questions to elicit displays of verbal prowess seems to be a predominantly middle-class Anglo phenomenon (Bernstein, 1977; Gay & Abrahams, 1973). The parent, who is already privy to the information requested, asks, "How many piggies were there in the story?" In such ways, middle-class children learn that elaborated verbal performance is inherently valued. Working-class black youngsters, in contrast, find that verbal performance is rewarding as an instrument for avoiding parents' sanctions. In such cases, the child's response often has the effect of circumlocuting or switching topics (Heath, 1982a). Nonmainstream students often have little exposure to the kinds of quasi-questions that teachers employ simply for testing language skills: "How would you tell that story in your own words?" "Who can tell me what we talked about in class yesterday?"

Heath (1982a, 1982b) has done extensive cross-cultural ethnographies in the functions of questions at home and at school. Observing in the homes of middle-class Anglo elementary school teachers, she found that in interacting with their own children, teachers posed a virtual torrent of questions. Most of these were quasi-questions to which the parent already possessed the answer. A large number were clarification questions asking the child to refine or explain the preceding response. Another large proportion were unanswerable "I wonder" questions that presumably modeled for the children the use of higher-order question types. Of course these parents also used questions as directives and to regulate the children's behavior.

In a neighboring black working-class community, Heath found, first of all, that questions constituted a far lower proportion of the utterances that adults addressed to their children. Imperatives were a dominant form (see also Cook-Gumperz, 1973). There were fewer quasi-questions asking children to label features of their environment. Instead, children were posed a great many analogy questions such as "What's that like?" and "Who's he acting like?" but less frequently, "What's that?" or "Who is he?" The children were never asked to explain the bases for their analogies. Another use of questioning common in the black households but absent in the Anglo ones functioned to initiate an extended narrative events: "Did you see Maggie's dog yesterday?" "No, but I saw it the day before." "Well, yesterday that dog got in a heap of trouble." Heath's observations also indicate that black working-class children had less experience with questions functioning as directives.

Significantly, what little direct instruction those children received a propos to questioning taught them to ignore or avoid the questions of strangers—especially white strangers—who might be entering the community on such invasive missions as reading gas meters or selling insurance. Gay and Abrahams (1973) note that this learning readily generalizes to the questions of white teachers.

In a white working-class community, Heath (1982b) notes that a great many quasi-questions were used, especially during story reading events, but that these questions were limited largely to labeling objects out of context. These parents did not ask questions encouraging children to synthesize information, or to extend knowledge into other contexts (e.g., a kitty in a story was not related to a kitty in the street). Questions were rarely used for instructional purposes, except as directives or behavior regulators. Even in these cases, a preponderance of imperative forms was evident.

In examining questioning events in school, Heath found a strong correspondence with the sorts of questions she observed in the middle-class Anglo homes: questions functioning as face-saving directives, quasi-questions asking for labeling or for evaluable verbal perfor-mances, questions extending events in stories to new contexts, questions asking for explanations or refinements of previous responses, questions used for integrating constructs by means of higher-order cognitive operations.

For the most part, the working-class black and white youngsters had few bases for properly construing the functions of these questions. Interestingly, Heath found that the working-class white children obtained some advantage from the out-of-context labeling questions to which they had been exposed. Their early reading achievement was standard. But their achievement fell off rapidly when reading materials asked children to go beyond the information given, to speculate about characters in new contexts, and the like. The kind of analogical perception in which the working-class black children had been trained was of litle service to them in school. Their frequently divergent responses were ignored or punished, and their inability to explain the bases for their analogies precluded any redemption in the eyes of their teachers.

TOWARD MULTICULTURAL REFORM
OF CLASSROOM TALK:
ETHICS AND STRATEGIES

It is naive to suppose that education is value-free. Throughout the grades, throughout the subject matters, schooling projects a "hidden curriculum" that supports the values of the dominant culture (Apple,

1979). The hidden curriculum is most evident in consideration of the *content* of tests and lessons. Thus, for example, educators are concerned about eliminating dominant culture sex-role stereotypes from student reading materials (Weitzman & Rizzo, 1980).

When the content of a teacher's question contains culturally foreign material, students from ethnic minority cultures are needlessly disadvantaged. Boggs (1972) notes the tragic absurdity of low achieving Hawaiian children struggling with reading test questions about igloos. Matluck (1978) discusses the difficulty of native Chinese students in sequencing a standard series of pictures involving a child with paint brushes spilling paint at an easel. The Chinese children were familiar with art materials of a very different nature, and while they understood the properties of sequence, they could not recognize the content of the pictures. Similarly, one observer in an ethnically homogenous Anglo school witnessed a well-intentioned classroom discussion about what one does at the seashore, in which children from upper-middle-class homes enthusiastically volunteered information while their peers from working-class backgrounds sat in total passivity. Located some 300 miles from the nearest ocean, the more affuent members of the class enjoyed annual vacations at the beach. But the seashore was a mere abstraction to those children for whom a vacation was simply a break from school.

While it requires the motivation to do so, ferreting out culturally biased content in classroom lessons is a relatively easy task. What this chapter has been discussing is the far more elusive problem of cultural bias in the *form* of classroom interaction. Classroom questioning events, functioning as they do in the manner described in this exposition, incorporate a number of culture-bound and ethnocentric assumptions which serve to subtly espouse mainstream values.

Classroom questions ask students to conform to mainstream values favoring volubility and elaboration. Classroom questions ask students to accept skilled verbal performance as an end in itself. They demand that students decontextualize experience, label objects, transform them into new settings, and explain analogical reasoning. Questioning in the schools forces students to dissociate themselves from the collectivity, to recognize certain privileges of designated leaders in directing group members, and to become obligated to the call-response contract of conversational interaction.

One of the most enigmatic aspects of the problem of ethnocentricity and cultural bias in classroom questioning is that, from the point of view of the professional educator, the values just enumerated seem rather attractive. In a literate, technological, specialized yet interdependent society, these values are quite functional (Ong, 1971). They are just the sorts of orientations needed, for example, in learning to write, and to produce autonomous, cohesive, and linear discourse (Cook-Gumperz & Gumperz, 1981).

And yet, to the degree that the values implicit in classroom questioning events violate nonmainstream ethnic children's rules for competent communicating, they further undermine chances for academic success. As the examples cited throughout this essay illustrate, many nonmainstream children simply have few bases for participating in the dominant mode of school learning. The form of interaction demanded is utterly unfamiliar. Classroom questioning events constitute an insidious form of cultural bias because they are so pervasive, because their inherent value orientation is generally so invisible to us, and because they sentence to failure just those children most in need of the knowledge and skills which they are intended to impart.

Wrestling with the moral dilemma of cultural orientations in the structure of curricula, Egan (1979) advocates that educators openly select that model which best conforms to the nature of Western industrialized society. If this stance is accepted (and it is not accepted universally), then it would be dysfunctional to abandon our present forms of classroom discourse. But at the risk of perpetuating the cycle of school failure, nonmainstream ethnic students must not simply be left adrift to cope—usually through silence and alienation. Indeed, by making provision for multicultural variation in styles of discourse, we may find ourselves enriching the learning opportunities of even mainstream students.

Strategies for Multicultural Adaptation

Some aspects of the solution require that teachers alter fairly discrete behaviors with no adverse effects on any members of the classroom community. For example, if the function of questions as directives is confusing to some children and threatening to others, then teachers can simply use more direct forms of request. Instead of asking, "Where do we put our coats in this classroom?" or "Can you put your coat away?" a teacher might state, "I would like you to hang your coat in the closet," or "Hang your coat in the closet, please, Linda." If Cazden's (1979) analysis is correct, these more direct requests might yield the beneficial side effect of conveying greater solidarity with the students.

If certain groups within a class are nonresponsive in the face of decontextualizing and labeling questions, teachers might pose question types more similar to those used at home. Rather than "What is this?" a teacher might ask "Where do you see this?" or "What's this like?" Heath (1982a) reports a pilot intervention study in which black working-class children were tape-recorded as they successfully answered the more familiar questions of the second type. The students' images of themselves as members of the classroom speech community improved markedly. In addition, the teachers interspersed models of the less familiar labeling questions and encouraged use of these tapes in a learning center. Finally, teachers provided direct instruction in school talk: "These are the kinds of questions we sometimes ask in school. They're different in some ways from the questions you're used to at home."

When appropriate for teaching concepts, teachers might make some allowances for behavioral modes of response rather than decontextualizing verbal responses. For example, if a teacher wants to ascertain a child's concept of square, this testing could be accomplished by means of quasi-questions: "How many sides does a square have?" "What do those sides have to be?" Alternatively, the teacher might say, "Show me a square somewhere in this room." "Now show me something in the room which is like a square, but isn't a square."

Philips's (1970) and Dumont's (1972) descriptions of successful Native American classrooms suggest yet more profound adaptations that create alternate approaches to structuring discourse and participant relations. In these classes, students either worked in small groups of peers or else the entire class behaved much as a small group. The dominance of the teacher in regulating talk was reduced, and collective student responses were permitted, if not encouraged. In other words, the nonmainstream ethnic student may benefit from a more equal distribution of the communication network throughout the classroom speech community. In such a classroom, the teacher is a co-learner, an integrated member of the community, rather than an alien force imposed upon the group. While some educators may fear that such participant relations will undermine the teacher's authority, it is worth bearing in mind that, in many nonmainstream classrooms, the teacher may have recognized authority but very little power. For while authority can be assigned, power—for example, the power to motivate student learning—is awarded by the group.

Finally, and most profoundly, multicultural classrooms need what all classrooms need—teachers who can convey a sense of receptiveness.

Some students do not respond to questions posed before the entire class. Yet they may voluntarily approach the teacher for one-to-one sharing and instruction. Some students are alienated and reserved in the face of quasi-questions. The same students, however, may become highly animated by true inquiry questions that demonstrate teachers' interest in their unique contributions. Many students remain impassive when teachers' questions are veiled attempts to control behavior or to evaluate performance. These students can become participating members of the learning community when, instead, teachers make it clear that their questions are being used to foster learning.

REFERENCES

Apple, M. W. (1979). *Ideology and curriculum.* Routledge & Kegan Paul.

Banks, W. C., McQuatar, G. V., & Hubbard, J. L. (1978). Toward a reconceptualization of the social-cognitive basis of achievement orientations in blacks. *Review of Educational Research, 48,* 381-397.

Barnes, D. (1969). *Language, the learner and the school.* Hardmondsworth: Penguin.

Bernstein, B. (1962). Social class, linguistic codes and grammatical elements. *Language and Speech, 5,* 31-46.

Bernstein, B. (1973). A brief account of the theory of codes. In H. P. Dreitzel (Ed.), *Recent sociology No. 5: Childhood and socialization.* New York: Macmillan.

Bernstein, B. (1977). Foreword. In D. Adlam (Ed.), *Code and context.* London: Routledge & Kegan Paul.

Bloom, B. S., Krathwolh, D. R., & Masia, B. B. (1956). *The classification of educational goals, Handbook I: Cognitive domain.* New York: David McKay.

Boggs, S. T. (1972). The meaning of questions and narratives to Hawaiian children. In C. B. Cazden, V. P. John, & D. Hymes (Eds.), *Functions of language in the classroom.* New York: Teachers College Press.

Brophy, J. E., & Good, T. L. (1974). *Teacher-student relationships: Causes and consequences.* New York: Holt, Rinehart & Winston.

Brown, P., & Levinson, S. (1978). Universals in language: Politeness phenomena. In E. Good, (Ed.), *Questions and politeness. Cambridge: Cambridge University Press.*

Cazden, C. (1979). Language in education: Variation in the teacher-talk register. In J. E. Atlatis & G. R. Tucker (Eds.), *Georgetown University Round Table on Languages and Linguistics 1979.* Washington, DC: Georgetown University Press.

Cook-Gumperz, J. (1973). *Social control and socialization.* London: Routledge & Kegan Paul.

Cook-Gumperz, J., & Gumperz, J. J. (1981). From oral to written culture: The transition to literacy. In M. F. Whiteman (Ed.), *Variation in writing: Functional and linguistic-cultural differences.* Hillsdale, NJ: Lawrence Erlbaum.

Day, R. R. (1981). Silence and the ESL child. *TESOL Quarterly, 15,* 35-39.

Dillon, D., & Searle, D. (1981). The role of language in one first-grade classroom. *Research in the Teaching of English, 15,* 311-328.

Dore, J. (1977). "Oh them sheriff": A pragmatic analysis of children's responses to questions. In S. Ervin-Tripp & C. Mitchell-Kernan (Eds.), *Child discourse.* New York: Academic Press.

Dumont, R. V. (1972). Learning English and how to be silent: Studies in Sioux and Cherokee classrooms. In C. B. Cazden, V. P. John, & D. Hymes (Eds.), *Functions of language in the classroom.* New York: Teachers College Press.

Egan, K. (1979). *Educational development.* Chicago: University of Chicago Press.

Ervin-Tripp, S. (1976). Is Sybil there? The structure of some American English directives. *Language in Society, 5,* 25-66.

Flanders, N. A. (1970). *Analyzing teaching behavior.* Reading, MA: Addison-Wesley.

Gall, M. D. (1970). The use of questions in teaching. *Review of Educational Research, 40,* 707-720.

Gay, G. (1981). Interactions in culturally pluralistic classrooms. In J. A. Bales (Ed.), *Education in the 80's: Multiethnic education.* Washington, DC: National Educational Association.

Gay, G., & Abrahams, R. D. (1973). Does the pot melt, boil, or brew? Black children and white assessment procedures. *Journal of School Psychology, 11,* 330-340.

Glasman, N. S., & Biniaminov, I. (1981). Input-output analyses of schools. *Review of Educational Research, 51,* 509-539.

Gleason, J. (1973). Code-switching in children's language. In T. E. More (Ed.), *Cognitive development and the acquisition of language.* New York: Academic Press.

Goody, E. (1978). Towards a theory of questions. In E. Goody (Ed.), *Questions and politeness: Strategies in social interaction.* Cambridge: Cambridge University Press.

Green, J. L. (1982). *Research on teaching as a linguistic process: A state of the art.* (NIEP-81-0084), Washington, DC: National Institute of Education.

Green, J. L., & Wallat, C. (1981). Mapping instructional conversations—A sociolinguistic ethnography, In J. L. Green & C. Wallat (Eds.), *Ethnography and language in educational settings.* Norwood, NJ: Ablex.

Heath, S. B. (1982a). Questioning at home and at school. A comparative study. In G. Spindler (Ed.), *Doing ethnography: Educational anthropology in action.* New York: Holt, Rinehart & Winston.

Heath, S. B. (1982b). What no bedtime story means: Narrative skills at home and at school. *Language in Society, 11,* 49-76.

Hunkins, F. P. (1972). *Questioning strategies and techniques.* Boston: Allyn & Bacon.

Hymes, D. (1974). *Foundations in sociolinguistics: An ethnographic approach.* Philadelphia: University of Pennsylvania Press.

Katz, I. (1976). The socialization of academic motivation in minority group children. In D. Levin (Ed.), *Nebraska Symposium on Motivation.* Lincoln: University of Nebraska Press.

Labov, W. (1972). *Language in the inner city.* Philadelphia: University of Pennsylvania Press.

Matluck, J. H. (1978). *Cultural norms and classroom discourse: Communication problems in the multiethnic school setting.* Paper presented at the annual meeting of the American Educational Research Association, Toronto, Canada.

Mehan, H. (1979). *Learning lessons.* Cambridge, MA: Harvard University Press.

Morris, M. (1981). *Saying and meaning in Puerto Rico: Some problems in the ethnography of discourse.* Oxford: Pergamon.

Ogbu, J. U. (1981). School ethnography: A multilevel approach. *Anthropology and Education Quarterly, 12,* 3-29.

Ong, W. (1971). *Rhetoric, romance and technology.* Ithaca, NY: Cornell University Press.

Philips, S. U. (1970). Acquisition of rules for appropriate speech usage. In J. F. Alatis (Ed.), *Bilingualism and language contact: Antropological, linguistic, psychological, and sociological aspects.* (Monograph Series on Languages and Linguistics, No. 23). Washington, DC: Georgetown University Press.

Philips, S. U. (1970). Acquistion of rules for appropriate speech usage. In J. F. Alatis *Language in Society, 5,* 81-95.

Philipsen, G. (1975). Speaking "like a man" in Teamsterville: Culture patterns of role enactment in an urban neighborhood. *Quarterly Journal of Speech, 61,* 13-22.

Rosen, H. (1974). *Language and class: A critical look at the theories of Basil Bernstein.* Bristol, England: Falling Wall Press.

Sacks, H., Schegloff, E., & Jefferson, G. (1974). A simplist systematics for the organization of turn-taking in conversation. *Language, 50,* 696-735.

Searle, J. R. (1969). *Speech acts.* London: Cambridge University Press.

Sinclair, J. M., & Coulthard, R. M. (1975). *Towards an analysis of discourse,* New York: Oxford University Press.

Tannen, D. (1981). Indirectness in discourse: Ethnicity as conversational style. *Discourse Processes, 4,* 221-238.

Weitzman, L. J., & Rizzo, D. (1980). Images of males and females in elementary school textbooks in five subject areas. In E. H. Weiner (Ed.), *Sex-role stereotyping in the schools.* Washington, DC: National Educational Association.

Wells, G. (1981). *Learning as interaction.* Cambridge: Cambridge University Press.

Western, R. (1974). *Development in children's understanding of form-function ambiguity.* Unpublished dissertation, University of Minnesota.

Wilkinson, L. C. (1981). Analysis of teacher-student interaction-expectations communicated by conversational structure. In J. L. Green & C. Wallat (Eds.), *Adult-child conversation.* New York: St. Martin's Press.

Willes, M. (1981). Learning to take part in classroom interaction. In P. French & M. Maclure (Eds.), *Adult-child conversation,* New York: St. Martin's Press.

Williams, F., & Narremore, R. C. (1969). On the functional analysis of social class differences in modes of speech. *Speech Monographs, 36,* 77-102.

10

Interethnic Communication in Children's Own Dance, Play, and Protest

JUDITH LYNNE HANNA ● *University of Maryland*

Children express themselves through visual kinetic images in a school setting. A developmental theory of cognitive and affective expression, a symbolic interaction/semiotic perspective, and a holistic study of the anthropology of dance, together inform an argument about children's use of aesthetic/play as a means to symbolize and to mediate black-white interactions. Observations during a year-long study of an urban desegregated elementary school suggest that children's spontaneous individual and group dance movements in the classroom and hall and organized dances on the playground may be vehicles of we/they marking, defensive structuring, sympathetic magic, and playing with antistructure or aspirations in a stratified society. Dance/play appears as "serious business" in public schools, stages where many tensions and conflicts in America are acted out, when children dramatize concepts and patterns of and for social life. Implications for theory, research method, teaching, and learning are discussed.

The purpose of this chapter is to call attention to a neglected but important phenomenon: children's symbolic expression through visual kinetic imagery in a school setting. A developmental theory of cognitive and affective expression, a symbolic interaction/semiotic perspective, and an anthropological theory of dance as nonverbal communication inform the discussion. The ramifications of the dance nonverbal mode are significant to communication and cognition theory and method in general and to understanding interethnic communication in schools in particular.

AUTHOR'S NOTE: *The support of the Pacesetter study from the Richardson Independent School District, Pacesetter School, and National Endowment for the Humanities Fellowship at American Enterprise Institute for Public Policy Research is gratefully acknowledged. This article is a revision and synthesis of papers presented earlier at the conference of the American Anthropological Association (1979), the Eighteenth Interamerican Congress of Psychology, Dominican Republic (1981), the International*

THEORETICAL BACKGROUND

Several psychologists have provided relevant theoretical and empirical work on children's creative symbolization. In 1908 Freud wrote, "Every child at play behaves like the creative writer, in that he creates a world of his own, or rather, rearranges the things of his world in a way that pleases him"(1958, p. 45). As a form of play, children's spontaneous dance is a vehicle for intuition and fantasy. Jean Piaget (in Levy, 1978) believed that play acts are characterized by the primacy of assimilation over accommodation. Accommodation refers to a child modifying his or her behavior to the outside world, for example, following the teacher's instructions. Assimilation means the child incorporates elements of the outside world into his or her own personal view of reality and standards. Play, according to Jerome Bruner and his colleagues, is problem solving (1976, p. 244 and passim). Rudolf Arnheim calls the creativity found in children's dance "a kind of reasoning . . . either intellectual or perceptual" (1972, p. 287).

Gardner (1973) translates two major views of human development, the cognitive approach of Piaget and the affective view of Erikson (who extended the work of Freud), into a model for the emergence of artistry. With Wolf (Wolf & Gardner, 1980), he posits four major approximate phases, as well as their intervening pivotal crises, that characterize the child's development toward symbolic expression in the arts. Because this model is embedded in western culture, cross-cultural research may require some modification(s). The child is first a direct communicator; then gains an understanding of symbols; gradually becomes proficient, self-conscious, and peer-oriented in the use of symbols; and eventually is able to think hypothetically and confront choices.

Pertinent to understanding children's symbolic capability through dance/play is the third phase: 5- to 11-year-olds who can give aesthetic form to thoughts and feelings. These youngsters have passed through infancy when children experience themselves as movers and social actors; their exchanges with adults anticipate ways in which they will relate to others through dance. By the time children have reached the

Conference on Dance and the Child (1982), and the Association for the Anthropological Study of Play/Society for Applied Anthropology, Washington, D.C. (1985). The comments made by Larry Warren, Jill Sweet, JoAnn Magdoff, Charles Keil, Thomas Kochman, Carol Robertson, Remi Clignet, Phyllis May, William John Hanna, Harry Wolcott, and reviewers for the International and Intercultural Communication Annual *on earlier drafts are appreciated.*

third phase, they have playfully used symbols and mastered the body to acquire a highly articulate gestural, postural, and motor vocabulary. Now highly individual symbols give way to socially validated signifiers in accordance with peer group values, and the youngsters become craftspersons. "The product . . . must 'speak for itself' even to strangers. It must . . . capture not the individual child's response but something of the basic structure of object or event, the concrete palpable characteristics of experience" (Wolf & Gardner, 1980, p. 67).

Can dance carry such messages? It is possible because this expressive form is languagelike, complete with semantics, syntax, pragmatics, competence, performance, and devices and spheres of encoding and decoding meaning. I have spelled out this capability elsewhere (Hanna, 1979a, 1979b). However, it is appropriate here to point out that dance, for the most part, is more like poetry than prose. Tenets of the theory of dance as symbolic action will be discussed in relation to illustrative empirical cases.

METHOD AND EXPLANATION

This article is based on material from a year-long ethnographic study of a school located in a black neighborhood in the Richardson Independent School District in Dallas, Texas. The school had a court-mandated 50-50 black-white ratio in each classroom. Data for the entire study include participant-observations; video, film, and tape recordings; historical records; and open-ended interviews with a probability sample of 120 students stratified on the basis of sex, race,[1] and grade. (Grades 2, 4, and 6 were chosen to reflect different levels of cognitive and social development.)

Within the theoretical perspectives of symbolic interaction and semiotics, the present exploratory study focuses on the creation, meaning, structure, and utilization of symbolic behavior in social relations. Social interaction is a dynamic that is affected by prior experiences and values, information and assessment of a situation (constraints and dictates), anticipated responses to actions, and accidents. Analysis follows Victor Turner's (1969) approach of considering what people say, what they do, and how both verbalizations and actions fit into the cultural and social context.

Of course, it is possible to overanalyze behavior or attribute meaning that is not present. This is especially the case in dealing with nonverbal communication that is often difficult for actors, and certainly children, to explain verbally. In fact, the field of nonverbal communication gained impetus from the mental health professions. Patients/clients verbally said one thing or nothing while their bodies "said" the opposite (see Davis & Skupien, 1982). The famous modern dancer Isadora Duncan put it this way, "If I could *tell* you what I mean, there would be no point in dancing." However, an individual can be trained to read and describe body behavior in the same way that a student learns to analyze visual art or music.

Although all children were observed, only black children were seen spontaneously dancing in the school. Black psychologists Alfred Pasteur and Ivory Toldson (1982) point out, "Blacks seem to perceive the environment and respond to it with . . . movement (dance and athletics) . . . more frequently than do Westerners, who are more dependent on . . . words and numbers in their search for consonance with the world" (p. 52). Katrina Hazzard-Gordon (1983a, 1983b),on the basis of field work and secondary sources, reports that among working class blacks, dance is an aspect of black personal identity, cultural integrity, and boundary marking to distinguish one's ingroup from the outgroup. "Dance becomes a litmus test. . . . Proper Afro-American dance demands the demonstration of certain postures and gestures held in esteem in black culture. . . . Inability to dance indicates that one's cultural base is not black, that one has taken on another cultural identity." Afro-Americans feel a "deep-seated bitterness" when they directly witness the violation of attributes they recognize as culturally theirs. Relevant to my observations is this statement: "Dance is the arena in which black confronts white and wins. It is the province over which black rule has prevailed relatively unchallenged. When whites attempt to dance black, they pose what is perceived in the black mind as a challenge to that rule" (1983a, p.24).

Within the tradition of anthropology, the school is considered not as an isolated entity but as an institution that meshes with and serves other social organizations. Specializing in transforming some immigrant groups for mainstream society's assimilation, schools generally affirm the middle and upper classes' "destiny" to manage and lead, and channel children from low income groups into menial jobs. Schools attempt to induce students willingly to accept adult role responsibilities, including those in the world of work. Although children are to some extent creatures of their schooling, it is important to point out that each is also a creatively adapting individual with his or her own mind, sensory apparatus, and historical time of growing up.

In light of the myriad forms of communication in a recently desegregated urban school, some black children's dance movements and complete dances (such as those described by Brady, 1975; Eckhardt, 1975; Jones & Hawes, 1972; White & Michels, 1983) appears to reflect problems of ethnic relations and urban education. Dances seem (1) to symbolize and mediate current desegregation dynamics as an assertion of identity (a vehicle of we/they marking and defensive structuring) and (2) to play with a reversal of social ranking (much like sympathetic magic in enacting, in one realm, wished-for results in another). Dance events, themes, and participants comment on ethnic relations as do many of the other arts of blacks (see Keil, 1966; Levine, 1977). Indeed, exclusively black dance events, themes, and performers are by their very existence a reflection of and a comment on a divided society. For generations blacks were excluded from studying and professionally performing some theater dance forms. Black American modern dance choreographers such as Talley Beatty, Alvin Ailey, George Faison, Eleo Pomare, and Donald McKayle have portrayed themes of white oppression. As will be illustrated, the dances of blacks, like the dances of other ethnic groups in heterogeneous urban areas, may be at once educational, a symbol of ethnic identity, a form of group assertion, and a means to influence social relations.

With the above sketch of the guiding theories and the methodological approach, the next section presents (from field notes and audiovisual records) three examples that most dramatically characterize a larger universe of dance and movement observed in Pacesetter School. The detailed ethnographic approach, broader context of social relations, and variety of forms of communication in the school are reported elsewhere.[3] The discussion draws upon qualitative data: observations of youngsters' actions, their informal comments, the interviews, and the relationship of the exegetic and behavioral to the broader cultural and social context.

THREE EXAMPLES

Illustration 1

One day, during an unusual 40-minute second-grade classroom period before the teacher had established control, several black children yelled out remarks and walked about the room. They played with furniture pretending it was gymnastic, musical, or military equipment, and pushed, pulled, or hit others. A black boy tried to cut a white girl's blond hair. A black girl kept talking loudly. In response to the white teacher's question, "Would you like to go out?" the youngster got up from her chair and walked into the aisle, where she stood, feet apart and knees bent. She brought her knees together and apart four times while crossing her hands together and apart in unison with the knees in a Charleston step. Then she scurried back to her assigned seat and sat down. Moments later she skipped to the door, opened it, picked up a book lying outside, and ran back to her place. Then she stood upon the chair seat and performed what in ballet is called an arabesque. Standing on the ball of one foot, she lifted the other leg backward as high as she could, one arm held diagonally up and forward, the other diagonally down. From this position she laughingly lost her balance and fell to the floor. The teacher picked her up and carried her out of the classroom. During the girl's performance, her peers gave her their undivided attention.

Illustration 2

At least once a week I saw one to six black children at a time spontaneously dance a few steps in short sequences in a variety of situations both inside and outside the classrooms in ways that did not disrupt formal teaching and learning. For example, as a second-grade class was being dismissed, one black boy exited performing a Charleston step three times. This was the same step the black girl performed in the first illustration. After the first boy exited, a second black boy followed performing the same movement phrase. The sequence occurred repeatedly until six black boys had left the classroom. In a fourth-grade music class, several black boys "bebopped" to the admiring looks of their peers. One black boy walked with exaggerated hip shifts, the upper and lower torso moving in opposition; another boy walked about while shimmying his shoulder blades. A third sat snapping his fingers and then got up and performed a step-kick walking dance sequence. A fourth boy shook his arms and rippled his torso. As a sixth-grade class was going through the halls to the cafeteria, several black boys and girls performed a variety of dance movement phrases.

Illustration 3

During recess outdoors on a warm sunny day, groups of black girls spontaneously organized dance cheers, ring-plays, and line-plays that combine dance and song. Using the spatial form of children's dances probably of British origin and learned from white Americans, black children meshed the African style of loose, flexible torso, extending and flexing knees, with an easy breathing quality, shuffling steps, and pelvic swings and thrusts. Thus, they created syncretistic dances of the sort that Jones and Hawes describe as ring and line plays (1972, pp. 67-68). A leader either sang a phrase that the group answered or the leader led the performers. Movements accompanied and accented the song text or illustrated it. Hand clapping or other body percussion punctuated the performance to create a syncopated rhythm within the song and dance. In one instance, when a white girl wished to join the black girls in one of the dances, a black girl stepped back, put her hands on her hips, and looked the white girl up and down about the hips and feet. Then with a quizzical look and scowl, she said loudly for all to hear: "Show me you can dance!" Everyone watched as the white girl withdrew to the side-lines.

Later, a different white girl joined the "Check Me" ring play in which the name of each participant in the circle was singled out in turn, going to the right. One girl's name was called by the girl standing to her immediate left; she identified herself, sang a refrain, and then called on the next girl to her right.

Check <clap>, check <clap>, check <clap>
My name is Tina,
I am a Pisces.
I want you to <clap>
check, check, check,
to check out Bridgette.
Check <clap>, check <clap>, check.
My name is Bridgette. . . .

When it was the white girl's turn to be called, the black girl just passed her by and called the next black girl. Rejected, the white girl called out, "I can do it, too!" No one paid attention.

THE SCHOOL CONTEXT

The illustrations suggest how a child can play to peers, disrupt the classroom, and defy school decorum through dance, how children dance for what may be self-expression or relaxation, and how children may pridefully express ethnic cohesion. The situational context should be briefly described here in order to assess the possible meanings of the dancing. Schools tend, in part, to reflect and reinforce the values and experiences of the communities that send students to them, in keeping with the American tradition of local community involvement in public education. We turn to history to help explain creative behavior that can exist for its own pleasure or as a defensive reaction.

Prior to desegregation, blacks in Dallas were forced to live in segregated places and were often permitted some self-governance. When whites in Dallas realized the value of black areas for roads, airports, and white residences, or when blacks became residentially too proximate, whites pushed the blacks out. Verbal intimidation, water well destruction, home bombing, and rezoning laws encouraged black relocation.

Pacesetter School is located in a black community created in the 1950s as a consequence of white terrorism and fire bombing of black homes purchased or being built in formerly all-white residential areas. At the time there was a housing shortage. The efforts of a biracial group of civic leaders led to a segregated housing project for blacks located within city limits so that residents could receive government regulatory services. Later the blacks had their own small shopping center, churches, and school.

Desegregation took away the blacks' control of the school. A five-year U.S. Justice Department civil rights effort culminated in a court case against Richardson Independent School District. The presiding judge accepted a plan for whites to be bused voluntarily to the community school centrally located in the school district. No student was to have more than a thirty-minute bus ride. Because the black community was originally composed of middle-class home-owners, school leaders assumed that the values of blacks and whites would be similar. The plan was to attract (thus the use of the label *magnet school*) whites from their own neighborhood schools to one with a 50-50 black-white ratio through the compelling factor of educational excellence: master teachers, low student-teacher ratios; special computer, art, music, and physical education facilities and programs; and individualized instruction.

Although the black community was originally middle class, it had become primarily lower class. There was a disparity between the black and white student family incomes, education, and occupations (Estes & Skipper, 1976). Whites' income and educational level were above the national average; blacks were below.

Black-white proximity in the past led to harassment of blacks; as a result, the black community was not unanimously in favor of having a desegregated magnet school. Feeling mistrust and anxiety, some blacks feared mistreatment and embarrassment yet again. They were wary of the whites who "took over their school." Although black children born during an era of "black power" assertiveness in the late 1960s and 1970s may not have been discriminated against in face-to-face situations, members of their families were. According to black teacher aides who lived in the community, some parents told their children not to let whites push them around. And the nationwide telecasting of *Roots* during the 1977-1978 school year further heightened young children's awareness of discrimination of blacks by whites and made the youngsters sensitive to anything that could possibly be interpreted as racism.

The black community was unhappy to lose most of the black teachers who had been at the school before desegregation. There were black and white co-principals and counselors; however, there were only two black teachers out of a total of 40 and one black assistant teacher out of 20. Some black children felt that the white volunteers, who tended to come from civil-rights-oriented families and to invite interracial friendships, were invading black turf. Because the territory occupied by blacks was historically small and precarious, it has been especially treasured (see Baldassare, 1978, p. 44; Isaacs, 1975, p. 51, on group attachment to place). Thus the history of the segregated community and its school, and children's use of space, including their cutting shapes in space through dance, become especially endowed with meaning.

Desegregation at Pacesetter brought together black and white, working and underclass (mostly black) and middle-class (mostly white) youngsters, and also neighborhood networks and individual volunteers who were strangers to each other and the black children. The majority of blacks had been together since preschool. Like friendship networks elsewhere, they did not readily accept strangers, even if they were black. For example, a sixth-grade black girl who moved into the Pacesetter neighborhood said,

Sometimes they wont' talk or play with you. When I first came here, it happened to me. Then after the second year was over it . . . was easier to get along because we had known each other for about a year then. Well, I am fully black, but it just seemed like I was from somewhere else that they treated me like that: like from outer space.

There was little interracial mixing evident when black children could choose seats or partners for an activity.

One assumption in most desegregation policies across the nation was that low-income blacks would find a model of middle-class white academic achievement and follow this example. A related assumption was that low-income children wished to emulate the model of academic success (see Wolf, 1981). Nationwide, however, the majority of low-income black children are two achievement grade levels behind middle-class whites and blacks (Wax, 1980). Many low-income youngsters neither value the pursuit of academic excellence nor do what is necessary to earn high marks. Indeed, at Pacesetter, some children devalued and belittled the ethics and activities of formal schooling. Not caring about academic work was a way they denied the school authorities power to confer negative evaluations through report cards that affected their self-image.

A sixth-grade boy expressed a commonly held view of academic academically but attempted to disrupt their effort. William Grier and Price Cobbs point out that "intellectual achievement is regarded as elevating oneself to a higher plane and removing oneself from the black brotherhood" (1968, p. 144). This attitude appears to be a class-related pattern. Richard Sennett and Jonathan Cobb (1973) describe the same kind of feeling toward academic success held by working-class white ethnics in Boston. Paul Willis (1977) reports similar attitudes among working-class whites in England. Due to limited employment opportunities for blacks, education did not have the same pay-off for them as it did for whites. Consequently, some blacks considered schooling worth little. Today there are black youngsters who do not way to fill the inferior roles in the world of work that white society historically slotted for them.

DEFENSIVE STRUCTURING

In spite of the low esteem some black children have for academic success, they are nonetheless sensitive to public revelation, such as in oral recitation, of their inadequate school work. This leads some of them to face-saving behavior, or what Bernard Seigel (1970) described as defensive structuring that occurs among groups under stress and with limited resources. They seek arenas in which they can dominate and gain recognition. They attempt to establish a prideful group identity when they perceive external threats to that identity. This process involves the subordination of the individual to the group as it cooperatively masters challenges.

Expressive symbolic behavior, such as dance or athletics, are acceptable arenas for mastery. This behavior reinforces an individual's sense of being the kind of person the significant others—his or her peers—esteem. Through dance themes, participation criteria, and places of performance in a white-controlled school, youngsters identify themselves as distinct from the "shuffling black" stereotypes of earlier historical periods and the whites of today. They declare a wished-for privileged status and, in a sense, they attain it.

What were the participants' views of black children's spontaneous dancing? Children and adults generally recognized black children's superior performance in certain realms, such as those involving the body. During Black History Week the school celebrated black athletes and entertainers. When dancing disrupted the classroom, youngsters who usually interrupted the teacher's control were delighted, middle-class youngsters who admired the audacity of a peer were fascinated, and academically oriented children feared that the whole class would be punished for the misbehavior of a few. When dancing was not disruptive, children smilingly acknowledged a peer's skill or ignored a peer's unexceptional movement.

On one hand some white girls and boys waited to be allowed to join in the dances on the playground. When on an occasion a teacher suggested to the black girls that they invite the volunteers to join them, each black girl ran to bring a white girl into the circle to try to follow along. Not all volunteers, however, appreciated the dancing. When asked what was going on, a white boy said, "They always do that crap!"

Teachers did not object to the dancing if it allowed classroom activities to proceed.[4] They expected dancing from black children. "They're more physical," reported the white principal. Over the course of a year, teachers—and even children—echoed this refrain in regard to pushing, hitting, and dancing. But if a white child tried to imitate a black peer, in a way that did not disrupt the lesson, the teacher would tell the youngster to be still. Teachers admonished white and middle-class black children for expressive physical activity in the classroom, halls, or auditorium.

IMPORTANCE OF THE BODY AND DANCE

Although white students at Pacesetter were generally more successful in the school's formal academic performance activities, many blacks asserted themselves in alternate intellectual and physical performance arenas. Dance is one such arena for creative and reactive behavior. What are some of the bases of dance as a form for creativity, compensation, or defensive structuring?

The primordial and most vital marker of identity consists of the ready-made set of endowments that each individual shares at birth with members of the group: the body itself "is at once the most intimate and inward and the most obvious and outward aspect of how we see ourselves, how we see others, and how others see us" (Isaacs, 1975, p. 47). The body in motion arrests even greater attention, for it implies a change in environmental conditions that may require reaction for one's safety. Easily perceptible, dancing attracts notice.

If one has few material possessions and little power in the adult world, as is the case with oppressed minorities and with children, the body and its use are likely to become particularly important. The significance of the Afro-American "body in motion" has roots in Africa, the American slave auction block, and antebellum labor markets (see Levine, 1977; Mergen, 1981; Rawick, 1972; Wiggins, 1980; Yoffie, 1947). Many African societies from which Afro-Americans originally came view the body in motion, especially in dancing, as predicting an individual's personality, work capability, creativity, and innovation (Hanna, 1979b). On the slave auction block a muscular, healthy-looking body reflected the individual's capability for strenuous, physical work. Since the slavery era most jobs open to blacks required manual labor. When sports opened up to them beginning in the 1940s, they achieved socioeconomic success through athletics. Performing arts became another avenue of social mobility.

Because children generally learn that "the spoken word can be held against . . . [them] as self-incriminating evidence" (Long, Morse, & Newman, 1976), they often use body language to express what is considered inappropriate. As is the case with adult knowledge, children's knowledge, not always explicit, is based on unspoken assumptions shared among friendship and reference groups.

The dance form of body language appears to be a form of communication that protects children's and minority groups' thoughts and actions from the negative sanctions of the teacher or other school authority (see Rich, 1974, p. 148). In many Afro-American communicative acts, the sender has control of the situation at the receiver's expense. Purposefully ambiguous, the sender of the message reserves the prerogative to insist on a harmless interpretation rather than a provocative one (Mitchell-Kernan, 1972, p. 169).

Dance and song often encode messages from such patterns of social relations as hierarchy, inclusion-exclusion, and exchanges across social boundaries (Hanna, 1979d). Dance may also function as swearing—as a form of release (Montagu, 1967). The nonverbal mode, according to many researchers, is more powerful than the verbal for expressing such fundamental feelings and contingencies in social relationships as liking, disliking, superiority, timidity, fear, and so on.

ANTISTRUCTURE AND PROTOSTRUCTURE

Black children's spontaneous dancing at Pacesetter reverses usual society roles. Anthropologists have described regularly recurring, temporary power reversals as "rituals of rebellion" (Gluckman, 1954). Brian Sutton-Smith (1976) and Morris Peckham (1975), among others, have viewed play and art activities as social antistructure set off in a compensatory or cathartic relationship to the rest of the culture. Through the dance medium, blacks at Pacesetter become dramatically dominant in a white-dominated society. Bodily energy and thought are liberated as performers play with alternative social dominance patterns.

The school administration was aware of a few black students' use of body language to defy teachers. Several weeks before I approached one of the co-principals about conducting a study of communication patterns, she had been working with a group of black girls about what teachers called their "insolent" body behavior toward white teachers. A girl would, for example, turn one shoulder away from the teacher, thrust her chin toward the adult, or stand with hands on hips, one extended away from the teacher, the leg also extended, while the other leg was forward and bent.

In the first illustration, the black girl's dance movements can be construed as dramatically defying the white teacher by acting inappropriately during a formal lesson. The child broke rules of both the white-dominated school[5] (which she later readily described) and of traditional ballet style. She mocked the teacher by leaving her assigned seat and walking into the aisle to perform a Charleston movement—part of the repertoire of several black African groups[6] and part of her Afro-American ethnic identity. Then, again, out of the appropriate time and place, she performed an arabesque movement—part of the white ethnic ballet tradition. To add a further incongruity, the black girl performed a dance movement—usually on a stage floor—on the seat of a classroom chair. Feet were placed where the buttocks are supposed to be. Breaking these rules, the child sassed the teacher in a display of insubordination. Her deliberately clumsy fall, performing a movement that traditionally requires the dancer to assume a basic pose and then change the body support on one leg with elegant and graceful body control, was more than mere clownlike action.

This performance suggested once again the historical pattern of blacks parodying white behavior (Hansen, 1967; Levine, 1977); it appeared as a metaphor for the teacher's inability to control her classroom generally and the black children in particular. Note that radio and television coverage of Arthur Mitchell in Dallas made common knowledge the history of ballet as a European tradition and formerly studied, performed, and viewed by whites. News commentators repeatedly said that until Mitchell founded the Dance Theatre of Harlem, there were few black ballet dancers. Mitchell came to Dallas periodically to teach, and Pacesetter school offered extracurricular ballet classes. In this way blacks learned the ballet rules well enough not only to execute them but to break them (see Finnan, 1982).

The incident in the first case also appears similar to sympathetic magic in the sense of an individual symbolically enacting, through body motion, wished-for behavior in another realm. The girl collapsed her arabesque pose in lieu of concluding it with the traditional ballet aplomb. Thus she seemed to symbolize or, with the compelling power of metaphor, to effect the white teacher's complete downfall from authority. Symbolic actions are often meant to bring about what they express. Many children disliked the teacher for yelling and fussing at them too much. Children complained as they exited the classroom and in response to these interview questions: "What is your idea of a nice teacher?" "What is your idea of a mean teacher?" "If a child misbehaves, what do you think a teacher should do?" The principal began to work with the teacher to help her find better ways to establish control of her classroom.

In the second illustration, what specifically triggered the children's dance movements in the classrooms and halls was uncertain. The youngsters appeared to enjoy dancing to gain their peer's admiration. For some children who find structured classroom activities incompatible with their capabilities or moods, dancing may be a release of pent-up energy after adhering to a formal academic regime. In black folklore, the arts have a long history of providing solace and support. About black people black dancer Jones said, "We'd dance awhile to rest ourselves" (1972, p. 124).

Dancing may be a way for children to say something about themselves to themselves and to others—students and teacher—as part of defensive structuring. For white children, dancing, rarely part of their spontaneous play, is a more segmented aspect of life with special times, places, and clothes; it is not, as Jones and Hawes say, "all mixed in with life" (1972, p. 124).

Besides being a commentary against the way society and school are structured or serving as a means of catharsis, dance can be viewed as the source of new cultural and social patterns. In the third illustration, black pride, identity, boundaries, and neighborhood loyalty seemed to coalesce in the dances most black Pacesetter girls performed to assert camaraderie, provide fun, and work through problems in a world they do not control. The dancers could have been what Claire Farrer (1981) calls "contesting," discovering the paradigm of rules in existence and hence gaining the advantage by redefining the paradigm and its rules. By recognizing only blacks, the participants in this case may have redefined the rule of turn-taking according to one's place in the circle. Alternatively, it could be that the fixed rules included only blacks as legitimate participants.

The dances distinguish the insider neighborhood children from the outsider volunteers who belong to a variety of other elementary school neighborhood communities. Occasionally black boys joined in the dances. However, the few black newcomers who were not yet part of the school neighborhood group were excluded as were the white girls who tried to participate in the dances. Yet most black children clearly identified with specific dance and music. During free time in a classroom, there was an argument over which record would be played. A black child insisted on a black selection, declaring, "You in soul country now!"

Dance themes, events, and participation criteria reflect general attitudes that have been held among blacks for generations (see Jones &

Hawes, 1972), as well as newer attitudes. Although children learned some dances from their mothers and older folks, they also made up songs and dances to express their own realities of the era of "black power" and desegregation (see Spindler & Spindler, 1982, on learning theory). A fourth-grade girl said she made up the words to the song called "Walking over people, I don't care, shampoo, shampoo." Girls formed a line, arms about each other's waists, and moved briskly about the play area singing and dancing. "Sock It" and "Power" are other favorites called "cheers." These were blends of ring and line dances with high school, college, and professional football cheer leader dance routines.

The dances reflect one individual or group versus another in a game and/or real life. Ambiguous meaning creates the excitement. The black girls' performances appear to be ingroup bonding in an arena in which they can excel as a response to their awareness of past white oppression and exclusion of black people. Their dancing suggests a future of racial separation possibly carried on as in the past—or even a reversal of power relations, blacks superior to whites. The white audience is put on its mettle. Perhaps the black girls' dances are similar to the slave animal trickster tales in which the weaker animal bests the stronger through its wits. The tales afforded their creators psychic relief, an arena of mastery, and a vision of a possible future.

Children often do not feel comfortable participating in arenas where they sense that they are not welcome, they are unlikely to perform well, or the competition is unfairly matched. Thus they stake out their own turf as ethnic minorities have always done.[7] One consequence of the black dances is that the white children have the "outsider" status in informal children-delineated performance arenas at Pacesetter that blacks have had in broader arenas of life. By focusing on power through high-energy dance movements and song texts, the girls suggest role reversal in the wider society. What the national context offers in prestige for whites, the local arena offers in recognition and power for blacks. In this desegregated setting the children's expressed power takes center stage.

IMPLICATIONS

To summarize, we have been considering children's symbolic expression through visual kinetic images. A discussion of cognitive developmental theory, dance as nonverbal communication, and the school's historical setting and contemporary situation laid the groundwork for understanding the three illustrations of children's spontaneous dance. This cognitive and affective mode seems to capture the dynamics of black versus white, along with low income versus middle income, insider versus outsider, and child versus adult. In the first illustration, a child disrupted the classroom with antischool attention-getting behavior. Nancy Henley points out that "the power of disruption is the ultimate power of the powerless" (1977, p. 83). A black girl challenged a white adult authority figure through palpably asserting her defiance and black childhood identity by dancing a Charleston step. Then, she symbolically deflated the elevated superordinate by demeaning and mocking a ballet dance movement. The young girl's dance movements broke the rules for classroom decorum, child-adult and student-teacher relations, and appropriate time, place, structure, and style for Afro-American dance and ballet performance. In the second illustration, black children spontaneously performing short dance movement sequences both inside and outside the classrooms seemed to be a form of release and identity marker. In the third illustration, black girls asserted black power, ingroup exclusivity and superiority, and the possibility of reversed black/white power relations.

Most Pacesetter teachers dismissed spontaneous dance movements in the classroom and halls and organized plays and cheers on the playground as frivolous, validating their perception that blacks are more physical than whites. Dance/play is, however, "serious business" in dramatizing concepts and patterns of and for social life. Consequently, children's spontaneous activities in the school setting warrant more consideration.

Public schools are stages where many tensions and conflicts in American society are acted out: slavery, segregation, white harassment of blacks, a legacy of black-white suspicion, the black power movement of the 1960s and 1970s, and desegregation. It seems reasonable to conclude that the black children's dance movements, contexts, and participation criteria symbolize and mediate existing and possible social relationships made visibly vital with prophetic yearnings. The children's social world embodies the image of possible adult life. Dancing at Pacesetter is concerned with respect and mutual recognition that positions of relative power and influence may be reversed or at least moderated. At Pacesetter this behavior did not mirror the concepts necessary to legitimize a social system of structured inequality in which they would be unequal to whites. Dancing is thus a balanced play of accommodative/assimilative responses in the Piagetian sense, a bending of self to reality and a bending of reality to self (see Levy, 1978, pp. 110-116)—an adaptive coping pattern for human dignity, respect, and opportunity.[8] The dance/play process is more important than the product, providing a temporary moratorium on frustration and being self-initiated.

What are the theoretical and methodological implications of this exploratory study? Although there have been systematic cognitive development studies of symbolic encoding/decoding using several of the arts, there has been none for dance. Revelation of nonverbal expressive behavior at Pacesetter points to the need for cognitive theories to extend their purview and empirical work to be undertaken. We know little about children's developmental and cultural patterns in nonverbal communication or their interpretations of it.

Children's nonverbal communication could be filmed or videorecorded to develop a catalog or repertoire of their behavior. Selected segments with distinct social interactions could be transferred to a film or videotape to elicit interpretations of the interactions using a systematically stratified sample. Who communicates what to whom, where, when, why, how, and with what meaning and effect? Initiators, followers, active and passive respondents, territorial markers, turn-taking signals, and cues which gain and establish an activity could be noted. Communicators, communicatees, and samples of students and adults could be asked open-ended questions about their understanding of dance activity from interactions presented on videotape. For example, what is happening? How do you know? What are the clues? Where is it appropriate? Is it friendly or angry? Good or bad?

It is useful to identify meanings that are not shared in a heterogeneous setting. Misinterpreted or out-of-conscious awareness messages may reduce the effectiveness of individuals of one culture who interact with another and hinder positive interethnic relations among students, as well as between them and teachers and other community members. Understanding and coping with face-to-face interactions is central to human social conduct. Participants in the communication process mutually affect each other. Gestural forms often precede interethnic encounters and thus become the first warning received of the subsequent course of action.

What are the practical implications of awareness of children's communication through dance/play? Educators talk about taking children from where they are to where the school wants them to go. There is substantial evidence in support of the usefulness of bilingual education for non-English-speaking youngsters (McLaughlin, 1982). There is also a case to be made for bimodal education, that is, using a form of communication familiar to children to teach them other modes of communication. The argument for teaching foreign languages can be made for introducing movement expression to children whose movement expression potential was stifled. Examples of how this can be done are readily available (Blatt & Cunningham, 1981).

Although nationwide low income black children are two years behind grade level in measure of academic achievement, many of these youngsters appear to display above average development in kinetic symbolic behavior. Dance draws upon cognitive ability not widely recognized. We have seen how children creatively use the body in time and space and with energy to kinetically conceptualize attitudes, feelings, and ideas. Similar evidence was presented at the international conference on Dance and the Child (1982). A principal presented examples of German children's dances—which no teacher had shown them—that visualized the youngsters' own thoughts and values (Segler, 1982). A Flemish priest described his work in Cali, Colombia, with a group that tries to educate poor youth through dancing (De Pauw, 1982).

Bicultural education has only begun to use dance as a resource. Reddy Singha (1982), an East Indian who lives in Canada, reports how she became aware of the difficulties of being both a cultural and a physical minority (she has a deaf daughter). Drawing upon her training as a classical Indian dancer and geographer, she created the Cultural Clues Approach to Learning to help immigrants and the hearing-impaired. The program, which uses folk dances and related activities, has led to change in ethnic attitudes among majority youngsters as Ijaz (1980) demonstrated.

Teachers could diagnostically observe children's dance to discover their concerns, and they may learn ways to harness children's enjoyment of movement to academic learning. Instructors might permit children to dance out their essays in social studies, English, and science. Schools tend to use dance games only in the early grades. Maybe this is a mistake.

As children progress through the different phases of development, they acquire an increasingly sophisticated capability for symbolic expression. Dance is a potential resource for education to utilize a form of knowing, to promote multiethnic understanding, and to enrich curriculum and teaching methods. We have explored some instances of dance as play and protest and of the relation of dance to society. Certainly further theoretical and empirical work is warranted.

NOTES

1. The word *race* is used in its political sense. The terms *culture* or *class* are more accurate.

2. Youngsters' dancing could have been dismissed as "fooling around" except for the fact that, since 1963, this researcher has been studying relations between dance and society, especially in Africa (Hanna, 1979b, 1980, 1983a, 1986).

3. Research findings appear in Hanna, 1979c (recorded dance songs), 1982, 1984, and 1987.

4. Gilmore found dance behavior in a Philadelphia all-black, low-income school that was similar to the dancing at Pacesetter. Children danced at recess and continued doing steps when they returned to the classroom. However, at the school Gilmore studied, the black administration banned the dances as lewd and disrespectful (1983). In an article on teen-age pregnancy and motherhood, Dash (1986) reported on Washington, D.C. children's cheers that reflect a positive attitude toward sexual promiscuity that their mothers disliked. Groups of girls from housing projects or neighboring buildings competed at community events. "They also held secret competitions attended only by other children and teenagers, where some cheerleaders wore short skirts and no underpants while doing flips and chanting sexually suggestive cheers that went like this: I did it once/I did it twice/I took my time/I did it right."

5. Sieber found that when teacher surveillance stops, elementary school children engage in all manner of normally forbidden activities, including dancing, that violate the norms of "acting right" (1980, p. 58).

6. See Hanna (1979b). Alternatively, as Charles Keil has suggested (personal communication), the Charleston could be a putdown of Roaring Twenties whites if the girl had watched Donald O'Connor or Debbie Reynolds on television.

7. Black boys defined football fields and restrooms at Pacesetter School as their turf. Few whites played football because many of the blacks fought over the rules and did not throw the ball to them.

8. See Hanna (1979b) for a discussion of psychobiological bases of dance.

REFERENCES

Arnheim, R. (1972). *On inspiration: Toward a psychology of art.* Berkeley: University of California Press.

Baldassare, M. (1978). Human spatial behavior. *Annual Review of Sociology, 4,* 29-56.

Blatt, G., & Cunningham, J. (1981). *It's your move: Expressive movement activities for the language arts class.* New York: Teachers College Press.

Brady, M. K. (1975). This little lady's gonna boogaloo: Elements of socialization in the play of black girls. In *Black girls at play: Folkloric perspectives on child development* (pp. 1-56). Austin, TX: Early Elementary Program, Southwest Educational Development Laboratory.

Bruner, J. S., Alison, J., & Sylva, K. (Eds.). (1976). *Play—its role in development and evolution.* New York: Basic Books.

Dash, L. (1986). Motherhood the hard way. *Washington Post,* pp. 1, 8-9.

Davis, M., & Skupien, J. (1982). *Body movement and nonverbal communication: An annotated bibliography, 1971-1980.* Bloomington: Indiana University Press.

De Pauw, C. (1982). Dance groups of the Cruzada de la Amistad. *Papers II, International Conference on Children and Youth Dancing* (pp. 90-95). Stockholm: Swedish Division of DACI, Dansmuseet.

Eckhardt, R. (1975). From handclap to line play. In *Black girls at play: Folkloric perspectives on child development* (pp. 57-101). Austin, TX: Early Elementary Program, Southwest Educational Development Laboratory.

Estes, R., & Skipper, K. (1976). *Comprehensive evaluation of the Pacesetter program.* Richardson, TX: Richardson Independent School District contracted report.

Farrer, C. R. (1981). Contesting. In A. T. Cheska (Ed.), *Play as context* (1979 Proceedings of the Association for the Anthropological Study of Play, pp. 195-208). West Point, NY: Leisure Press.

Finnan, C. R. (1982). The ethnography of children's spontaneous play. In G. Spindler (Ed.), *Doing the ethnography of schooling* (pp. 356-380). New York: Holt, Rinehart & Winston.

Freud, S. (1958). *On creativity and the unconscious: Papers on psychology, art, literature, love, religion* (selected with introduction and annotation by Benjamin Nelson). New York: Harper & Row.

Gardner, H. (1973). *The arts and human development.* New York: Wiley.

Gilmore, P. (1983). Spelling "Mississippi": Recontextualizing a literacy-related speech event. *Anthropology and Education, 14,* 235-255.

Gluckman, M. (1954). *Rituals of rebellion in South-East Africa.* Manchester: Manchester University Press.

Grier, W. H., & Cobbs, P. M. (1968). *Black rage.* New York: Basic Books.

Hanna, J. L. (1979a). Toward semantic analysis of movement behavior: Concepts and problems. *Semiotica, 25*(1-2), 77-110.

Hanna, J. L. (1979b). *To dance is human: A theory of nonverbal communication.* Austin: University of Texas Press.

Hanna, J. L. (1979c). *American folk dance.* In H. Cohen (Ed.), *American folklore cassette lecture series.* Daland, FL: Everitt Edwards.

Hanna, J. L. (1979d). Movements toward understanding humans through the anthropological study of dance. *Current Anthropology, 20,* 313-339.

Hanna, J. L. (1980). African dance research: Past, present, and future. *Africana Journal, 11*(1), 103-104.

Hanna, J. L. (1982). Public social policy and the children's world: Implications of ethnographic research for desegregated schooling. In G. Spindler (Ed.), *Doing the ethnography of schooling: Educational anthropology in action* (pp. 316-355). New York: Holt, Rinehart & Winston.

Hanna, J. L. (1983a). The mentality and matter of dance. In M. Engle (Ed.), *Art Education* (Art and the mind), *36*(2), 42-46.

Hanna, J. L. (1983b). *The performer-audience connection: Emotion to metaphor in dance and society.* Austin: University of Texas Press.

Hanna, J. L. (1984). Black/white nonverbal differences, dance and dissonance: Implications for desegregation. In A. Wolfgang (Ed.), *Nonverbal behavior: Perspectives, applications, intercultural insights* (pp. 349-385). Toronto, C. J. Hogrefe.

Hanna, J. L. (1986). Dance. In T. A. Sebeok (Ed.), *Dictionary of semiotics*. Berlin: Mouton-deGruyter.

Hanna, J. L. (1987). Disruptive school behavior—in a desegregated magnet school and elsewhere. New York: Holmes & Meier.

Hansen, C. (1967). Jenny's toe: Negro shaking dances in America. *American Quarterly, 19,* 554-563.

Hazzard-Gordon, K. (1983a). Afro-American core culture social dance: An examination of four aspects of meaning. *Dance Research Journal, 15*(2), 21-26.

Hazzard-Gordon, K. (1983b). *Atibas a comin': The rise of social dance formations in Afro-American culture.* Unpublished doctoral dissertation, Cornell University, Ithaca, NY.

Henley, N. (1977). *Body politics, power, sex and nonverbal communication.* Englewood Cliffs, NJ: Prentice-Hall.

Isaacs, H. R. (1975). *Idols of the tribe.* New York: Harper & Row.

Ijaz, A. M. (1980). *Ethnic attitudes of elementary school children toward blacks and East Indians and the effect of a cultural program on these attitudes.* Unpublished doctoral dissertation, University of Toronto, Ontario Institute for Studies in Education.

Jones, B., & Hawes, B. L. (1972). *Step it down: Games, plays and stories from the Afro-American heritage.* New York: Harper & Row.

Keil, C. (1966). *Urban blues.* Chicago: University of Chicago Press.

Levine, L. W. (1977). *Culture and black consciousness: Afro-American folk thought from slavery to freedom.* New York: Oxford University Press.

Levy, J. (1978). *Play behavior.* New York: Wiley.

Long, N. J., Morse, W. C., & Newman, R. G. (1976). *Conflict in the classroom: The education of emotionally disturbed children* (3rd ed.). Belmont, CA: Wadsworth.

McLaughlin, B. (1982). *Language learning in bilingual instruction: Literature review.* Washington, DC: National Institute of Education.

Mergen, B. (1981). *Children slave and free.* Paper presented at the 7th Annual Meeting of the Association for the Anthropological Study of Play, Ft. Worth, Texas.

Mitchell-Kernan, C. (1972). Signifying and marking: Two Afro-American speech acts. In J. J. Gumperz & D. Hymes (Eds.), *Sociolinguistics: The ethnography of communication* (pp. 161-179). New York: Holt, Rinehart & Winston.

Montagu, A. (1967). *The anatomy of swearing.* New York: Macmillan.

Pasteur, A. B., & Toldson, I. L. (1982). *Roots of soul: The psychology of black expressiveness.* Garden City, NY: Anchor Press/Doubleday.

Peckham, M. (1965). *Man's rage for chaos: Biology, behavior and the arts.* Philadelphia: Chilton.

Rawick, G. P. (Ed.). (1972). *The American slave: A composite autobiography* (19 vols.). Westport, CT: Greenwood.

Reddy Singha, R. (1982). Global awareness through dance. *Papers II, International conference on children and youth dancing* (pp. 151-161). Stockholm: Swedish Division of DACI, Dansmuseet.

Rich, A. (1974). *Interracial communication.* New York: Harper & Row.

Segler, H. (1982). Dances of children from the southern part of lower Saxony. *Papers II, International conference on children and youth dancing* (pp. 143-150). Stockholm: Swedish Division of DACI, Dansmuseet.

Sennett, R., & Cobb, J. (1973). *The hidden injuries of class.* New York: Knopf.

Sieber, R. T. (1979). Classmates as workmates: Informal peer activity in the elementary school. *Anthropology and Education Quarterly, 10,* 207-235.

Siegel, B. J. (1970). Defensive structuring and environmental stress. *American Journal of Sociology, 76*(1), 11-32.

Spindler, G., & Spindler, L. (1982). Do anthropologists need learning theory? *Anthropology and Education Quarterly, 13*(2), 109-124.

Sutton-Smith, B. (1976). *The dialectics of play.* Schoerdorff, West Germany: Verlag Hoffman.

Turner, V. (1969). *The ritual process.* Chicago: Aldine.

Wax, M. (Ed.). (1980). *When schools are desegregated: Problems and possibilities for students, educators, parents, and the community.* New Brunswick, NJ: Transaction Books.

White, B., & Michels, B. (1983). *Apples on a stick: The folklore of black children.* New York: Coward-McCann.

Wiggins, D. K. (1980). The play of slave children in the plantation communities of the old South, 1820-1860. *Journal of Sport History, 7,* 21-39.

Willis, P. E. (1977). *Learning to labour: How working class kids get working class jobs.* Farnborough, England: Saxon House.

Wolf, D., & Gardner, H. (1980). Beyond playing or polishing: A developmental view of artistry. In J. J. Hausman (Ed.), *Arts and the schools* (pp. 47-78). New York: McGraw-Hill.

Wolf, E. (1981). *Trial and error: The Detroit school segregation case.* Detroit: Wayne State University Press.

Yoffie, L.R.C. (1947). Three generations of children's singing games in St. Louis. *Journal of American Folklore, 60,* 1-51.

III

ETHNICITY IN THE DEVELOPMENT
OF INTERPERSONAL RELATIONSHIPS

11

Ethnicity, Types of Relationship, and Intraethnic and Interethnic Uncertainty Reduction

WILLIAM B. GUDYKUNST • *Arizona State University*

This study examines the influence of ethnicity, gender, dyadic composition, and type of relationship on self-disclosure, perceived similarity, and attributional confidence in intraethnic and interethnic relationships. It also explores differences between intraethnic and interethnic relationships. Results revealed that ethnicity and type of relationship have a significant impact on the dependent variables, but gender and dyadic composition do not. The data further indicate that there are differences in intraethnic and interethnic self-disclosure, perceived similarity, and attributional confidence. These differences are influenced by type of relationship but not ethnicity, gender, or dyadic composition. The data support Axiom 4 and Theorem 15 of Berger and Calabrese's (1975) theory under all conditions, and Axiom 6 in the white intraethnic data, the black interethnic data, and in the analyses of the black and the white differences.

Since the early 1970s there have been several analyses of interethnic communication (e.g., Rich, 1973; Ross, 1978; Smith, 1973). Inherent in these analyses is the assumption that interethnic communication is different from intraethnic communication. While there is some empirical evidence supporting this assumption, no theoretical explanation that specifies how and why differences exist has been advanced. The purpose of this chapter is to begin to fill this void by comparing selected aspects of intraethnic and interethnic communication from the perspective of uncertainty reduction theory (Berger & Calabrese, 1975; Berger & Bradac, 1982). By applying this theory to the area of interethnic communication, the present inquiry advances theory in intercultural communication and specifies scope and boundary conditions for uncertainty reduction theory.

INFLUENCES ON UNCERTAINTY REDUCTION

Research to date on uncertainty reduction theory has focused upon specific contexts (i.e., initial interactions, romantic relationships) with few comparisons across types of relationships—either acquaintance/friend or cultural similarity/dissimilarity. This research, with rare exceptions, also has been limited in that it has focused the influence of only one type of similarity; namely, attitude similarity. Both of these foci limit the generalizability of the theory. Although the original formulation of the theory (Berger & Calabrese, 1975) was to lay the foundation for a developmental theory of interpersonal communication, few comparisons of uncertainty reduction processes have been made in different types of relationships. Limiting research to attitude similarity is expected given the emphasis on the similarity construct by Berger and Bradac (1982). Bishop (1979) pointed out that "To understand the ways in which the perception of similarity influences interpersonal relations, it is necessary that the problem be approached from the point of view of a wide variety of types of similarity" (p. 461). One type of similarity of particular interest in the United States is ethnic similarity/dissimilarity.[1]

The present study is part of a line of research with two interrelated objectives: (1) to develop a theoretical explanation for interethnic and intercultural differences in communication and (2) to specify scope and boundary conditions for uncertainty reduction theory. Early research in this line revealed differences in uncertainty reduction processes in high and low context cultures (Gudykunst, 1983b) as well as differences in perceptions of North American intracultural and intercultural communication (Gudykunst, 1983a) in initial interactions. Gudykunst and Nishida (1984) extended these exploratory studies finding differences in Japanese and North American uncertainty reduction processes in intracultural and intercultural initial encounters. Gudykunst and associates (1986) further studied the influence of language spoken (Japanese versus English) on Japanese-Japanese and Japanese-North American initial interactions. A comparison of black and white use of uncertainty reduction strategies in initial interactions was conducted by Gudykunst and Hammer (1984). More recently, Gudykunst, Yang, and Nishida (1985) demonstrated that uncertainty reduction theory provides an adequate explanation of communication in acquaintance, friend, and dating relationships in Japan, Korea, and the United States. Finally, Gudykunst (1985) elaborated the line of research examining the influence of cultural similarity/dissimilarity and kind of relationship on uncertainty reduction processes in acquaintances and friendships.

It is impractical to examine all aspects of uncertainty reduction theory across kinds of relationships and in the presence of ethnic similarities/dissimilarities at the same time. For the purpose of the present study, nine specific variables were selected for inclusion: ethnicity, ethnic similarity/dissimilarity, gender, dyadic composition, kind of relationship, attributional confidence, self-disclosure, perceived similarity, and length of relationship. These variables were included because they are central to uncertainty reduction theory or are factors useful in specifying scope and boundary conditions for the theory. The literature on ethnicity, gender, dyadic composition, and relationship development provides the foundation for the specification of hypotheses regarding the effects of these independent variables on self-disclosure, perceived similarity, and attributional confidence in intraethnic and interethnic communication. Since there is no previous research on the effects of the independent variables on differences in intraethnic and interethnic communication, research questions and hypotheses are posed.

Intraethnic and Interethnic Communication

Previous analyses suggest there are significant differences between intraethnic and interethnic communication (Davis & Triandis, 1971; Gumperz, 1982a, 1982b; LaFrance & Mayo, 1978; Levitt & Abner, 1971; Pennington, 1979; Rich, 1973; Ross, 1978; Shuter, 1982; Simard, 1981; Smith, 1973; Stanback & Pearce, 1981; Turner & Giles, 1981; Word, Zanna, & Cooper, 1974). Simard (1981), for example, found that when considering potential friends from another ethnic group, both Francophone and Anglophone subjects in Canada "perceive it as more difficult to know how to initiate a conversation, to know what to talk about during the interaction, to be interested in the other person, and to guess in which language they should talk, than when they considered a person from their own group" (p. 179). Similarly, Shuter's (1982) research revealed that both males and females vary their patterns of asking questions in initial interactions depending upon the ethnic group of the person with whom they are communicating.

While research supports the existence of general differences between intraethnic and interethnic communication, there is no specific research that has examined similarities and/or differences in self-disclosure, perceived similarity, or attributional confidence. A research question, therefore, is posed:

Question: Are there significant differences between intraethnic and inter-ethnic self-disclosure, perceived similarity, and attributional confidence?

Ethnicity

In the last two decades there have been several descriptions of black patterns of communication (e.g., Abrahams, 1970, 1976; Baughman, 1971; Daniel, 1974; Daniel & Smitherman, 1976; Kochman, 1972; Smitherman, 1977). There also have been numerous comparisons of blacks and whites (for an overview of work in international perspective, see Kleinberg, 1971). Jones (1983), for example, found that there were 133 social psychological studies comparing blacks and whites published in the major journals between 1968 and 1980 (for a review of earlier studies see Dreger & Miller, 1968). The vast majority of these studies, however, were concerned with prejudice and not directly with the behavioral aspects of communication. Nevertheless there has been research comparing black and white patterns of communication behavior. One recent study is particularly instructive. Ickes (1984) studied unstructured initial black-white encounters, concluding

> that in the context of initial, same-sex interracial dyads, (a) race (black vs. white) is an important variable influencing behavior and perceptions at the within-dyad level; (b) when interracial contacts between blacks and whites are situationally mandated, whites are likely to display more interactional involvement than their black partners, but at the same time may experience greater social stress; (c) individual dispositions of whites to initiate or avoid interaction with blacks appear to moderate these effects; but (d) these dispositional influences may be clearly manifested in interaction behavior only when the interracial nature of the interaction is made salient by virtue of the white subjects' distinctiveness within the social context. (p. 340)

Other work also has compared message interpretation (Burgoon, 1970), interaction in job settings (Triandis & Malpass, 1971), perceptions of the social environment (Triandis, 1976), nonverbal communication (Fugita, Wexley, & Hillery, 1974; LaFrance & Mayo, 1976, 1978; Word, Zanna, & Cooper, 1974), physiological reactions to interethnic encounters (van der Kolk, 1978), friendship formation (Bochner & Orr, 1979), speech convergence and divergence (Giles & Johnson, 1981), communication styles (Kochman, 1981; Miller, 1982), patterns of question asking (Shuter, 1982) satisfying communication (Hecht & Ribeau, 1984), and the use of uncertainty reduction strategies in general (Gudykunst & Hammer, 1984).

Although the area of black and white differences in self-disclosure has been given only cursory attention in the research published to date, the findings which have emerged are consistent. Specifically, previous research indicates that blacks tend to disclose at lower rates than whites (Diamond & Hellcamp, 1969; Jourard, 1958; Lasakow, 1958; Littlefield, 1974; Wolken, Moriwaki, & Williams, 1973). While the patterns of differences are consistent, there is a possibility that they may be attributable to social class rather then ethnicity. This interpretation is suggested by Jaffee and Polansky's (1962) research, which revealed no significant differences between lower-class blacks and lower-class whites. Partial support for this explanation is provided by Mayer (1967), who found that middle-class women tend to disclose more about marital problems than working-class women.

Uncertainty reduction theory (i.e., Berger & Calabrese, 1975) suggests that self-disclosure is correlated positively with attributional confidence (Axiom 4), that similarity also is correlated positively with attributional confidence (Axiom 6), and that self-disclosure and similarity are correlated positively (Theorem 15). All three relationships were supported in Gudykunst and associates' (1985) study of acquaintance, friendship, and dating relationships. In addition, the relationship between self-disclosure and attributional confidence was supported in Gudykunst and Hammer's (1984) study of black and white initial interactions. Since there are data to suggest that black-white differences in self-disclosure exist and that self-disclosure is associated highly with perceived similarity and attributional confidence, it follows that ethnicity should influence the other two variables as well. The lack of previous research, however, does not allow specification of a directional hypothesis. Also, as noted above, there is no basis to hypothesize whether ethnicity influences differences in intraethnic and interethnic communication. The following hypothesis and research question, therefore, are proffered:

> *Hypothesis 1*: Ethnicity (black versus white) influences intraethnic and interethnic self-disclosure, perceived similarity, and attributional confidence?
>
> *Question 2*: Does ethnicity influence differences in intraethnic and interethnic self-disclosure, perceived similarity, and attributional confidence?

Gender and Dyadic Composition

There are numerous studies of gender differences in self-disclosure. Cline (1983) reviewed a total of 49 studies using self-reports of disclosure and 40 studies using behavioral measures. Of the 89 studies that had examined gender differences in disclosure, 47 (28 self-report and 19 behavioral) found no significant differences (no statistical power analysis was made of these studies) and 42 (21 self-report and 21 behavioral) found significant differences. In those studies that found significant differences, females consistently disclosed at higher rates than males. Cline's review also revealed that females received more disclosure than males. With respect to dyadic composition, females tended to disclose more to females, but gender of partner had little impact on male disclosure. The literature, thus, indicates a greater likelihood of intimate disclosure by females than males and greater intimacy toward female than male partners. In combination, results suggest the greatest disclosure for female-female dyads (Cline, 1983, p. 399).

In addition to the general studies reviewed by Cline (1983), one specific study has examined black and white intraethnic and interethnic interaction in same and opposite sex dyads (Shuter, 1982). Shuter found significant effects for gender and dyadic composition on all three of his dependent variables: type of questions asked, amount of questions asked, and the length of time talked. The results indicated that "blacks and whites significantly changed their interaction depending on the composition of the dyad" (Shuter, 1982, p. 50).

Previous research on gender and dyadic composition, although not unequivocal, does suggest that these factors should influence self-disclosure. Since self-disclosure is theoretically and empirically linked to the other two dependent variables, two nondirectional hypotheses and two research questions appear to be justified:

Hypothesis 2: Gender influences intraethnic and interethnic self-disclosure, perceived similarity, and attributional confidence.

Hypothesis 3: Dyadic composition influences intraethnic and interethnic self-disclosure, perceived similarity, and attributional confidence.

Question 3: Does gender influence differences in intraethnic and interethnic self-disclosure, perceived similarity, and attributional confidence?

Question 4: Does dyadic composition influence differences in intraethnic and interethnic self-disclosure, perceived similarity, and attributional confidence?

Type of Relationship

Most writing on interpersonal relationship development (e.g., Altman & Taylor, 1973; Knapp, 1978; Miller & Steinberg, 1975) suggests that there should be differences in communication processes as relationships increase in levels of intimacy. Altman and Taylor's social penetration theory, for example, gives central importance to the concept of disclosure and hypothesizes that interpersonal exchange gradually progresses from superficial, nonintimate areas to more specific, intimate, and central areas of the personalities of the actors in a relationship. As relationships develop, increased amounts of interpersonal exchange (breadth of penetration) as well as increasingly intimate levels of exchange (depth of penetration) take place.

Altman and Taylor (1973) posit four stages of relationship development: orientation, exploratory affective exchange, affective exchange, and stable exchange. The exploratory affective exchange stage is the equivalent to acquaintance relationships. This stage involves interaction at the periphery of the personality and, therefore, does not include high levels of disclosure or attributional confidence vis-à-vis the behavior of others in a relationship. The affective exchange stage, in contrast, is reached in friendships. Interaction at this stage is "characterized by a definite increase in communication in very private or central areas of the personality" (Altman & Taylor, 1973, p. 140). The theoretical changes hypothesized by social penetration theory were supported by Won-Doornink's (1979) research.

Once relationships between people of different ethnic groups reach the stage of friendship, there may be little difference between these relationships and those between people of the same ethnic group. Altman and Taylor (1973) argue that in the affective exchange stage "Cultural stereotypy is broken down in these more intimate areas and there is a willingness to move in and out of such exchanges" (pp. 139-140). This position is consistent with Miller and Steinberg's (1975) contention that, in developed relationships, the majority of predictions are based on psychological data, not cultural or sociological data. Research by Gudykunst (in press) partially supports the conclusion drawn from developmental theory. Specifically, he found moderate to high correlations between intracultural and intercultural perceived similarity and social penetration in close friendships.

Given the extensive research (e.g., Duck & Gilmour, 1981a, 1981b) supporting changes in patterns of communication as relationships develop, the following hypothesis and question are proffered.[2]

Hypothesis 4: The type of relationship (acquaintance versus friend) influences intraethnic and interethnic self-disclosure, perceived similarity, and attributional confidence. Specifically, there will be higher levels of self-disclosure, perceived similarity, and attributional confidence in friendships than in acquaintances for both intraethnic and interethnic relationships.
Question 5: Does the type of relationship influence differences between intraethnic and interethnic self-disclosure, perceived similarity, and attributional confidence?

METHODS

Subjects

The subjects for the study were all students at a medium-sized northeastern university. All subjects were solicited from the general student population and volunteered to participate in the research outside of class. A total of 326 subjects, 163 whites (81 males and 82 females) and 163 blacks (82 males and 81 females), returned completed questionnaires. There were no differences between the blacks and whites or males and females on demographic variables assessed (i.e., year in school).

Research Design

A 2 × 2 × 2 (Ethnic group × Gender × Dyadic composition) multivariate analysis of variance (MANOVA) design was employed. In addition to these three variables, type of relationship was assessed and utilized as an independent variable in the analysis. Subjects were first assigned randomly to one of the two dyadic composition conditions—reporting about their communication with a person of the same sex or of the opposite sex. Once assigned to this condition each subject was asked to select a person from the other ethnic group whom they knew. Specifically, blacks selected a white person and whites selected a black person. The subjects were then asked to select a person of the same ethnic group as themselves of the same as the first person that they had known for approximately the same length of time as the first person selected. The subjects' responses regarding their communication with these two people constituted the operationalization of interethnic and intraethnic communication respectively. The responses are, therefore, self-reports of behavior in actual relationships.

Measurement

Self-disclosure was measured using a shortened version of Jourard's (1964) 60-item questionnaire.[3] The original instrument consists of ten questions in each of six topical areas. Each question asked the subjects to indicate the degree to which they had disclosed certain types of information; for example, "My feelings about how parents ought to deal with children" and "What I find to be the worst pressures and strains in my studies." Three items were selected randomly from each of the six topical areas: (1) attitudes and opinions (numbers 1, 7, and 10); (2) tastes and interests (5, 8, and 9); (3) work or studies (1, 7, and 9); (4) money (1, 6, and 9); (5) personality (6, 9, and 10). Jourard's response scale was used in its original form (0 = no disclosure about item, 1 = disclosure in general terms, 2 = full disclosure about item). The 18 items were combined into an overall scale yielding an alpha of .88 for both intraethnic and interethnic disclosure. Difference scores were obtained by subtracting the overall interethnic score from the overall intraethnic score.

Perceived similarity was operationalized using McCroskey, Richmond, and Daly's (1975) measure of perceived homophily. Responses for the 16 items were made on a 1 to 7 scale; the higher the response, the more similarity perceived. Examples of endpoints of these items include "Doesn't think like me"-"Thinks like me"; "Morals unlike mine"-"Morals like mine"; and "Economic situation different than mine"-"Economic situation similar to mine." The combination of the 16 items yielded acceptable alphas (intraethnic = .83; interethnic = .76). Difference scores were obtained by subtracting the interethnic score from the intraethnic score.

Attributional confidence was assessed using Clatterbuck's (1979) CL7 scale, with responses ranging from 0 to 100%. This scale asks the respondents to indicate the degree to which they can predict the other person's behavior, attitudes, feelings, and attraction to the respondent. The first item, for example, read "How confident are you of your general ability to predict how he/she will behave?" Combination of the seven items provided an alpha of .89 for both the intraethnic and interethnic scales. Difference scores were computed in the same manner as with the other two scales.

RESULTS

Manipulation Check

Subjects were asked to select intraethnic and interethnic relationships that had lasted approximately the same length of time. Given the constraint that both relationships had to be with a person of the same or opposite sex, it was expected that the length of time they had known the two people would vary. In order to check this assumption, subjects were asked the actual length of time they had known the selected persons. The average length of the intraethnic relationships was 45.56 months, while the average length of the interethnic relationships was 36.86 (t = 4.50, 322 df, p < .001). To determine if the difference in length was due to different types of relationships (i.e., acquaintance versus friend), the t-tests were computed controlling for type of relationship: acquaintance, t = 1.99, 104 df, p < .05 (intra = 27.16, inter = 22.64); friend, t = 2.12, 97 df, p < .05 (intra = 66.15, inter = 58.55).[4]

To rule out that the difference in the length of time might be attributed to one of the other independent variables, a three-way analysis of variance was computed on the difference scores (intra—inter). This analysis yielded no significant effect for any of the dependent variables: ethnicity, F(1,313) < 1, p = ns (white = 8.68, black = 11.11; power = .87 for small effect size of .15 with p = .01);[5] gender, F(1,313) < 1, p = ns (males = 10.38, females = 9.34); dyadic composition, F(1,313) = 2.18, p = ns (same sex = 12.92, opposite sex = 6.82). Because there were differences in the lengths of the relationships and they were not explained by any of the independent variables, length was treated as a covariate in all other analyses.

To rule out the potential confounding influence of social class, the prestige of the subjects' parents' occupations were compared using the National Opinion Research Center's occupational prestige scale.[6] There were no significant differences for prestige by ethnicity, F(1,268) = 2.58, p = ns (blacks = 49.66, whites = 52.36); or gender F(1,268) < 1, p = ns. Any difference by ethnic group obtained in the analysis, therefore, should be attributable to ethnicity, not social class.

Tests of Hypotheses

Intraethnic Communication. All hypotheses were tested using multivariate analysis of covariance, with length of relationship used as the covariate. Table 11.1 displays the means and standard deviations for all variables. Results revealed a Bartlett's test of sphericity = 39.95 (3 df, p < .001) indicating that multivariate analysis was warranted. The within cells regression for the covariate yielded no significant effect (Hotelling's T^2 = .00, $F(3,276)$ < 1, p = ns), suggesting that length of relationship did not have an impact on the dependent variables. Power for this and all other multivariate tests was .86 for a small effect size of .25 (Stevens, 1980).

Only one multivariate interaction effect was significant—ethnicity × type of relationship × dyadic composition (Hotelling's T^2 = .04, $F(3,276)$ = 3.61, p < .01). The only dependent variable to display a univariate interaction effect was perceived similarity: $F(1,278)$ = 7.64, p < .01. Analysis of the mean scores suggests that there is little difference (.26) in perceived similarity by type of relationship for white same-sex dyads, but there is a large difference (.90) for white opposite-sex dyads. In contrast there is a larger difference (.84) in perceived similarity for black same-sex dyads than for opposite-sex dyads (.10).

The analysis did not reveal significant multivariate effects for dyadic composition (Hotelling's T^2 = .01, $F(3,276)$ < 1, p = ns) or gender (Hotelling's T^2 = .02, $F(3,276)$ = 1.86, p = ns). In contrast, both ethnicity (Hotelling's T^2 = .04, $F(3,276)$ = 4.11, p < .01) and type of relationship (Hotelling's T^2 = .39, $F(3,276)$ = 36.02, p < .001) had significant multivariate effects. All three dependent variables revealed significant univariate effects by type of relationship: self-disclosure, $F(1,278)$ = 81.29, p < .001 (friends > acquaintances); perceived similarity, $F(1,278)$ = 20.77, p < .001 (friends > acquaintances); attributional confidence, $F(1,278)$ = 51.47, p < .001 (friends > acquaintances). These results support the prediction made in Hypothesis 4; that is, friends perceive themselves as more similar, self-disclose more, and are more confident in predicting each others' behavior than are acquaintances. Only self-disclosure yielded a significant univariate effect by ethnicity: $F(1,278)$ = 10.45, p < .001 (blacks > whites). The finding that blacks self-disclose more than whites runs counter to previous research and will be discussed in detail.

Interethnic Communication. The Bartlett's test of sphericity yielded a value of 39.84 (3 df, p < .001), indicating multivariate analysis was warranted. The within-cells regression for the covariate, length of relationship, did not yield a significant effect (Hotelling's T^2 = .01, $F(3,274)$ < 1, p = ns), suggesting again that it does not influence the dependent variables. The only multivariate interaction effect found to

TABLE 11.1
Means and Standard Deviations by Independent Variables

	Ethnicity				Sex				Dyadic Composition				Relationship Type			
	Whites		Blacks		Males		Females		Same		Opposite		Acquaintance		Friend	
	M	SD	M	SD	M	SD	M	SD	M	SD	M	SD	M	SD	M	SD
Intradisclosure	.86	.35	.97	.39	.91	.35	.93	.39	.98	.35	.86	.38	.67	.34	1.05	.31
Interdisclosure	.73	.38	.93	.43	.81	.39	.83	.43	.85	.40	.80	.43	.70	.37	.89	.42
Disclosure difference	.13	.38	.05	.47	.10	.44	.09	.43	.13	.38	.06	.48	.06	.35	−.08	.36
Intrasimilarity	4.43	.97	4.45	.90	4.46	.87	4.41	.99	4.49	.93	4.38	.93	4.11	.89	4.63	.91
Intersimilarity	3.48	.72	3.60	.90	3.62	.80	3.47	.81	3.62	.78	3.48	.84	3.46	.87	3.61	.77
Similarity difference	.96	1.18	.81	1.26	.85	1.19	.92	1.24	.88	1.27	.89	1.16	.66	1.13	.68	1.08
Intraconfidence	72.60	17.53	72.20	20.16	74.76	17.77	70.61	19.64	75.18	17.88	70.18	19.38	62.43	17.46	78.14	17.04
Interconfidence	56.63	19.99	59.12	24.68	59.23	22.09	57.30	22.73	59.13	22.43	57.40	22.34	55.58	20.86	59.72	23.12
Confidence difference	15.97	20.56	13.08	21.91	15.46	22.60	13.31	19.72	15.99	20.99	12.78	21.26	10.41	16.54	8.10	15.83

be significant was the four-way interaction (Hotelling's T^2 = .04, $F(3,274)$ = 3.22, p < .05). None of the univariate four-way interaction effects, however, were significant. This suggests that the interaction effects should not confound the interpretation of other results.

The analysis did not reveal significant multivariate effects for dyadic composition (Hotelling's T^2 = .01, $F(3,274)$ < , p = ns) or gender (Hotelling's T^2 = .01, $F(3,274)$ = 1.16, p = ns). Neither variable, therefore, has an influence on the set of dependent variables. Both ethnicity (Hotelling's T^2 = .10, $F(3,274)$ = 8.75, p < .001) and kind of relationship (Hotelling's T^2 = .50, $F(3,274)$ = 46.09, p < .001) revealed significant multivariate effects on the set of dependent variables. The only significant univariate effect by ethnicity displayed was on self-disclosure: $F(1,276)$ = 25.32, p < .001 (blacks > whites). These results are consistent with the intraethnic findings and will be discussed. All three dependent variables yielded univariate effects by kind of relationship: self-disclosure, $F(1,276)$ = 100.88, p < .001 (friends > acquaintances); perceived similarity, $F(1,276)$ = 10.19, p < .01 (friends > acquaintances); attributional confidence, $F(1,276)$ = 80.65, p < .001 (friends > acquaintances). The results are consistent with predictions from research on the development of interpersonal relationships.

Summary. These analyses revealed that ethnicity had significant multivariate effects in both intraethnic and interethnic tests; therefore, the data supported Hypothesis 1. With respect to gender and dyadic composition there were not significant effects in either analysis. This indicates that neither Hypothesis 2 nor Hypothesis 3 was supported. Finally, there were significant multivariate effects by type of relationship for both analyses, suggesting that Hypothesis 4 was supported.

Test of Research Questions

The first research question posed concerned the general differences between intraethnic and interethnic communication. In order to examine this question, t-tests were computed between intraethnic and interethnic responses. These analyses revealed significant differences for all three variables: self-disclosure, t = 4.01 (318 df), p < .001 (intra = .92, inter = .82); perceived similarity, t = 12.70 (302 df), p < .001 (intra = 4.43, inter = 3.56); attributional confidence, t = 12.12 (318 df), p < .001 (intra = 72.61, inter = 58.25). These results suggest that, with respect to the first question, there are differences between intraethnic and interethnic communication.

The second, third, and fourth questions dealt with the potential effects of ethnicity, gender, and dyadic composition on these differences. These questions were addressed using MANOVA, with differences in the lengths of the relationships treated as a covariate. The Bartlett's test of sphericity (189.25, 3 df, $p < .001$) was high enough to warrant use of MANOVA. The multivariate within-cells regression for the covariate was not significant (Hotelling's $T^2 = .02$, $F(3,279) = 2.15$, $p = ns$), indicating that length of relationship does not have an influence on differences in intraethnic and interethnic communication for the set of dependent variables. There were no significant multivariate interaction effects.

The multivariate main effects of the three independent variables were all insignificant: ethnicity, Hotelling's $T^2 = .01$, $F(3,279) = 1.21$, $p = ns$; gender, Hotelling's $T^2 = .01$, $F(3,279) < 1$, $p = ns$; dyadic composition, Hotelling's $T^2 = .00$, $F(3,279) < 1$, $p = ns$. These results suggest that ethnicity, gender, and dyadic composition do not have an impact upon differences in intraethnic and interethnic communication.

The possible effect of kind of relationship on differences in intra- and interethnic communication (Question 5) was assessed separately in order not to reduce the degrees of freedom in the above analyses. The Bartlett's test of sphericity was sufficiently high to warrant multivariate analysis (53.88, 3 df, $p < .001$). The multivariate within-cells regression for the covariate was not significant (Hotelling's $T^2 = .02$, $F(3, 173) < 1$, $p = ns$), suggesting again that length does not influence the dependent variables. Type of relationship did have a significant multivariate effect: Hotelling's $T^2 = .05$, $F(3,173) = 2.73$, $p < .05$. The only variable that differences in kind of relationship had a significant effect on was the self-disclosure difference scores: $F(1,175) = 7.62$, $p < .01$ (intra $>$ inter for acquaintances; inter $>$ intra for friends). These results indicate that there is more self-disclosure in intraethnic acquaintances than interethnic ones; in contrast, there is more self-disclosure in interethnic friendships than intraethnic ones.

DISCUSSION

Tests of Hypotheses

The present data supported Hypotheses 1 and 4, but not Hypotheses 2 and 3. With respect to the first hypothesis, the findings are consistent with most research on ethnicity. That is, ethnicity has an impact upon communication. Specifically, for both the intraethnic and interethnic analyses, ethnicity had a multivariate effect on the three dependent variables, as well as an independent effect on self-disclosure. Blacks reported disclosing more in both intraethnic and interethnic relationships than whites. Blacks and whites perceived their similarity to be almost exactly the same in their intraethnic relationships, but blacks perceived more similarity in interethnic relationships than whites. Similarly, the degree of attributional confidence in intraethnic relationships was almost exactly the same for blacks and whites, although blacks perceived greater attributional confidence in interethnic relations than whites. The greater perceived similarity and attributional confidence reported by blacks in interethnic relationships can be explained by the greater amount of interethnic contact in which blacks engage. Since blacks engage in more interethnic contact than whites, they have more opportunity to observe black-white similarities and to learn to predict whites' behavior. Such an explanation is consistent with Rose's (1981) discussion of cognitive and dyadic processes in interethnic contact situations.

While black-white differences in self-disclosure are consistent with previous research (e.g., Diamond & Hellcamp, 1969; Jourard, 1958; Littlefield, 1974; Wolken et al., 1973), the specific finding that blacks disclosed more than whites is inconsistent. There are three plausible explanations for this difference. First, as indicated earlier, previous studies may have compared middle-class whites with lower-class blacks. The present study, in contrast, included only middle-class subjects. It may be that middle-class whites disclose more than lower-class blacks, but middle-class blacks disclose more than middle-class whites because of overcompensation to middle-class norms. Second, previous research has focused on adolescents (Littlefield, 1974), high school students (Diamond & Hellcamp, 1969), or was specific to therapeutic situations (Wolken et al., 1973), while the present analysis examined college students in developed relationships. The inconsistencies in the findings, therefore, may be due to age differences in subjects or the context of disclosure. Third, there may have been changes as a function of time. Because the previous studies were all conducted prior to 1974, the ten years that have elapsed may have impacted upon black and white patterns of disclosure. Differentiating among these three explanations requires additional research.

The lack of support for Hypothesis 2, the posited influence of gender, is not totally surprising. As indicated earlier, Cline's (1983) review of research on gender and self-disclosure revealed that a majority of the studies (47 out of 89, 28 self-report and 19 behavioral) reported no significant difference between males and females, even though she went on to argue that there probably were differences due to gender and dyadic composition. Gudykunst and Hammer's (1984) comparison of blacks and whites also found no significant multivariate effect by gender on behavioral intentions in initial interactions. The present results also are consistent with Ickes's (1984) findings that there were few gender differences in initial interracial interactions. Following Ickes, the lack of gender differences in the interethnic condition may be "due partly to the unique presence of the interracial variable, an aspect of interactions that appeared to be so compelling that it tended to override all but the strongest influences of sex composition" (1984, p. 337).

Even though Hypotheses 2 and 3 were not supported, there was an interaction effect involving gender and dyadic composition. Specifically, there was a four-way multivariate interaction effect in the interethnic analysis. This interaction effect, however, explained little variance (i.e., less than 1%). Analysis of the mean scores where interaction did occur suggests that blacks and whites vary their communication depending on their gender and the composition of the dyad. This finding is consistent with Shuter's (1982) research on question asking in initial interactions.

The multivariate analyses supported Hypothesis 4 in both the intraethnic and interethnic conditions. In both conditions there was greater self-disclosure, greater perceived similarity, and greater attributional confidence in friendships than in acquaintance relationships. These findings are consistent with predictions that would be made from developmental theory (e.g., Altman & Taylor, 1973; Knapp, 1978; Miller & Steinberg, 1975), as well as previous research (e.g., that cited in Duck & Gilmour, 1981b). These results suggest that in future work examining similarities and differences in intraethnic and interethnic communication, the stage of the relationship must be taken into consideration.

Tests of Research Questions

Results for the first question revealed that there is significantly more disclosure, perceived similarity, and attributional confidence in intraethnic relationships than in interethnic ones. These results are consistent with general analyses of interethnic communication (Rich, 1973; Smith, 1973), as well as analyses from sociolinguistic (Gumperz, 1982a, 1982b) and social psychological (Turner & Giles, 1981) perspectives. The specific results for perceived similarity are consistent with Simard's (1981) research with Francophones and Anglophones in Canada.

The findings with respect to self-disclosure are different from those in Gudykunst and Nishida's (1984) study of North Americans and Japanese. These researchers found a greater intent to disclose in culturally dissimilar initial interactions than in culturally similar ones. The differences in these two studies may be attributed to one of two factors. First, self-disclosure may vary due to the nature of the dissimilarities. More self-disclosure may take place when cultural dissimilarities are present, less when the communicators are culturally similar but differ in ethnic group membership. Second, the differences may be due to stage of relationship. Gudykunst and Nishida examined initial interactions, while the present analysis focused on more developed relationships. Partial support for the second explanation is found in the analysis of the difference scores by kind of relationship. This analysis revealed that there was more disclosure in intraethnic acquaintances than in interethnic ones, but greater disclosure in interethnic than intraethnic friendships. Differentiating between these two explanations in future research is considered important for the development of theory to explain interethnic and intercultural communication, as well as specifying boundary conditions for uncertainty reduction theory.

With respect to Questions 2, 3, and 4, the results revealed that ethnicity, gender, and dyadic composition did not effect differences in intraethnic and interethnic communication. The only factors found to be related to differences in intra- and interethnic communication were kind of relationship. The influence of kind of relationship is consistent with previous work on relationship development (e.g., Altman & Taylor, 1973).

Implications for Uncertainty Reduction Theory

The present data allowed for a test of two axioms (4 and 6) and one theorem (15) from Berger and Calabrese's (1975) theory outside the initial interaction context. Results for Axiom 4—"High levels of uncertainty in a relationship cause decreases in the intimacy level of communication content. Low levels of uncertainty produce high levels of intimacy" (p. 103)—indicate that the axiom is supported in both black and white samples in all three conditions. The highest correlations obtained in the white (.72) and black (.60) samples were between disclosure and attributional confidence difference scores. These correlations are consistent with those obtained by Gudykunst and Hammer's (1984) study of black and white intentions in an initial interaction context.

Results for Axiom 6—"Similarities between persons reduce uncertainty, while dissimilarities produce increases in uncertainty" (p. 106)—are not consistent across situations. This axiom is supported in the white intraethnic data, the black interethnic data, and in both black and white difference analyses. It, however, is not supported in black intraethnic and white interethnic data. Perceived similarity (in terms of attitudes, values, appearance, and background) does not appear to reduce uncertainty in black intraethnic communication. It may be that ethnic similarity reduces uncertainty in these relationships. The data also suggest that these types of similarity do not lead to attributional confidence for whites in interethnic communication. Ethnic dissimilarities appear to override attitude, value, appearance, and background similarities for whites in interethnic situations. The results for whites are consistent with the research of Triandis and Davis (1965) and Bishop (1979). The differences found here suggest boundary conditions for this axiom.

Theorem 15—"Intimacy level of communication content and similarity are positively related" (p. 109)—is supported in all three conditions. Berger and Calabrese reported no previous research supporting this theorem, but Prisbell and Anderson (1980) found that attitude-value similarity was related to depth of self-disclosure.

Results of the correlation analysis with the percentage of intraethnic communication networks also supports a recent elaboration of uncertainty reduction theory. Parks and Adelman (1983) found that shared networks was related to attributional confidence in romantic relationships. While the "network" variable used in the present analysis is not the same as the one used by Parks and Adelman, it does yield results consistent with predictions that would be made based upon their research. Specifically, the network variable was related positively with intraethnic attributional confidence and negatively with interethnic attributional confidence for both blacks and whites. These results suggest that intra- and/or interethnic networks should be incorporated into any elaborated version of uncertainty reduction theory designed to explain both intra- and interethnic communication.

CONCLUSION

The present study revealed that ethnicity and type of relationship have a significant impact upon both intraethnic and interethnic communication, while gender and dyadic composition do not. The data also showed differences in intraethnic and interethnic self-disclosure, perceived similarity, and attributional confidence. The only factor to influence these differences was type of relationship. Ethnicity, gender, and dyadic composition did not have a significant impact upon differences between intraethnic and interethnic communication. Findings of the present study supported Axiom 4 and Theorem 15 of Berger and Calabrese's (1975) theory under all conditions, and Axiom 6 under the majority of conditions.

The present study supports Bishop's (1979) argument that ethnic/cultural similarities/dissimilarities must be taken into consideration if interpersonal relationships are to be explained adequately. These findings, when taken together, further suggest that while there are differences in the use of self-disclosure, perceived similarity, and attributional confidence in intraethnic and interethnic relationships, the differences do not yeld different interrelations among the variables. The interrelations in both situations are consistent with those that would be predicted from uncertainty reduction theory. Uncertainty reduction theory, therefore, appears to be a useful perspective for explaining interethnic communication, as well as intraethnic communication. Future work using this perspective should focus upon specifying theoretical elaborations, as well as scope and boundary conditions necessary for it to adequately explain intraethnic and interethnic communication.

NOTES

1. Montagu (1972) argued that substituting the term *ethnic group* for *race* decreases the "negative" connotations associated with racial terms and will lead to increased study. Vora and Asante (1979) make a similar point, but suggest using *culture* instead of *ethnic group*. Because it is more descriptive of the differences examined, *ethnicity* is used wherever possible here.

2. As discussed later, subjects were asked to match intraethnic and interethnic relationships in terms of length of time, not type of relationship. Because type of relationship was not controlled rigidly (i.e., subjects labeled relationships at the end of the

questionnaire rather than being asked to select from a specific category) some intraethnic and interethnic relationships selected by the same subjects (about one-third) were not labeled the same. This becomes problematic only in examining the difference scores. To answer the question posed here, it will be necessary to use only those respondents who selected relationships of the same type. This question will be analyzed separately so as not to decrease the N for the remaining analyses.

3. Jourard's (1964) instrument has been criticized for lack of predictive validity (e.g., Cozby, 1973). It has been shown, however, that total scores are correlated with amount and intimacy of self-disclosure on written self-descriptions (Pederson & Breglio, 1968). Further, scores of the instrument in its original form (where scores reflected subjects' past history of disclosure to parents and individuals labeled "best same-sex friend" and "best opposite-sex friend") were correlated with "actual disclosure" measured by subjects' disclosure "to an experimenter or to peers the subject had never met" (Cozby, 1973, p. 74). The instrument used here assessed disclosure to specific people, not labeled categories. The method of administration, therefore, corresponds closely with Jourard's (1971) revised scale, which according to Cozby, does have predictive validity.

4. The drop in degrees of freedom here is because comparisons were made only for those subjects who selected intraethnic and interethnic relationships that fell in the same categories. If a subject labeled one relationship acquaintance and the other friend, he or she was omitted from this analysis.

5. The power is the same for all other analyses. Power for small effect size was selected because as Cohen (1977, p. 25ff) points out, initial studies outside the laboratory can be expected to produce only small effect sizes.

6. This scale was developed by North and Hatt (1947) and updated for the census occupational codes in 1960 (Hodge, Siegel, & Rossi, 1964), and in 1970 (Siegel, 1971). Several recent reviews of indicators of social class (e.g., Haug, 1977; Powers, 1982; Trieman, 1977) conclude that occupation is the best single indicator of class.

REFERENCES

Abrahams, R. (1970). *Positively black*. Englewood Cliffs, NJ: Prentice-Hall.

Abrahams, R. (1976). *Talking black*. Rowley, MA: Newbury House.

Altman, I., & Taylor, D. (1973). *Social penetration*. New York: Holt, Rinehart & Winston.

Baughman, E. E. (1971). *Black Americans: A psychological analysis*. New York: Academic Press.

Berger, C. R., & Bradac, J. J. (1982). *Language and social knowledge*. London: Edward Arnold.

Berger, C. R., & Calabrese, R. J. (1975). Some explorations in initial interactions. *Human Communication Research, 1*, 99-112.

Bishop, G. (1979). Perceived similarity in interpersonal attitudes and behavior. *Journal of Applied Social Psychology, 9*, 446-465.

Bochner, S., & Orr, F. (1979). Race and academic status as determinants of friendship development. *International Journal of Psychology, 14*, 37-46.

Burgoon, M. (1970). The effects of response set and race on message interpretation. *Speech Monographs, 37,* 264-268.

Clatterbuck, G. (1979). Attributional confidence and uncertainty in initial interactions. *Human Communication Research, 5,* 147-157.

Cline, R. (1983). The acquaintance process as relational communication. In R. Bostrom (Ed.), *Communication yearbook 7* (pp. 396-413). Beverly Hills, CA: Sage.

Cohen, J. (1977). *Statistical power analysis for the behavioral sciences* (rev. ed.). New York: Academic Press.

Cozby, P. G. (1973). Self-disclosure: A literature review. *Psychological Bulletin, 79,* 73-91.

Daniel, J. (Ed.). (1974). *Black communication: Dimensions of research and instruction.* New York: Speech Communication Association.

Daniel, J., & Smitherman, G. (1976). How I got over: Communication dynamics in the black community. *Quarterly Journal of Speech, 62,* 26-39.

Davis, E. E., & Triandis, H. C. (1971). An experimental study of black-white negotiations. *Journal of Applied Social Psychology, 1,* 240-262.

Diamond, R. E., & Hellcamp, D. T. (1969). Race, sex, ordinal position of birth, and self-disclosure in high school students. *Psychological Reports, 25,* 235-238.

Dreger, R. M., & Miller, K. S. (1968). Comparative psychological studies of Negroes and whites in the United States: 1959-1965. *Psychological Bulletin Monograph Supplement,* no. 7.

Duck, S., & Gilmour, R. (Eds.). (1981a). *Personal relationships 1: Studying personal relationships.* London: Academic Press.

Duck, R., & Gilmour, R. (Eds.). (1981b). *Personal relationships 2: Developing personal relationships.* London: Academic Press.

Fugita, S. S., Wexley, K. N., & Hillery, J. M. (1974). Black-white differences in nonverbal behavior in an interview setting. *Journal of Applied Social Psychology, 4,* 343-350.

Giles, H., & Johnson, P. (1981). The role of language in ethnic group relations. In J. Turner & H. Giles (Eds.), *Intergroup behavior* (pp. 199-243). Chicago: University of Chicago Press.

Gudykunst, W. B. (1983a). Similarities and differences in perceptions of initial intracultural encounters. *Southern Speech Communication Journal, 49,* 40-65.

Gudykunst, W. B. (1983b). Uncertainty reduction and predictability of behavior in high and low context cultures. *Communication Quarterly, 31,* 49-55.

Gudykunst, W. B. (1985). An exploratory comparison of close intracultural and intercultural friendships. *Communication Quarterly, 33,* 270-283.

Gudykunst, W. B. (1985). The influence of cultural similarity and type of relationship on uncertainty reduction processes. Communication Monographs, 52, 203-217.

Gudykunst, W. B., & Hammer, M. R. (1984). *The effect of ethnicity, gender, and dyadic composition on uncertainty reduction.* Paper presented at the Speech Communication Association convention, Chicago, IL.

Gudykunst, W. B., & Nishida, T. (1984). Individual and cultural influences on uncertainty reduction strategies.*Communication Monographs, 51,* 23-36.

Gudykunst, W. B., Nishida, T., Koike, H., & Shiino, N. (1986). The influence of language on uncertainty reduction in initial Japanese-Japanese and Japanese-North American interactions. In M. McLaughlin (Ed.), *Communication Yearbook 9* (pp. 555-575). Newbury Park, CA: Sage.

Gudykunst, W. B., Yang, S. M., & Nishida, T. (1985). A cross-cultural test of uncertainty reduction theory: Comparisons of acquaintances, friendships, and dating relationships in Japan, Korea, and the United States. *Human Communication Research, 11*, 407-454.

Gumperz, J. (1982a). *Discourse strategies.* Cambridge: Cambridge University Press.

Gumperz, J. (Ed.). (1982b). *Language and social identity.* Cambridge: Cambridge University Press.

Haug, M. E. (1977). Measurement in social stratification. *Annual Review of Sociology, 3*, 51-79.

Hecht, M., & Ribeau, S. (1984). Ethnic communication: A comparative analysis of satisfying communication. *International Journal of Intercultural Relations, 8*, 135-152.

Hodge, R. W., Siegel, P., & Rossi, P. (1964). Occupational prestige in the United States, 1925-1963. *American Journal of Sociology, 70*, 286-302.

Ickes, W. (1984). Compositions in black and white: Determinants of interaction in interracial dyads. *Journal of Personality and Social Psychology, 47*, 330-341.

Jaffee, L. D., & Polansky, N. A. (1962). Verbal inaccessibility in young adolescents showing delinquent trends. *Journal of Health and Social Behavior, 3*, 95-111.

Jourard, S. (1958). A study of self-disclosure. *Scientific American, 198*, 77-82.

Jourard, S. (1964). *The transparent self.* New York: Van Nostrand Reinhold.

Jourard, S. (1971). *Self-disclosure.* New York: Wiley.

Jourard, S., & Lasakow, P. (1958). Some factors in self-disclosure. *Journal of Abnormal and Social Psychology, 56*, 91-98.

Jones, J. M. (1983). The concept of race in social psychology. In L. Wheeler & P. Shaver (Eds.), *Review of Personality and Social Psychology* (pp. 117-150). Beverly Hills, CA: Sage.

Kleinberg, O. (1971). Black and white international perspective. *American Psychologist, 26*, 119-128.

Knapp, M. (1978). *Social intercourse: From greetings to goodbye.* Boston: Allyn & Bacon.

Kochman, T. (Ed.). (1972). *Rappin' and stylin' out: Communication in urban black America.* Urbana: University of Illinois Press.

Kochman, T. (1981). *Black and white: Styles in conflict.* University of Chicago Press.

LaFrance, M., & Mayo, C. (1976). Racial differences in gaze behavior during conversations: Two systematic observational studies. *Journal of Personality and Social Psychology, 33*, 547-552.

LaFrance, M., & Mayo, C. (1978). Gaze direction in interracial dyadic communication. *Ethnicity, 5*, 167-173.

Levitt, D. W., & Abner, E. V. (1971). Black-white semantic differences and interracial communication. *Journal of Applied Social Psychology, 1, 263-277.*

Littlefield, R. P. (1974). Self-disclosure among Negro, white, and Mexican-American adolescents. *Journal of Counseling Psychology, 21*, 133-136.

Mayer, J. E. (1967). Disclosing marital problems. *Social Casework, 48*, 342-391.

McCroskey, J. C., Richmond, V. P., & Daly, J. A. (1975). The development of a measure of perceived homophily in interpersonal communication. *Human Communication Research, 1*, 323-332.

Miller, G. R., & Steinberg, M. (1975). *Between people.* Chicago: Science Research Associates.

Miller, L. D. (1982). Attraction and communication style as determinants of interpersonal relationships: Perceptual comparisons between blacks and whites. In N. Jain (Ed.),

International and intercultural communication annual (Vol. VI, pp. 49-62). Annandale, VA: Speech Communication Association.

Montagu, A. (1972). *Statement on race.* New York: Oxford University Press.

North, C. C., & Hatt, P. H. (1947). Jobs and occupations: A popular evaluation. *Public Opinion News, 9,* 3-13.

Parks, M., & Adelman, M. (1983). Communication networks and the development of romantic relationships: An expansion of uncertainty reduction theory. *Human Communication Research, 10,* 55-80.

Pederson, D. M., & Breglio, V. J. (1968). The correlation of two self-disclosure inventories with actual disclosure: A validity study. *Journal of Psychology, 68,* 291-298.

Pennington, D. L. (1979). Black-white communication. In M. Asante, E. Newmark, & C. Blake (Eds.), *Handbook of intercultural communication* (pp. 383-402). Beverly Hills, CA: Sage.

Powers, M. G. (Ed.). (1982). *Measures of socioeconomic status.* Boulder, CO: Westview Press.

Prisbell, M., & Anderson, J. (1980). The importance of perceived homophily, level of uncertainty, feeling good, safety, and self-disclosure in interpersonal relationships. *Communication Quarterly, 28,* 22-33.

Rich, A. L. (1973). *Interracial communication.* New York: Harper & Row.

Rose, T. L. (1981). Cognitive and dyadic processes in intergroup contact. In D. Hamilton (Ed.), *Cognitive processes in stereotyping and intergroup behavior* (pp. 259-302). Hillsdale, NJ: Lawrence Erlbaum.

Ross, E. L. (Ed.). (1978). *Interethnic communication.* Athens: University of Georgia Press.

Shuter, R. (1982). Initial interaction of American blacks and whites in interracial and intraracial dyads. *Journal of Social Psychology, 117,* 45-52.

Siegel, P. (1971). Prestige in the American occupational structure. Unpublished doctoral dissertation, University of Chicago.

Simard, L. (1981). Cross-cultural interaction. *Journal of Social Psychology, 113,* 171-192.

Smith, A. L. (1973). *Transracial communication.* Englewood Cliffs, NJ: Prentice-Hall.

Smitherman, G. (1977). *Talkin' and testifyin': The language of Black America.* Boston: Houghton Mifflin.

Stanback, M., & Pearce, W. B. (1981). Talking to "the man": Some communication strategies used by members of subordinate social groups. *Quarterly Journal of Speech, 67,* 21-30.

Stevens, J. (1980). Power of the multivariate analysis of variance test. *Psychological Bulletin, 8,* 728-737.

Treiman, D. J. (1977). *Occupational prestige in comparative perspective.* New York: Academic Press.

Triandis, H. C. (Ed.). (1976). *Variations in black and white perceptions of the social environment.* Urbana: University of Illinois Press.

Triandis, H. C., & Davis, E. E. (1965). Race and belief as determinants of behavioral intentions. *Journal of Personality and Social Psychology, 2,* 715-725.

Triandis, H. C., & Malpass, R. S. (1971). Studies of black and white interaction in job settings. *Journal of Applied Social Psychology, 1,* 101-117.

Turner, J. C., & Giles, H. (Eds.). (1981). *Intergroup behavior.* Chicago: University of Chicago Press.

Van Der Kolk, C. (1978). Physiological reactions of black, Puerto Rican, and white students in suggested ethnic encounters. *Journal of Social Psychology, 104,* 107-114.

Vora, E., & Asante, M. K. (1979). The impact of the concept of race versus that of culture on communication. In W. Davey (Ed.), *Intercultural theory and practice* (pp. 156-157). Washington, DC: Society for Intercultural Education, Training, and Research.

Wolken, G. H., Moriwaki, S., & Williams, K. J. (1973). Race and social class as factors in the orientation toward psychotherapy. *Journal of Counseling Psychology, 20,* 312-316.

Won-Doornink, M. J. (1979). On getting to know you: The association between stage of relationship and reciprocity of self-disclosure. *Journal of Experimental Social Psychology, 15,* 229-241.

Word, C., Zanna, M., & Cooper, J. (1974). The nonverbal mediation of self-fullfilling prophecies in interracial interaction. *Journal of Experimental Social Psychology, 10,* 109-120.

12

The Influence of Ethnic and Attitude Similarity on Initial Social Penetration

MITCHELL R. HAMMER • University of Wisconsin/Milwaukee

One factor that has been found to influence relationship development is the degree of perceived similarity between communicators. Most of this research, however, investigated the influence of attitude similarity on interpersonal attraction. Few studies examined the differential effects of attitude and ethnic similarity on social penetration during initial interactions. It was this concern that the present study addressed. A multivariate analysis of variance design was used to assess the influence of ethnic similarity (white American, similar to subject; black American, dissimilar to subject) and attitude similarity (attitudes similar to subject; attitudes dissimilar to subject) on intentions to engage in social penetration. Results revealed a significant main effect by attitude similarity on social penetration, indicating subjects' intention to engage in significantly greater social penetration with attitudinally similar others than with attitudinally dissimilar others. These results suggest that attitude similarity may be more important than ethnic similarity in influencing social penetration in nonintimate initial interactions.

Each person has a fundamental need for social interaction. Social and personal relationships provide the basic structure through which social contact and interpersonal intimacy are realized. Relationships do not develop, however, through random happenstance. Rather, organized and coordinated behavior occurs between two communicators from the opening phases of their initial interaction (Miller, Hintz, & Couch, 1975) to the final stages of relationship termination (Knapp, 1978).

One theoretical perspective that attempts to describe and explain the process of relationship development is social penetration theory devel-

AUTHOR'S NOTE: *An edited version of this chapter was presented at the International Communication Association Annual Convention, San Francisco, May 1984.*

oped by Altman and Taylor (1973). Central to this theory is the role disclosure assumes in escalating/de-escalating relational intimacy; relationships are posited to develop from superficial exchanges of information to more intimate personal communication. This process is seen as involving both increased frequency of interpersonal communication (termed breadth of penetration) and increasingly intimate levels of disclosure (termed depth of penetration). The rate and degree to which relationships proceed to more frequent and intimate levels depends upon the subjective assessments each interactant makes concerning the cost and rewards for engaging in disclosive behavior.

Based on this perspective, Altman and Taylor (1973) suggest that interpersonal relationship development tends to proceed through four stages: orientation, exploratory affective exchange, full affective exchange, and stable exchange. The orientation stage represents the least social penetration and the stable exchange stage represents more frequent and intimate disclosure.[1]

One factor that has been found to influence the relationship development process is the degree of perceived similarity between communicators. The majority of research in this area, however, has examined the influence of attitude similarity on interpersonal attraction (Byrne, 1971; Rokeach, 1960) with little attention given to other aspects of the relationship development process. Further, research has neglected to investigate the comprehensive effects of other forms of similarity (e.g., cultural, ethnic) on the relationship development process.[2] As Bishop (1979, p. 461) comments:

> These results suggest previous research has been much too narrow in emphasizing belief similarity. It is clear that other types of similarity are important and need to be investigated. To understand the ways in which the perception of similarity influences interpersonal relations, it is necessary that the problem be approached from the point of view of a wide variety of types of similarity.

Bishop goes on to argue that ethnic similarity is one major type of similarity that should be examined. Therefore, it is the purpose of the present study to examine the influence of ethnic similarity on the frequency and intimacy of interpersonal disclosures (social penetration) during initial interactions.

INFLUENCES ON SOCIAL PENETRATION

Much of the research on the role of similarity in interpersonal relations has focused on attitude similarity and its effects on attraction in initial interactions. Results from studies conducted within the cross-cultural arena, as well as the plethora of research completed in the United States, consistently indicates that the greater the attitude similarity between communicators: (1) the greater the degree of initial attraction (Brewer, 1968; Byrne, 1971; Rokeach, 1960; Yabrudi & Diab, 1978); (2) the more positive others are rated (Santee & Jackson, 1978; Veitch & Piccione, 1978); and (3) the more intimate interpersonal relations become (Lazarsfeld & Merton, 1954; Verbrugge, 1977).

In addition to research focusing on the effects of attitude similarity on attraction and intimacy, a number of studies have also examined the influence of ethnic similarity on attraction and intimacy. Research by Jones and Diener (1976), Allen (1976), Stephan (1977), and Ting-Toomey (1981) suggests that ethnic similarity is positively related to interpersonal attraction and relational intimacy. Simard (1981), in examining the influence of ethnic similarity/dissimilarity between Francophones and Anglophones in Canada, found that both groups perceived it as "more difficult to know how to initiate a conversation, to know what to talk about during the interaction, to be interested in the other person, and to guess in which language they should talk" when communicating with ethnically dissimilar others compared to ethnically similar others (p. 183). Research by Gudykunst (1983), consistent with results of the Simard (1981) study, found that respondents preferred to talk less and perceived their conversation flow as more difficult in initial interaction with culturally dissimilar others compared to culturally similar others. Overall, these results suggest that ethnic similarity does have an influence during initial interactions on attraction and interpersonal intimacy.

A few studies have simultaneously investigated the differential effects of both attitude and ethnic similarity on interpersonal attraction. Research by Rokeach, Smith, and Evans (1960); Byrne and Wong (1962); and Stein, Hardyck, and Smith (1965) suggests that attitude similarity is more predictive of interpersonal attraction than ethnic similarity while work by Triandis (1961) indicates that ethnic similarity is more influential than attitudinal similarity on attraction. In attempting to reconcile these apparently contradictory findings, Triandis and Davis (1965) conclude that ethnic similarity may be more important in influencing attraction during intimate interactions (e.g., close friendships) while attitudinal similarity may be more important in influencing attraction in nonintimate interactions (e.g., initial encounters). Subsequent studies by Triandis, Loh, and Levin (1966) and Goldstein and Davis (1972) lend support to Triandis and Davis's (1965) proposition, as does Insko, Nacoste, and Moe's (1983) recent review of studies concerned with belief congruence and outgroup rejection.

Overall, research results suggest that both attitude and ethnic similarity are important influences on interpersonal attraction and interpersonal intimacy and that their relative importance, when both are operative, depends on whether the interaction is of the nonintimate or intimate variety. While no study has specifically examined the differential effects of attitude and ethnic similarity on social penetration in initial (nonintimate) interactions, the results from the literature on attraction and interpersonal intimacy previously cited suggest the following two hypotheses for the present study:

H$_1$: There is significantly greater intention to engage in initial social penetration in attitudinally similar dyads than in attitudinally dissimilar dyads.

H$_2$: There is no significant difference in initial social penetration between ethnically similar dyads and ethnically dissimilar dyads.

Because previous research suggests that ethnic similarity/dissimilarity should not influence initial social penetration, the second hypothesis is worded as the null hypothesis. In order to test this hypothesis, Beta level or Type II error (rather than Alpha level or Type I error which is appropriate for testing the first hypothesis) is examined.

METHODS

Design and Subjects

A 2 × 2 independent groups design, with two levels of ethnic similarity (white American, similar to subject; black American, dissimilar to subject) and two levels of attitude similarity (attitudes similar to subject; attitudes dissimilar to subject), was used to test the two hypotheses.[3] A total of 240 white American students in communication courses at a major midwestern university participated in the study. Of this group, 125 (52%) were males and 115 (48%) were females.

Stimulus Material

Based on Byrne's (1961) bogus stranger technique, four treatment conditions were presented to 60 subjects randomly assigned to each condition. The scenario involved the subjects reading about a social situation in which each subject is about to be introduced by a friend to an individual of the same sex as the subject who is either ethnically similar/dissimilar and attitudinally similar/dissimilar.[4] After reading the scenario, the subjects completed a questionnaire concerning their behavioral intentions toward disclosing information to the identified individual.

Although use of the bogus stranger technique and behavioral intentions is not as desirable as direct observation of behavior, the focus on behavioral intentions is consistent with Triandis's (1976) comparative study of black and white perceptions of the social environment. Triandis (1977) argues that actual behavior is a function of behavioral intentions and that intentions "are good predictors of overt action" (p. 202). Whether intentions lead to behavior is influenced by "facilitating conditions"; for instance, the person's ability to carry through the behavior he/she intends to perform (e.g., do they have the necessary skill to perform the behavior?).

Measures

Subjects' willingness to disclose various kinds of information to the identified stimulus person was assessed from the perspective of social penetration theory (Altman & Taylor, 1973). From this theoretical framework, Taylor and Altman (1966a, 1966b) developed an extensive questionnaire to measure the degree of social penetration in interpersonal relationships. They developed 671 intimacy-scaled topics of conversation grouped into 13 categories.

In the present study, 36 randomly selected items from the original Taylor and Altman (1966a, 1966b) questionnaire were used. Frequency (breadth) of social penetration was measured (in a slightly modified form) by asking subjects to indicate, on a 9-point behavioral differential scale, the degree to which they would or would not discuss the topic with the stimulus person (0 = least frequent, 8 = most frequent). Intimacy (depth) of social penetration was assessed by having subjects rate the intimacy of each item (0 = superficial, 6 = very intimate). The social penetration measure was obtained by multiplying the frequency rating by the intimacy rating for each item, adding the resultant scores, then dividing this number by the number of items that make up each scale.

Three items randomly selected from 12 of the 13 dimensions of social penetration identified by Taylor and Altman (1966a, 1966b) made up the 36-item questionnaire used in the present study. The 12 dimensions, along with their reliability coefficients (Alpha) obtained in the present study, were (1) relationship with others, that is, opinions regarding interaction with others in social situations (.50); (2) interests and hobbies, that is, opinions concerning leisure time activities and interests of respondents (.67); (3) parental and family, that is, opinions about topics relevant to respondents' family (.54); (4) religion, that is, religious ideas, activities, and beliefs (.75); (5) money and property, that is, opinions about money and property (.45); (6) attitudes and values, that is, opinions about life and living (.33); (7) love, dating, and sex, that is, opinions regarding respondents' own experiences in these areas (.67); (8) own marriage and family, that is, relationship with actual or potential spouse and/or children (.57); (9) politics and social issues, that is, opinions concerning government, politics, and social issues (.39); (10) school and work, that is, opinions about past or present school or work experiences (.76); (11) emotions and feelings, that is, respondents' feelings and emotions (.62); and (12) physical condition and attractiveness, that is, respondents' personal likes/dislikes about appearance (.54). The "biographical" dimension (items of a personal/demographic nature) was omitted in the present study. Overall, the original Taylor and Altman (1966a, 1966b) questionnaire has been found to be both an accepted (Chelune, 1979) and currently valid (Solono, 1981) measure of social penetration.

The following five dimensions had alpha levels of .60 or better and were used as the dependent measures in the analysis of social penetration: (1) interests and hobbies; (2) religion; (3) love, dating, and sex; (4) school and work; and (5) emotions and feelings. One plausible explanation for the rather low reliabilities (below .60) obtained for 7 of the 12 dimensions is that these topics are subjects generally not discussed in initial interactions, and therefore generate varying and inconsistent responses.

RESULTS

A 2 × 2 multivariate analysis of variance (MANOVA) was used in the present study (ethnic similarity/dissimilarity; attitudinal similarity/dissimilarity).

Multivariate Analysis

Bartlett's test of sphericity was calculated in order to determine the degree of relatedness among the dependent variables for social penetration (frequency × intimacy of disclosure). Sufficiently high correlations among the dependent variables were obtained to warrant multivariate analysis (240.32; df = 10; p ≤ .001; determinant = .35). Bartlett's Box F statistic was employed to test for homogeneity of variance among the dependent measures. No significant differences were observed on three of the five dependent measures. Significant differences were found, however, on the dimensions of school and work (3.22; p ≤ .03) and emotions and feelings (3.81; p ≤ .02).

A significant multivariate main effect was observed by attitude similarity/dissimilarity on the set of dependent variables (Hotelling's trace = .05; Wilks' lambda = .95; F = 2.40; df = 5,232; p < .04), indicating that attitude similarity/dissimilarity had an influence on the degree of social penetration. Overall means for the attitude similarity condition across the five dependent measures was 11.64 compared to 10.80 for the attitudinally dissimilar condition, indicating that respondents intended to exhibit a higher degree of social penetration with attitudinally similar others than with attitudinally dissimilar others. Statistical power for this MANOVA was at least .78 for a small effect size of .25 (Stevens, 1980). Therefore, the first hypothesis was supported.

No significant multivariate main effects were found by ethnic similarity/dissimilarity on the set of dependent measures. Statistical power for this MANOVA was at least .78 for a small effect size of .25 (Stevens, 1980). Beta error for the MANOVA was not larger than .22, supporting the second (null) hypothesis of the study. That is, no significant difference was observed in social penetration between ethnically similar dyads and dissimilar dyads during initial interaction. In addition, no significant multivariate interaction effects were observed among the set of five dependent variables.[5]

Univariate Analysis

Table 12.1 presents the means and standard deviations for social penetration measures by attitude similarity/dissimilarity and ethnic similarity/dissimilarity. A significant univariate main effect by attitude similarity/dissimilarity was found on the dimension of love, dating, and sex (F = 5.12; df = 1,236; p ≤ .03). The mean response for the attitudinally similar condition was higher (12.67) than that for the attitudinally dissimilar condition (10.41). No significant univariate main effects by attitude similarity/dissimilarity were found on the other four dimensions (relationship with others, interests and hobbies, parental and family, and religion). Statistical power for these univariate analyses was at least .92 for an effect size of .15, with an alpha of .05 (Cohen, 1977).

DISCUSSION

The primary purpose of the present study was to investigate the influence of attitude and ethnic similarity/dissimilarity on social penetration during initial interactions. Results from the multivariate analysis indicate that respondents who intend to interact with attitudinally similar others exhibit a higher degree of social penetration than with attitudinally dissimilar others. Ethnic similarity/dissimilarity, however, appears to have no discernible effect on social penetration intentions. In drawing this conclusion, care must be taken since the power for the MANOVA was at least .78 with beta error of .22. This suggests there is a 22% chance of accepting a false null hypothesis. For this conclusion to be substantiated, future research must be conducted with sufficient power.

These results are consistent with research that has focused on the relationship between attitude similarity and attraction (e.g., Rokeach, 1960) and interpersonal intimacy (e.g., Lazarsfeld & Merton, 1954). Further, a significant multivariate main effect was not observed by ethnic similarity/dissimilarity on social penetration in the present study, consistent with the finding of Rokeach, Smith, and Evans (1960) and of Stein, Hardyck, and Smith (1965) that attitudinal similarity is more predictive of interpersonal attraction than ethnic similarity. In the present study, attitudinal similarity appears to be more predictive than ethnic similarity for social penetration as well.

TABLE 12.1
Means and Standard Deviations for the Social Penetration Measures

	Social Penetration Dimensions									
	Interests/Hobbies		Religion		Dating, Love, & Sex		School & Work		Emotions & Feelings	
Conditions	$\overline{X}$	(s.d.)	$\overline{X}$	(s.d.)	$\overline{X}$	(s.d.)	$\overline{X}$	(s.d.)	$\overline{X}$	(s.d.)
Attitude similarity	11.52	(8.40)	11.88	(9.31)	12.67	(7.95)	10.96	(7.98)	11.18	(6.77)
Attitude disdimilarity	11.44	7.31	10.23	(8.07)	10.41	(7.45)	12.33	(8.40)	9.58	(6.18)
Ethnic similarity	11.18	(7.37)	11.42	(8.28)	11.50	(7.66)	11.25	(7.16)	10.35	(5.55)
Ethnic dissimilarity	11.78	(8.34)	10.69	(9.10)	11.58	(7.74)	12.05	(9.23)	10.41	(7.45)

Because the present study focused on attitude and ethnic similarity/dissimilarity, simultaneously, the result is most directly consistent with Triandis and Davis's (1965) proposition. In their proposition, attitude similarity is viewed as more important than ethnic similarity in nonintimate interactions while ethnic similarity may be more important in intimate encounters. Because the present study focused only on initial (nonintimate) interactions, however, the results are supportive only of the greater importance of attitude similarity in nonintimate encounters.

The present findings suggest three issues to be addressed in future research. First, the differential effects of attitude and ethnic similarity/dissimilarity on social penetration should be investigated for both initial and more intimate interactions (e.g., close friendships). Only by examining both relational contexts can the effects of attitude and ethnic similarity/dissimilarity be comprehensively investigated.

Second, a number of recent studies have extended work on the effects of similarity/dissimilarity on attraction by examining the mediating influence of actual interaction. Sunnafrank and Miller (1981), for example, found no significant differences in subjects' attraction toward attitudinally similar and dissimilar others. Instead, they found that the amount of interaction actually increased (compared to preinteraction expectations) subjects' attraction toward attitudinally dissimilar others. Sunnafrank (1983) observed that "when individuals are allowed to go through a normal initial conversation prior to discussing attitudinal topics, the attitude similarity variable fails to exert a significant influence on attraction" (p. 284). It should be noted, however, that both studies focused only on attitude similarity and examined the mediating influence of actual interactions only on attraction. Future work needs to assess the differential effects of various similarities (e.g., attitude, ethnic), along with actual interaction, not only on attraction but on other aspects of the relationship development process (e.g., social penetration).

Finally, dissimilarities may, in and of themselves, be attractive. As Rogers and Shoemaker (1971) stated, moderate dissimilarities between communicators may create conditions of optimal heterophily that enhance interpersonal relations. Also, Broome (1983) found that the effects of dissimilarity between interactants are moderated by at least two variables: expectation of evaluation and message openness. Future research needs to examine the conditions under which dissimilarities may enhance the relationship development process.

NOTES

1. A recent elaboration of social penetration theory (Altman, Vinsel, & Brown, 1981) suggests that, through the conceptual mechanism of dialectics, social penetration may be more comprehensively viewed as a cyclical rather than a more linear (cost-reward) process. In this view, social relationships exhibit openness (willingness to disclose self to other) and closedness (unwillingness to disclose self to others), as well as stability (consistency) and change (variety). However, this elaboration is not directly relevant to the intent of this study, which is to focus on the influence of attitude and ethnic similarity/dissimilarity only on social penetration during initial interactions.

2. The term *ethnicity* is used throughout this chapter wherever possible. The use of ethnicity, rather than race, is based on Montagu's (1972) argument that potentially negative connotations associated with racial terms may be lessened by substituting the word ethnicity for race.

3. The gender of the subject may influence the subject's responses. It could have been incorporated into the present study as another independent variable.

4. A formal manipulation check was not included in the questionnaire. Discussion with the subjects during debriefing, however, supported the reliability of the manipulation; the subjects appeared to be thinking of ethnically similar/dissimilar and attitudinally similar/dissimilar individuals when they responded to the items, as instructed in the questionnaire.

5. MANOVAs were also run separately on the individual components of social penetration, namely, the frequency (breadth) and the intimacy (depth) of penetration. In contrast to the social penetration measure, no significant effects by attitude or ethnic similarity/dissimilarity on either frequency or intimacy of disclosure were found. Intuitively, this result is somewhat perplexing, but it is consistent with Altman and Taylor's (1973) social penetration theory. According to these authors, neither frequency nor intimacy alone is descriptive of the relationship development process. Rather, the combination of the two, that is, the degree to which individuals talk with one another more frequently about topics that are increasingly more intimate, reflects the nature of a relationship.

REFERENCES

Allen, B. P. (1976). Race and physical attractiveness as criteria for white subjects' dating choices. *Social Behavior and Personality. 4,* 289-296.

Altman, I., & Taylor, D. A. (1973). *Social penetration: The development of interpersonal relationships.* New York: Holt, Rinehart & Winston.

Altman, I., Vinsel, A., & Brown, B. B. (1981). Dialectic conceptions in social psychology: An application to social penetration and privacy regulation. *Advances in Experimental Social Psychology, 14,* 107-160.

Bishop, G. (1979). Perceived similarity in interpersonal attitudes and behavior. *Journal of Applied Social Psychology, 9,* 446-465.

Brewer, M. (1968). Determinants of social distance among East African tribal groups. *Journal of Personality and Social Psychology, 10,* 279-289.

Broome, B. J. (1983). The attraction paradigm revisited: Responses to dissimilar other. *Human Communication Research, 10 (1),* 137-151.

Byrne, D. (1961). Interpersonal attraction and attitude similarity. *Journal of Personality and Social Psychology, 62,* 713-715.

Byrne, D. (1971). *The attraction paradigm.* New York: Academic Press.

Byrne, D., & Wong, T. (1962). Racial prejudice, interpersonal attraction and assumed dissimilarity of attitudes. *Journal of Abnormal and Social Psychology, 65,* 246-253.

Chelune, G. J. (1979). Measuring openness in interpersonal communication. In G. J. Chelune (Ed.), *Self-disclosure.* San Francisco: Jossey-Bass.

Cohen, J. (1977). *Statistical power analysis for the behavioral sciences* (rev. ed.). New York: Academic Press.

Golstein, M., & Davis, E. E. (1972). Race and belief: A further analysis of the social determinants of behavioral intentions. *Journal of Personality and Social Psychology, 22,* 346-355.

Gudykunst, W. B. (1983). Similarities and differences in perceptions of initial intracultural and intercultural encounters: An exploratory investigation. *Southern Speech Communication Journal, 49*(1), 49-65.

Insko, C. A., Nacoste, R. W., & Moe, J. L. (1983). Belief congruence and racial discrimination: Review of the evidence and critical evaluation. *European Journal of Social Psychology, 13,* 153-174.

Jones, S., & Diener, E. (1976). Ethnic preference of college students for their own and other racial groups. *Social Behavior and Personality, 4,* 225-231.

Knapp, M. (1978). *Social intercourse.* Boston: Allyn & Bacon.

Lazarsfeld, P. & Merton, R. (1954). Friendship as a social process. In M. Berger et al. (Eds.), *Freedom and control in modern society.* New York: Octagon Books.

Miller, D., Hintz, R., & Couch, J. (1975). Elements and structure of openings. *Sociological Quarterly, 16,* 479-499.

Montagu, A. (1972). *Statement on race.* New York: Oxford University Press.

Rogers, E., & Shoemaker, F. (1971). *Communication of innovation: A cross-cultural approach* (2nd ed.). New York: Free Press.

Rokeach, M. (1960). *The open and closed mind.* New York: Basic Books.

Rokeach, M., Smith, P., & Evans, R. (1960). Two kinds of prejudice or one? In M. Rokeach, *The open and closed mind.* New York: Basic Books.

Santee, R. T., & Jackson, S. E. (1978). Similarity and positive self-description as determinants of estimated appraisal and attraction. *Social Psychology, 41,* 162-165.

Simard, L. (1981). Cross-cultural interaction. *Journal of Social Psychology, 113,* 171-192.

Solano, C. H. (1981). Sex differences and the Taylor-Altman self-disclosure stimuli. *Journal of Social Psychology, 115,* 287-288.

Stein, D., Hardyck, J. M., & Smith, M. (1965). Race and belief. *Journal of Personality and Social Psychology, 1,* 281-290.

Stephan, W. G. (1977). Cognitive differentiation in intergroup perception. *Sociometry, 40,* 50-58.

Stevens, J. C. (1980). Power of the multivariate analyses of variance tests. *Psychological Bulletin, 8,* 728-737.

Sunnafrank, M. (1983). Attitude similarity and interpersonal attraction in communication processes: In pursuit of an ephemeral influence. *Communication Monographs, 50*(4), 273-284.

Sunnafrank, M.J.M., & Miller, G. R. (1981). The role of initial conversations in determining attraction to similar and dissimilar strangers. *Human Communication Research, 8*(1), 16-25.

Taylor, S., & Altman, I. (1966a). *Intimacy-scaled stimuli for use in studies of interpersonal relations.* Naval Medical Research Institute, (Report No. 9) April.

Taylor, S., & Altman, I. (1966b). Intimacy-scaled stimuli for use in studies of interpersonal relations. *Psychological Reports, 19,* 729-730.

Ting-Toomey, S. (1981). Ethnic identity and close friendship in Chinese-American college students. *International Journal of Intercultural Relations, 5*(4), 338-406.

Triandis, H. (1961). A note on Rokeach's theory of prejudice. *Journal of Abnormal and Social Psychology, 62,* 184-186.

Triandis, H. (1976). *Variations in black and white perceptions of the social environment.* Urbana: University of Illinois Press.

Triandis, H. (1977). *Interpersonal behavior.* Monterey, CA: Brooks/Cole.

Triandis, H. C., & Davis, E. E. (1965). Race and belief as determinants of behavioral interactions. *Journal of Personality and Social Psychology, 2,* 715-725.

Triandis, H. C., Loh, W. D., & Levin, L. (1966). Race and belief as determinants of behavioral intention. *Journal of Personality and Social Psychology, 3,* 468-472.

Veitch, R., & Piccione, A. (1978). The role of attitude similarity in the attribution process. *Social Psychology, 41,* 165-169.

Verbrugge, L. (1977). The structure of adult friendship choices. *Social Forces, 56,* 576-597.

Yabrudi, P., & Diab, L. (1978). The effects of attitude similarity-dissimilarity, religion, and topic importance on interpersonal attraction among Lebanese university students. *Journal of Social Psychology, 106,* 167-171.

Name Index

Subject Index

About the Authors

ROSITA DASKAL ALBERT (Ph.D. in Social Psychology, University of Michigan) is originally from Brazil. Currently she is Associate Professor of Intercultural Communication in the department of Speech-Communication at the University of Minnesota. She has directed several federally and state-funded large-scale research programs, including a multiyear project on Hispanic-Anglo interactions in school and work settings. She has written two books, *Communication Across Cultures* and *Understanding North Americans,* and numerous articles based on her research on the intercultural sensitizer or culture assimilator as a method for intercultural training. Her work has appeared in the *International Journal of Intercultural Relations* and the *Handbook of Intercultural Training.* Her current interests include intercultural interactions in multinational companies.

LARRY G. COLEMAN (Ph.D., State University of New York, Buffalo) is a graduate assistant professor at Howard University in Washington, D.C. He teaches seminars in Afro-American Communication and Communication Theory and supervises and trains Teaching Associates. His research interests include Black rhetoric, folklore, sociolinguistics, mass media, comedy, and storytelling. Dr. Coleman formerly served as Research Associate in the Center for Ethnic Studies at the University of Texas and as Instructor in Afro-American Studies at the University of Pittsburgh. He is co-founder and Vice President of the International Association of Black Storytellers. He performs as a storyteller and conducts professional workshops on storytelling. His articles appear in the *Journal of Black Studies,* in *Black Lives,* and in a forthcoming anthology he has produced on the Jesse Jackson Presidential campaign.

C. J. DUVALL (M.S., Purdue University School of Science) is a Black industrial psychologist. He has been heavily involved in social, psychological, and organizational issues in various industrial settings. His major research interest is in intergroup relations and behaviors, specifically involving Black people.

ROBERT FORTIER, Ph.D., is Associate Professor of Psychology, Purdue University School of Science. Among his subject responsibilities in 19 years of teaching are clinical psychology; community psychology; and emotional, cognitive, and social problems in adults. He has also worked as consultant to numerous social agencies and institutions.

HOWARD GILES obtained his Ph.D. from the University of Bristol, England, in 1971 and in 1984 succeeded the late Henri Tajfel as Professor of Social Psychology in the same institution. In 1982, he became the Founding Editor of the *Journal of Language and Social Psychology,* and in 1985 co-organized the First International Conference on Social Psychology, Language and Ethnic Relations in Australia. He has published widely in the areas of the interface of bilingualism, intergroup relations, and cultural identity, with much of this in the context of his birthplace of Wales. He is currently engaged in establishing an international and interdisciplinary Centre for the Study of Communication and Social Relations at Bristol, part of which will be concerned with the relationships between ethnicity, communication, aging, and health.

WILLIAM B. GUDYKUNST (Ph.D., University of Minnesota) is Associate Professor of Communication at Arizona State University. His recent work includes editing *Intercultural Communication Theory* and *Intergroup Communication,* co-editing *Methods for Intercultural Communication Research* (with Young Yun Kim) and *Communication, Culture, and Organizational Processes* (with Lea Stewart and Stella Ting-Toomey) and co-authoring *Communicating with Strangers* (with Young Yun Kim). His research on extending uncertainty reduction theory to interethnic and intercultural situations has appeared in *Human Communication Research, Communication Monographs, Communication Quarterly,* and *The Southern Journal of Speech Communication.*

MITCHELL R. HAMMER (Ph.D., University of Minnesota) is Assistant Professor of Communication at the University of Wisconsin-Milwaukee (Milwaukee, Wisconsin). He teaches courses in the areas of intercultural and organizational communication. His research interests include intercultural communication effectiveness, the role of communication in intercultural adjustment and acculturation, the process of relationship development between people from different cultures, interethnic communication, and the analysis of cultural and communication processes in organizations. He has designed and conducted a variety of program evaluations for numerous client organizations. He co-authored the chapter on intercultural training design for the *Handbook of Intercultural Training* and has published articles in *Communication Yearbook,* the *International Journal of Intercultural Relations,* and *Communication Quarterly,* among others.

JUDITH LYNNE HANNA, an Associate Research Scholar at University of Maryland, and a Tutor (doctoral students) of International College, Los Angeles, was formally trained in education, political science, and anthropology (Ph.D., Columbia University). She works in the fields of arts and society, urban studies, Africa, and education and public policy. Author of *To Dance Is Human: A Theory of Nonverbal Communication* (University of Chicago Press reprint of 1979 original, 1987), *The Performer-Audience Connection: Emotion to Metaphor in Dance and Society* (University of Texas Press, 1983), *Dance, Sex, and Gender: Signs of Identity, Dominance, Defiance, and Desire* (University of Chicago Press, 1987), *Disruptive School Behavior—in a Desegregated Magnet School and Elsewhere* (Holmes & Meier, 1987), *Dance and Stress* (AMS Press, 1987), and co-author of *Urban Dynamics in Black Africa* (Aldine, 1981), she has also published more than fifty articles on communication in, for example, *Current Anthropology, Doing the Ethnography of Schooling, Journal of Communication, Nonverbal Behavior,* and *Semiotica.*

PATRICIA JOHNSON undertook her under- and postgraduate work in the Psychology Department at the University of Bristol, England, obtaining her Ph.D. in 1984. The investigations reported herein constitute, in abridged form, two of the empirical studies found in her doctoral dissertation. She has co-authored, on a number of occasions, with Howard Giles in the area of the social psychology of ethnolinguistics.

YOUNG YUN KIM (Ph.D., Northwestern University) is Professor of Communication at Governors State University. She teaches courses in communication theory and research, intercultural communication, and communication training. Her research interests include the role of communication in cross-cultural adaptation, the process of psychic and behavioral transformation of individuals vis-à-vis a new or changing sociocultural environment, and cognitive information processing and communication competence. She has conducted surveys in a number of Asian and Hispanic communities in Illinois, and has published articles in many communication journals and readers. She is the co-author of *Communicating with Strangers: An Approach to Intercultural Communication* and the co-editor of *Methods for Intercultural Communication Research* (both with William B. Gudykunst).

THOMAS KOCHMAN (Ph.D., New York University) is Professor of Communication at the University of Illinois at Chicago. He teaches courses in sociolinguistics, intercultural communication, and ethnography of communication. His research interests include the relationship between patterns of communication, culture and society; acculturation theory (specifically as it applies to Americanization); and the role of cultural differences in interpersonal conflict. He is the author of *Black and White Styles in Conflict* and editor of *Rappin' and Stylin' Out: Communication in Urban Black America*. He has contributed chapters to many edited collections and has published articles in such journals as *Language in Society, Language, Foundations of Language, Anthropological Linguistics, Society,* and *The International Journal of the Sociology of Language*.

STEVEN L. McNABB (Ph.D., Brown University) is a consulting anthropologist in Anchorage, Alaska. He is principal of the Social Research Institute and is a Research Associate with the John Muir Institute in Napa, California. During the past ten years he has conducted numerous studies for state, federal, and local government agencies; and Alaska Native organizations. His research on over one hundred Indian, Aleut, and Eskimo villages in Alaska investigated topics such as culture change, social organization, natural resource uses, linguistics, interethnic relations, social problems, and education. His main research interest is the effect of rapid social and economic change on relatively isolated and impoverished minority populations. Some of his recent work appears in the journals *Human Organization* and *The Journal of Ethnic Studies.*

ROBERT NEEL, Ph.D., is Professor of Psychology at Purdue University School of Science. He has had 33 years of teaching experience in personality theory and industrial psychology. He conducted research in the personnel-industrial area, spent three years in industry as a personnel psychologist, and spent a year abroad as a senior lecturer in the Fulbright Fellowship Program. He has published research articles and presented papers at both national and international levels in personality, industrial organization, and cross-cultural personality.

DONALD L. RUBIN (Ph.D., University of Minnesota) is Associate Professor in the Departments of Speech Communication and Language Education and in the Program in Linguistics, and is Research Fellow at the Institute for Behavioral Research at the University of Georgia. He teaches courses in language and communication, intercultural communication, and communication education. His research focuses on the development of oral and written communication and on the significance of linguistic variation. His work appears in several monographs and book chapters and in such journals as *Child Development, Research in the Teaching of English, Language and Speech, Language and Communication,* and *Written Communication.*

WILLIAM J. STAROSTA (Ph.D., Indiana University) is Graduate Professor and Academic Coordinator for Communication Arts at Howard University (Washington, D.C.). He teaches doctoral seminars in Intercultural/Interracial Communication and Rhetorical Criticism. He conducted field research three times in South Asia under Fellowships from Fulbright-Hays, the American Institute for Indian Studies, and the Wisconsin-Berkeley Year-in-India Program. Dr. Starosta has frequently served on editorial boards, written chapters, and published articles on intercultural communication and rhetoric for journals including *The Quarterly Journal of Speech,* the *Journal of Black Studies,* and the *International and Intercultural Communication Annual.* He currently serves on the editorial board of *World Communication.*

STELLA TING-TOOMEY (Ph.D., University of Washington) is Assistant Professor of Communication at Rutgers University. Her primary teaching and research interests are in intercultural communication and interpersonal communication. Her publications have appeared in *Human Communication Research, International Journal of Intercultural Relations, International and Intercultural Communication Annual,* and *Communication Quarterly,* among others. She is the co-editor of *Communication, Culture, and Organizational Processes* (with W. Gudykunst and L. Stewart) and *Communication, Gender, and Sex Roles in Diverse Interaction Contexts* (with L. Stewart). Her current research foci are cross-cultural relational development and intercultural adaptation processes and communication.

OLIVER C. S. TZENG (Ph.D., University of Illinois) is Professor of Psychology and Director of the Osgood Laboratory for Cross-Cultural Research at Purdue University School of Science at Indianapolis. He teaches courses in graduate quantitative methodologies, social problems, and intercultural sociology and personality. His research interests include cross-cultural social and behavioral studies, research methodologies, interpersonal relations, and implicit personality theories. Since 1981, he has been entrusted with the complete documents, research data, conference notes, references, working papers, and the *Atlas of Affective Meaning* data to which Professor Osgood devoted the past 20 years.

ROGER WARE, Ph.D., is Associate Professor of Psychology at Indiana University—Purdue University at Indianapolis. He has a wide range of experience in teaching, research, and consulting. His major research interests include organizational relationships, group dynamics, and humanistic psychology. He is currently involved in several cross-cultural studies of human love relationships and personality assessment.